Entrepreneurship in Africa

This book presents current research by leading experts from around the globe on entrepreneurship in Africa, focusing on how entrepreneurship is central to the economic development of many of the economies on the African continent. Collectively, the contributors identify the frontier of impactful research on entrepreneurship and provide a glimpse into both the opportunities and the challenges for entrepreneurship in Africa.

This book was originally published as a special issue of the *Africa Journal of Management*.

Bruce T. Lamont is the Jim Moran Eminent Scholar of Business Administration at Florida State University, Tallahassee, USA.

Hermann A. Ndofor is Assistant Professor at the Kelley School of Business, Indiana University, Bloomington, USA.

Entrepreneurship in Africa

Opportunities for Both Africa and Entrepreneurship Research

Edited by

Bruce T. Lamont and Hermann A. Ndofor

LONDON AND NEW YORK

First published 2018 by Routledge

2 Park Square, Milton Park, Abingdon, Oxfordshire OX14 4RN
52 Vanderbilt Avenue, New York, NY 10017

Routledge is an imprint of the Taylor & Francis Group, an informa business

First issued in paperback 2020

British Library Cataloguing-in-Publication Data
A catalogue record for this book is available from the British Library

ISBN13: 978-0-8153-5922-7 (hbk)
ISBN13: 978-0-367-53066-2 (pbk)

Typeset in Minion Pro
by codeMantra

Publisher's Note
The publisher accepts responsibility for any inconsistencies that may have arisen during the conversion of this book from journal articles to book chapters, namely the possible inclusion of journal terminology.

Disclaimer
Every effort has been made to contact copyright holders for their permission to reprint material in this book. The publishers would be grateful to hear from any copyright holder who is not here acknowledged and will undertake to rectify any errors or omissions in future editions of this book.

Contents

Citation Information

The chapters in this book were originally published in the *Africa Journal of Management*, volume 2, issue 3 (September 2016). When citing this material, please use the original page numbering for each article, as follows:

Chapter 1
Entrepreneurial Intentions: A Cultural Perspective
Ian K. Alexander and Benson Honig
Africa Journal of Management, volume 2, issue 3 (September 2016) pp. 235–257

Chapter 2
Entrepreneurial Opportunities and Poverty in Sub-Saharan Africa: A Review & Agenda for the Future
Jacob A. L. Vermeire and Garry D. Bruton
Africa Journal of Management, volume 2, issue 3 (September 2016) pp. 258–280

Chapter 3
Leaving a Social Venture: Social Entrepreneurial Exit among the Maasai in Northern Tanzania
Alexander Tetteh Kwasi Nuer, Miguel Rivera-Santos, Carlos Rufín and Gert Van Dijk
Africa Journal of Management, volume 2, issue 3 (September 2016) pp. 281–299

Chapter 4
Network Bricolage as the Reconciliation of Indigenous and Transplanted Institutions in Africa
Kevin McKague and Christine Oliver
Africa Journal of Management, volume 2, issue 3 (September 2016) pp. 300–329

Chapter 5
Positive Impact of Entrepreneurship Training on Entrepreneurial Behavior in a Vocational Training Setting
Michael M. Gielnik, Michael Frese, Kim Marie Bischoff, Gordon Muhangi and Francis Omoo
Africa Journal of Management, volume 2, issue 3 (September 2016) pp. 330–348

Chapter 6

Entrepreneurship in Africa: Identifying the Frontier of Impactful Research
Richard A. Devine and Moses N. Kiggundu
Africa Journal of Management, volume 2, issue 3 (September 2016) pp. 349–380

Notes on Contributors

Ian K. Alexander is Associate Professor at the Department of Food and Resource Economics, University of Copenhagen, Denmark.

Kim Marie Bischoff is based at the Leuphana Universität Lüneburg, Germany.

Garry D. Bruton is Professor at Texas Christian University, Fort Worth, USA.

Richard A. Devine is a Post-Doctoral Researcher at American University, Washington, DC, USA.

Michael Frese is Provost's Chair, Head of the Management & Organisation Department and Professor at National University of Singapore School of Design and Environment, Singapore.

Michael M. Gielnik is based at the Leuphana Universität Lüneburg, Germany.

Benson Honig is Professor of Human Resources and Management, and Teresa Cascioli Chair in Entrepreneurial Leadership, at McMaster University, DeGroote School of Business, Hamilton, Canada.

Moses N. Kiggundu is Professor of Management and International Business at the Sprott School of Business, Ottawa, Canada. He is cross-appointed to Carleton University's Institute of African Studies, Ottawa, Ontario.

Bruce T. Lamont is the Jim Moran Eminent Scholar of Business Administration at Florida State University, Tallahassee, USA.

Kevin McKague is Associate Professor at the Shannon School of Business, Cape Breton University, Sydney, Canada.

Gordon Muhangi is based at the Nakawa Vocational Training Institute, Kampala, Uganda.

Hermann A. Ndofor is Assistant Professor at the Kelley School of Business, Indiana University, Bloomington, USA.

Alexander Tetteh Kwasi Nuer is based at the Social Sciences Department, Wageningen University, The Netherlands.

Christine Oliver is Professor and Henry J. Knowles Chair in Organizational Strategy at the Schulich School of Business, York University, Toronto, Canada.

Francis Omoo is based at the Nakawa Vocational Training Institute, Kampala, Uganda.

Miguel Rivera-Santos is Associate Professor at Babson College, Babson Park, USA.

Carlos Rufín is Associate Professor at the Sawyer School of Business, Suffolk University, Boston, USA.

Gert Van Dijk is Distinguished Professor at the Social Sciences Department, Wageningen University, The Netherlands.

Jacob A. L. Vermeire is a Doctoral Researcher at Vlerick Business School, Gent, Belgium.

ENTREPRENEURIAL INTENTIONS: A CULTURAL PERSPECTIVE

Ian K. Alexander and Benson Honig

The theory of planned behaviour is widely used to measure entrepreneurial intentions. Thus, we investigate the possible moderating role of indigenous ethnic culture on the attitude-intention, subjective norm-intention and perceived behavioural control-intention relationships. In support of the theory of planned behaviour, attitude and perceived behavioural control have a positive influence on the odds of becoming a nascent entrepreneur. However, subjective norm was not a significant predictor. The inclusion of ethnicity significantly improved the predictability of entrepreneurial intentions. We found that, in comparison with students from the Kikuyu tribe, students from the Luhya and Luo tribes are less likely to have intentions becoming nascent entrepreneurs. Finally, our findings confirm significant moderating effects of ethnicity. We draw a number of implications for the theory and practice of entrepreneurship education.

INTRODUCTION

Prior research has demonstrated that entrepreneurship is influenced by contextual factors (e.g., Manolova, Eunni, & Gyoshev, 2008; Noorderhaven, Thurik, Wennekers, & Stel, 2004; Valdez & Richardson, 2013). Among these factors the role of culture has received much attention. According to Krueger, Liñán, and Nabi (2013: 703), 'a greater understanding of the relationship between cultural issues and entrepreneurial activity is important because of its implication for national and regional development and growth.' Research has shown that members of different cultures vary systematically in aspects of their interpretation of entrepreneurship, the importance they place on entrepreneurship, as well as their entrepreneurial behaviour (e.g., Hansen, Deitz, Tokman, Marino, & Weaver, 2011; Mueller & Thomas, 2001; Schlaegel, He, & Engle, 2013). It is assumed that persons are drawn toward entrepreneurship because it is compatible with values to which the individual was previously conditioned (Dana, 1995).

While past studies have provided evidence of the interplay between culture and entrepreneurship, there are still some noticeable gaps in the extant literature. For instance, Liñán, Urbano, & Guerrero (2011) note that cognitive models wishing to explain variations in entrepreneurial intentions among regions do not usually include environmental cognitive elements. Moreover, although the culture–entrepreneurial intentions relationship has been discussed previously (e.g., Liñán & Chen, 2009; Pruett, Shinnar, Toney, Llopis, & Fox, 2009), the issue of tribal and indigenous tribal identity has not been studied. Yet national culture is not the only type of culture that influences entrepreneurship. Instead, entrepreneurial behaviour is influenced by different levels of culture including religion, family and ethnic cultures, among others. For example, (Mungai, 2013) argues that in culturally heterogeneous societies, indigenous ethnic cultures play a more dominant role in moulding the values and perceptions of its citizens than national cultures. However, there is limited empirical research focusing on the influence of ethnic culture on entrepreneurship and even less examining its impact on entrepreneurial intention.

In this study, the influence of culture on entrepreneurial intentions is examined at the indigenous ethnic-group level within the domestic Kenyan context. Kenya is multi-ethnic and therefore multi-cultural and thus, a single national culture to represent a culturally heterogeneous society is likely to be inappropriate (Bochner & Hesketh, 1994). Moreover, given that indigenous ethnic groups can be considered as subcultures within a country, the study of culture by ethnicity within a domestic context is feasible and appropriate since each ethnic group will have its own unique set of cultural values (Kwok & Uncles, 2005). The central question underlying this research is: How and to what extent does indigenous ethnic culture influence entrepreneurial intentions models? To answer this question we utilize the theory of planned behaviour to measure entrepreneurial intentions among students. More specifically, we examine the differences, if any, in entrepreneurial intentions among four major ethnic groups, namely the Luo, Kikuyu, Kamba and Luhya. We also investigate whether the effects of attitude, subjective norm and perceived behavioural control are the same or different among the four ethnic groups.

This study makes several important contributions to theory and practice. Firstly, although intentions is becoming ubiquitous, the influences of culture has not been widely explored. Thus, by adopting a cultural perspective on entrepreneurial intention, this study addresses one of the limitations of previous studies and helps shed light on the utility of intention models in culturally heterogeneous settings. Secondly, this study is one of the few pieces of research on intentions that empirically measures culture at an indigenous ethnic group level. It aims to provide evidence for the assumption that cultural differences at this level could directly influence intention and/or mediate or moderate the relationships within the model. Thirdly, in terms of the practical utility of this study, few studies have examined entrepreneurial intention in the East African setting; consequently, there is limited empirical evidence to guide decision-makers looking to develop entrepreneurship programs. Most notably, the lack of understanding of motivational factors and barriers to entrepreneurship hinders the development of adequate intervention programs. Authors such as Liñán and Chen (2009) and Kibler (2013) believe that an understanding of the formation of entrepreneurial behaviour before there is any observable action is important, especially when trying to encourage enterprising activity. Thus, our study will contribute to this approach by examining factors that might be relevant in explaining the variance in entrepreneurial intention. Finally, the African continent is under renewed and widespread interest because of its relatively rapid development. In this setting, there is still a great need for research to shed further light on the dynamics and effects of entrepreneurship. We aim to contribute to this area.

THEORY DEVELOPMENT

Theory of Planned Behaviour

Intention models are commonly used to predict behaviour, especially as they are considered to offer a coherent, parsimonious, highly-generalizable, and robust theoretical framework for understanding and predicting behaviour (Krueger, Reilly, & Carsrud, 2000).Among these models, the theory of planned behaviour is one of the most widely cited (Krueger et al., 2000). The theory helps examine and interpret, from a social cognition perspective, key antecedents to performing behaviour. It is based on the premise that intention can be an effective predictor of actual behaviour and that behaviour is intentionally planned (Ajzen, 1991). The theory of planned behaviour is increasingly used in entrepreneurship research to predict entrepreneurial intention (e.g., Engle et al., 2010; Lüthje & Franke, 2003) and to explore the antecedents to entrepreneurial behaviour (e.g., Carr & Sequeira, 2007; Díaz-García & Jiménez-Moreno, 2010; Zhao, Seibert, & Hills, 2005). More so, entrepreneurial intention has been considered as the first step to entrepreneurship development (Krueger & Carsrud, 1993).

Given that the theory has been widely discussed in the extant literature, we only present a brief summary of its underlying constructs. The central construct of the theory of planned behaviour is the individual's intention to perform a certain behaviour (Autio, Keeley, Klofsten, Parker, & Hay, 2001). Ajzen (1991) contends that intentions capture the motivational factors that influence a behaviour; they are indications of how hard people are willing to try, of how much of an effort they are planning to exert, in order to perform the behaviour. The theory views the intention to start a new venture as being dependent on three contextual elements: (1) personal attitude toward outcomes of the behaviour; (2) perceived social norms; (3) perceived behavioural control. The first two constructs (attitude and subjective norms) reflect the perceived desirability of intentions and the third (perceived behavioural control) reflects perceived feasibility of intentions (Urban, Van Vuuren, & Owen, 2008).

Personal attitude towards outcomes of the behaviour is similar to expectancy and refers to the attractiveness of performing the behaviour (Krueger et al., 2000). Attitudes refer to 'the degree to which a person has a favourable or unfavourable evaluation or appraisal of the behaviour in question' (Ajzen, 1991: 188). As a general rule, the more favourable the attitude towards a behaviour, the greater the intention to perform that behaviour.

Perceived social norms taps perceptions of what important people in respondents' lives think about performing a particular behaviour (Krueger et al., 2000). Social norms refer to the perceived social pressure to perform or avoid a behaviour (Iakovleva, Kolvereid, & Stephan, 2011). Along this line of reasoning, social encouragement and support for entrepreneurship is an essential part of the relevant social capital necessary for graduates to become self-employed.

Perceived behavioural control captures the ability and feasibility to execute a target behaviour (Ajzen, 1991). It stems from one's belief in one's own ability (self-efficacy) and implies the belief that a task is achievable (confidence), due to one's own competences. Therefore, the belief in one's ability to leverage resources (human, social, financial, and other physical resources) to create a venture (controllability) is a key factor in determining whether one views self-employment as feasible or not.

> Hypothesis 1a: The higher the attitude with respect to self-employment, the stronger is the students' intention to become self-employed.

> Hypothesis 1b: The higher the subjective norm with respect to self-employment, the stronger is the students' intention to become self-employed.

> Hypothesis 1c: The higher the perceived behavioural control with respect to self-employment, the stronger is the students' intention to become self-employed.

Ethnicity and intentions

According to Mungai & Ogot (2012) cultural/ethnic values can play a critical role in determining who gets into entrepreneurship and what functional role individuals plays in this activity. Portes & Rumbaut (2006) suggest that ethnic group membership can help to explain entrepreneurial outcomes, including values, skills, social capital and resource mobilization. Likewise, Hirschman (1982) argues that an ethnic group's socioeconomic achievements are partly a function of the human capital of individuals in that group, and the motives and ambition they derive from being part of that group. Further, institutional completeness and internal solidarity give members of some ethnic groups an advantage in mobilizing resources (Aldrich & Waldinger, 1990).

In terms of entrepreneurial intentions, given the relationship between ethnicity and entrepreneurship, it seems reasonable to assume that ethnicity also affects entrepreneurial intentions. Research by Wilson, Marlino, & Kickul (2004) shows that significant differences in the self-efficacy and entrepreneurial intentions exist among teen girls of different racial and ethnic identities. Moreover, globally there have been an increasing number of studies that report self-employment intention differences among ethnic groups; however, most of these studies have adopted conducted comparisons national ethnic groupings (e.g., Kristiansen & Indarti, 2004; Liñán & Chen, 2009; Pruett et al., 2009). However, we assume that there will also be differences in entrepreneurial intentions between indigenous ethnic groups, and that national cultural classifications may mask important intra-cultural diversity within the study population (Bandura, 2001).

Aharonovitz & Nyaga (2008) compare seven major tribes in Kenya: Kikuyu, Luo, Luhya, Kamba, Kalenjin, Kisii, and Meru, and find that the Kikuyu show the highest level of risk taking and education, factors that are closely related to entrepreneurial intent. Further, they found that the Luhya and Luo tribes rated high on altruism and cooperation. Given that entrepreneurial talent is generally selfish (Baumol, 1996), it could be expected that tribes like the Luhya and Luo that rate high in altruism would have lower entrepreneurial intentions than those with a low rating on the altruism/compassion scale (e.g., the Kikuyu tribe). Being disinclined to compete, having consensual decision making, and putting family first are complex issues that do not necessarily sit easy with modern entrepreneurship (Lindsay, 2005). Further, Marris (1968) argues that many of the characteristics and values held by the Kikuyu tribes facilitate entrepreneurship, stimulating the need for it and weakening the inhibitions. These include their adaptability, openness to change and individualism. LeVine, Strangman, & Unterberger (1966) suggest that ethnic groups like the Kikuyu in

Kenya are responsive to the economic incentives around them and are likely to retain their status of being perceived as opportunistic and industrious for a long time.

> Hypothesis 2: There is a significant difference in the level of entrepreneurial intentions among the Kikuyu, Kamba, Luhya and Luo tribes in Kenya.

Moreover, it seems safe to assume that differences in entrepreneurial intentions among the ethnic groups may be due to the different effects of their attitude, subjective norms and perceived behavioural control. First, in terms of attitude, although little is known about differences in entrepreneurial intentions and attitudes among persons belonging to different cultures and ethnicities (Wilson et al., 2004), research has shown that attitudes towards entrepreneurship may also vary by ethnicity (Lindsay, 2005). Several reasons can be argued to explain the potential ethnic differences in a persons' attitude towards entrepreneurship. For instance, certain cultural values may enhance the positive attitudes towards entrepreneurship, as well as provide legitimacy for such attitudes (Davidsson, 1995) and research has shown that Hofstede's cultural dimensions may correlate with certain personal traits which may or may not lead to a positive attitude towards entrepreneurship. For example, it can be argued that individuals who value personal traits such as independence and autonomy, characteristics associated with individualistic societies, will have a more positive attitude towards entrepreneurship than those who do not value these traits. Douglas and Shepherd (2002) noted that the intention to start one's own business appears to be driven by more entrepreneurial attitudes to independence and risk. Likewise, individuals in societies high in uncertainty avoidance may place more emphasis on risk avoidance and would have a less favourable attitude towards entrepreneurship than those from societies with low risk avoidance (Liñán & Chen, 2009). Aharonovitz and Nyaga (2008) found that students from the Kikuyu tribe are expected to be more oriented towards risk-taking, whereas, the other tribes (Kamba, Luo, Luyha) are expected to avoid risk. Given that research has shown that individuals with a high risk-taking propensity are more likely to have a positive attitude towards entrepreneurship (e.g., Lüthje & Franke, 2003), we anticipate that the attitude towards entrepreneurship is greater for Kikuyu students than for any of the other tribes. Another reason for the ethnic differences in personal attitude might as a result of the self-efficacy of group members. Self-efficacy engenders a positive attitude toward entrepreneurship and individuals with high levels of confidence in their skills to start a business are more likely to have a positive attitude towards entrepreneurship. Furthermore, Izquierdo and Buelens (2011) argue that having strong self-efficacy stimulates people's motivation to succeed at a given task which, in turn, can have an effect on their attitudes toward a given object. We speculate that the tribal groups which are more entrepreneurial, in comparison to those that are not, are able to provide their members with the life experiences that can build self-efficacy, including different processes, such as enactive mastery, role modelling, social persuasion and judgments (Bandura 1977). Hence, members of these tribes will have greater confidence in their abilities to pursue entrepreneurship and, by extension, have a more positive attitude towards entrepreneurship. Based on these arguments we hypothesize the following:

> Hypothesis 3a: The effect of attitude on entrepreneurial intentions is different among the Kikuyu, Luo, Kamba and Luhya tribes.

Further, social norms, which are unwritten rules about how to behave, define appropriate behaviour for every social group and can also influence levels of entrepreneurial intention. It is assumed that the social influences on behaviour are more likely to be stronger among tribes that exhibit collectivistic behaviours than tribes which are more individualistic (Walker Courneya, & Deng, 2006; Moriano, Gorgievski, Laguna, Stephan, & Zarafshani, 2011). This is because people from collectivistic cultures are more likely to comply with the expectations of their immediate group (House, Hanges, Javidan, Dorfman, & Gupta, 2004). Thus, the level of conformity to social pressure is expected to differ among the Luhyas, Luos, Kamba and Kikuyu, given their differences in cultural characteristics such as individualism and collectivism. According to Aharonovitz and Nyaga (2008), individuals from the Kikuyu tribe are less altruistic/collaborative than other tribes such as the Kamba, Luo and Luhya, and may therefore rely more on their own beliefs for developing entrepreneurial intention. Consequently, the consideration of the expectation of close others and the motivation to comply with such expectations – in short, their subjective norm – will have a relatively weaker influence on the intention to become an entrepreneur than in more altruistic/collaborative cultures. Krueger et al. (2000) speculated that it is possible that social norms may only be important in ethnic groups that have strong traditions of entrepreneurship. Thus, members of the Kikuyu tribe, which has a culture of business-related activities and which is less rurally oriented than the Luo and the Luhya (Foeken & Owuor, 2001), may feel more social pressure to undertake entrepreneurial activities. Further, another reason why social norms may be important is based on the fact that the prestige that different social norms attribute to occupations can affect occupational choice (Giannetti & Simonov, 2004). Due to the fact that "the prestige that attaches to certain occupations and the lack of respect for others are likewise culturally manipulable" Sudarkasa (1982: 286), we expect certain tribes to hold entrepreneurship in higher esteem than others. Subsequently, we hypothesize:

> Hypothesis 3b: The effect of subjective norms on entrepreneurial intentions varies among the Kikuyu, Luo, Kamba and Luhya tribes.

Lastly, perceived behavioural control is a strong motivational factor that can help enhance entrepreneurial intentions. In past studies, perceived behavioural control has been closely linked to self-efficacy. In fact, according to (Godin & Kok, 1996), self-efficacy is viewed as a notion that is conceptually related to perceived behavioural control. People who exhibit high levels of self-efficacy strongly believe in their ability to complete a job or a specific set of tasks (Bandura 1977). Moreover, differences in self-efficacy may be due to cultural vagaries. Mau (2000) noted that the societies that are more individualistic are more conducive to fostering self-efficacy, while a collective-oriented culture may inhibit the development of self-efficacy. Moreover, in areas where uncertainty avoidance is higher, individuals would feel less capable of coping with the uncertainty of start-ups, even if they have the necessary skills. Thus, perceived behavioral control would be a weaker predictor of entrepreneurial intention in those areas than in areas of lower uncertainty avoidance (Liñán and Chen, 2009). It is argued that individuals with a high risk propensity are likely to anticipate experiencing less debilitating anxiety about an entrepreneurial career, perceive a greater sense of control over outcomes, judge the likelihood of receiving positive rewards more highly, and thus possess higher perceived behavioural control (Zhao et al., 2005). Along this line of reasoning, Kikuyu students who, according to the literature, are more oriented towards taking risks, are expected to have a greater likelihood of pursuing an entrepreneurial career than students from the Kamba, Luhya and Luo tribes because they feel more confident in their ability to be an entrepreneur due to their own competences. Additionally, self-efficacy is developed from several sources, including enactive mastery and role modelling (Bandura, 1977). According to Gushue (2006: 87) "culture may influence the kinds of learning experiences to which a young person has (or is encouraged to seek) access, which affect the development of career self-efficacy beliefs and outcome expectancies." It is assumed that the cultures which are more business-oriented are better able to provide these learning experiences than others. Empirical evidence supporting this argument is provided by Ketter and Arfsten (2015) who found that in Kenya there were significant differences among the ethnic communities in total entrepreneurial self-efficacy, with the Kikuyu participants having the highest scores. On the other hand, it is also possible that individuals from the tribes with more business experience are able to express more realistic perceptions of their control over becoming entrepreneurs due to having greater exposure to business activities. They may be less likely to exhibit overconfidence, which is an unrealistically positive self-evaluation (Greenwald, 1980). Research has shown that overconfidence decreases with experience (e.g., Menkhoff, Schmidt, & Brozynski, 2006). In contrast, it may be that individuals with less experience are more likely to exhibit overconfidence, which replaces lack of information by overestimating ability (Salamouris, 2013). Given these arguments and other evidence, we hypothesize the following:

> Hypothesis 3c: The effect of perceived behavioural control on entrepreneurial intentions varies amomg the Kikuyu, Luo, Kamba and Luhya tribes.

METHODS

Setting and participants

This study was conducted in Kenya in 2014. Given our major objective of identifying ethnic differences in entrepreneurial intentions, the Kenyan setting was appropriate due to its high level of cultural heterogeneity. For the purpose of this study, we investigated whether or not there are differences in entrepreneurial intentions among university students from four of the largest Kenyan tribes: Kamba, Kikuyu, Luhya and Luo. Together, these tribes account for approximately 60% of the Kenyan population. The Kikuyu tribe is the largest ethnic tribe in Kenya, representing about 22% of the country's population. Traditionally, they have enjoyed great economic success, are well educated and have adopted many aspects of modern culture. The Luhya are Kenya's second largest ethnic tribe and they account for 14% of the Kenyan population. Traditionally, they have been linked to agriculture, growing crops like sugarcane, maize and wheat. The Luo tribe is the third largest community in Kenya and makes up close to 13% of the entire population. In the rural area, freshwater fishing in Lake Victoria is the most important economic activity. The Kamba are the fifth largest tribe, accounting for about 11% of Kenya's total population. Traditionally, they have been involved in artistic works (for example, handcrafts) as well as activities such as hunting, farming and pastoralism.

We targeted students at a major Kenyan University. It is worthwhile to use students as a sample in pre-startup entrepreneurship research, given that students show a higher propensity towards firm creation (Liñán & Santos, 2007). De Clercq, Honig, & Martin (2013: 9) argue that "students are ideally suited to the study of entrepreneurial intentions, as opposed to actual entrepreneurial behaviours because reflections on the outcomes that they want to achieve in their future careers are likely in the forefront of their minds; they are relatively homogeneous with respect to their prior work experience; and compared with a general adult sample, they are less likely to have actual entrepreneurial experience – a factor which might confound the level of entrepreneurial intentions." Table 1 depicts the descriptive characteristics of the sample in terms of gender, age, experience, parental income and ethnicity.

Survey Instrument

The survey instrument was developed using as a frame of reference previously validated questionnaires. Before administering the questionnaire, a focus group interview was used to examine the validity of the instrument, in terms of wording, structure and clarity. Respondents' feedback was reincorporated into the survey instrument. We used multi-item measures to examine the study constructs. The use of multi-item measures is in keeping with recommendations by authors such as Nunnally and Bernstein (1994: 67) who note that 'measurement error averages out when individual scores are summed to obtain a total score.' Before the survey instrument was administered, we explained the relevance of the survey and that participation was voluntary. Furthermore, following the work of De Clercq et al. (2013: 10), precautions were taken in order to "minimize bias responses due to social desirability, acquiescence or consistency with 'assumed' research hypotheses." As such, respondents were given the opportunity to complete the survey anonymously. Also, they were guaranteed complete confidentiality and were constantly reminded in the survey instrument to answer the questions as honestly as possible, since there were no wrong or right answers.

Table 1. Descriptive statistics.

		Frequency	Percentage (%)
Gender	Male	261	63.04
	Female	153	36.96
Age	Below 20	37	8.92
	20–25	298	71.81
	Above 25	80	19.28
Exposure	No	148	35.75
	Yes	266	64.25
Parental monthly income	Low	60	15.08
	Middle	80	20.10
	High	258	64.82
Ethnicity	Kamba	73	17.59
	Kikuyu	209	50.36
	Luhya	57	13.73
	Luo	76	18.31

Construct Measures

Dependent variable. Behavioural intention was measured using three items (see Table 2) taken from Kolveried (1996). An average of these items was used to represent the intention index score.

Independent variables. We assessed attitudes towards a career as self-employed by adapting a belief-based scale proposed by (Kolveried, 1996). Our measure included indexes that represent reasons in favour of self-employment (challenge, autonomy and self-realization) and reasons favouring organizational employment (security and avoidance of responsibility). Following Kolvereid's instruction, an indicator attitude was calculated as the numerical difference between the average of the two index scores for self-employment attitude and the average of the two index scores for employment attitude. A high score indicated a favourable attitude towards becoming self-employed.

Subjective norm was measured using six items drawn from Kolveried's (1996) measurement scale. Three items measured the normative belief and three items represented the motivation to comply. Normative beliefs were measured by asking respondents to rate whether persons who are important to them think they should pursue a career as an entrepreneur. Motivation to comply was measured by assessing how willing the respondents were to comply with the wishes of people who are important to them. The overall belief-based measure of subjective norm was calculated by multiplying each participant's normative belief items by their respective motivation to comply items, and then averaging these scores

Perceived behavioural control was measured drawing from a scale developed by (Kolveried, 1996). We used three indicators that took into consideration different aspects of perceived behavioural control (self-efficacy and controllability). Self-efficacy was measured by making reference to perceived difficulty of performing the behaviour, while controllability was assessed by examining the level of control individuals had in enacting the behaviour. A composite score was generated by averaging these items

We also attempted to characterize respondents based on their ethnic/tribal background. For purpose of this study we examined differences among the four most-mentioned ethnic groupings.

Control variables. Age (Kautonen, Tornikoski, & Kibler, 2011; Lévesque & Minniti, 2006), gender (Haus, Steinmetz, Isidor, & Kabst, 2013; Wilson, Kickul, & Marlino, 2007), past exposure to business (e.g., Carr and Sequeira 2007; Kolvereid 1996;) and parental income (Bhandari, 2006; Kothari, 2013; Lindquist, Sol, & Van Praag, 2015) were used as control variables in order to account for two types of potentially confounding factors, those that affect the overall perception and those related to the underlying unobserved heterogeneity of individuals. These variables have been shown to exert direct and indirect effects on entrepreneurial intentions. Age was recorded as a continuous variable. A dummy variable was created to represent gender: male (1) and female (2). Past exposure was recorded as '0' without business exposure and '1' with business exposure. Monthly parental income was classified into three groups, namely in the lower (KSH 10,000 and below), middle (KSH 10,000–30,000) and upper (Above KSH 30,000) income brackets. The income brackets were created with the assistance of key informants embedded in the context. The lower income category was used as the reference category.

Reliability and validity of measures

We tested the reliability of the measurement scale using Cronbach's alpha which provides a measure of the internal consistency (i.e. the extent to which all the items in a test measure the same concept or construct). Additionally, we used Confirmatory Factor Analysis (CFA) to assess the soundness of the factorial structure of the measure (Goethner, Obschonka, Silbereisen, & Cantner, 2009; Kline, 2014). We used both convergent validity and discriminant validity to ensure the substantive validity of the model (Liñán & Chen, 2009). Convergent validity was assessed by examining the composite reliability of constructs and average variance extracted (AVE). Gefen, Straub, and Boudreau (2000) recommend that the composite reliability be higher than 0.70 and Hair, Black, Babin, and Anderson (2009) mention that the AVE should be above the recommended level of 0.50. Additionally, an item with *t*-value > 2.0 also provides evidence of convergent validity (Gerbing & Anderson, 1988). Discriminant validity was assessed looking at correlations. It is accepted that items should correlate more strongly with their own construct than they do with others. This is an indication that they are perceived as belonging to the same theoretical construct (Liñán & Chen, 2009; Messick, 1998). In Table 2, we list the measures used in our analyses, with their individual items, overall reliability estimates (Cronbach's alpha, composite reliability) and average variance extracted (AVE).

Model specification

To estimate our model, we conducted a linear regression analysis. We also used T-tests and Wald tests to check for statistically significant differences among the ethnic groups. Further, a potential dilemma from using five psychological and behaviour variables in a model is the possibility of multicollinearity. Therefore, to reduce the risk of suppressor effect, we tested for multicollinearity via the variance inflation factors (VIF). As a general rule, VIF below 10 indicates multicollinearity is insignificant (Hairs, Anderson, Tatham, & Black, 1998). Other authors, such as Allison (1999) suggest a threshold of 2.40 as the cut-off point beyond which multicollinearity might become an issue. Further, we checked for multicollinearity after running after the OLS regression.

RESULTS

In testing the validity and reliability of our measurement scale, we conducted a confirmatory factor analysis (CFA) using AMOS 21. The result showed factor loadings, greater than 0.40. Furthermore, our measurement model had good fit: $\chi^2 = 204.02$, goodness-of-fit index (GFI) = 0.96, Tucker-Lewis index (TLI) = 0.98, confirmatory fit index (CFI) = 0.98 and root mean squared error of approximation (RMSEA) = 0.03. Convergent validity (CR >.70; AVE >.50; T >2.0) was established (see Table 2). Discriminant validity between the constructs was also established, since the AVE estimates of the constructs are greater than the squared correlations between the corresponding pairs of constructs.

Table 2. Factor loadings, reliability and validity of the constructs.

Construct	Factor Loading	T-value
Entrepreneurial intention (a = 0.85; CR =0.86; AVE = 0.68):		
I am very interested in setting up my own business	0.89	–
I strongly consider setting up my own business	0.93	21.20
I am likely to set up my own business	0.64	14.40
Attitude towards the behaviour		
Security (a = 0.80; CR = 0.82; AVE = 0.70):		
Job security	0.97	–
Job stability	0.69	5.29
Avoid responsibility (a = 0.70; CR = 0.70; AVE = 0.53):		
To avoid responsibility	0.74	–
To not have too much responsibility	0.72	6.12
Challenge (a = 0.76; CR = 0.77; AVE = 0.62):		
To have an exciting job	0.71	–
To have an interesting job	0.86	7.68
Autonomy (a = 0.78; CR = 0.78; AVE = 0.64):		
Freedom	0.76	–
Independence	0.84	8.28
Subjective Norms		
Normative beliefs (a = 0.90; CR = 0 .90; AVE = 0.74):		
My closest family thinks that I should not pursue a career as self-employed.	0.81	–
My closest friends think that I should not pursue a career as self-employed.	0.90	22.94
People who are important to me think that I should not pursue a career as self-employed.	0.81	20.16
Motivation to comply (a = 0.91; CR = 0.90; AVE = 0.76):		
I care a lot about what my closest family thinks about whether or not to pursue a career as self-employed.	0.81	–
I care a lot about what my closest friends think about whether or not to pursue a career as self-employed.	0.92	21.86
I care a lot about what people who are important to me think about whether or not to pursue a career as self-employed.	0.89	21.18
Perceived Behavioural Control (a = 0.76; CR = 0.77; AVE = 0.52):		
If I wanted to, I could easily pursue a career as self-employed.	0.68	–
As self-employed, I would have complete control over my situation.	0.75	11.24
If I become self-employed, the chances of success would be very high.	0.73	11.15

Correlations, means, and standard deviations for all study measures are presented in Table 3. The results indicate that entrepreneurial intentions in this study were correlated with attitude (R = 0.14, $p < 0.01$), perceived behavioural control (R = 0.34, $p < 0.01$) and ethnicity (R = –0.09, $p < 0.10$). Among these significant correlative variables, perceived behavioural control was most important factor correlated with entrepreneurial intentions. In regards to the control variables, gender (R = –0.14, $p < 0.01$),

Table 3. Correlations, Means and Standard Deviations.

	1	2	3	4	5	6	7	8	9	Mean	SD
1. Entrepreneurial intentions	1									4.41	0.77
2. Attitude	0.14***	1								1.57	1.82
3. Subjective norm	−0.03	−0.25***	1							−3.95	14.46
4. Perceived behavioural control	0.34***	0.10*	0.06	1						3.84	0.91
5. Ethnicity	−0.09*	−0.02	0.03	−0.01	1					1.95	1.11
6. Gender	−0.14***	−0.09*	0.08	−0.04	−0.00	1				1.37	0.48
7. Age	0.11**	−0.07	0.19***	−0.00	−0.00	−0.02	1			21.75	2.40
8. Parental monthly income	−0.05	0.07	−0.16***	−0.04	−0.18***	0.07	−0.18***	1		2.50	0.74
9. Past experience	−0.09*	0.22**	−0.35***	−0.10*	−0.01	−0.08	−0.14***	0.14***	1	0.64	0.48

$^{*}p < 0.1$, $^{**}p < 0.05$, $^{***}p < 0.01$

age (R = 0.11, $p < 0.05$) and past business exposure (R = −0.09, $p < 0.10$) were significantly correlated with entrepreneurial intentions. Furthermore, in terms of multicollinearity, no variable violated the 0.40 threshold suggested by statisticians. The variance inflation factors were low (Table 4), alleviating our concerns with regards to multicollinearity.

The linear regression analysis results are shown in Table 5. The control variables were entered in Model 1. Of these, age, income and past business exposure were significant predictors of entrepreneurial intention. Females had lower entrepreneurial intentions than their male counterparts (β = −0.21, $p < 0.05$). Also, entrepreneurial intentions increased as a function of age (β = 0.03, $p < 0.10$). Further, in terms of income, in comparison to the reference group (low income group) individuals from the middle income bracket (β = −0.30, $p < 0.05$) had a lower intent to pursue an entrepreneurial career. Finally, the entrepreneurial intentions of persons who were exposed to business (β = −0.18, $p < 0.05$) was lower than those who did not have business experience.

In Model 2, the three proximal predictors and control variables were fitted. In terms of the controls, the results were similar to Model 1. As it regards the proximal predictors, we found that entrepreneurial intention was positively associated with attitude (β = 0.04, $p < 0.05$) and perceived behavioral control (β = 0.29, $p < 0.01$); hence, Hypotheses 1 and 3 were fully supported. In other words, the higher the attitude and perceived behavioural control with respect to entrepreneurship, the stronger is the students' intention to become entrepreneurs.

In Model 3, we tested the effect of ethnicity. In comparison to the Kikuyu tribe (reference group), students from the Luhya tribe (β = −0.24, $p < 0.05$) had lower entrepreneurial intention, after accounting for our control variables and controlling for the proximal variables (attitude, subjective norms and perceived behavioural control). The results indicate the possibility that significant differences exist in the entrepreneurial intentions of the ethnic groups. Thus, in order to verify such differences, we ran a two-sample *t*-test. The result of this analysis is presented in Table 6. While we saw differences, in most cases they were not statistically significant. However, we did find a significant difference in entrepreneurial intentions when comparing the

Table 4. Multicollinearity Analysis.

Variable	VIF	1/VIF
Attitude	1.12	0.89
Subjective norm	1.23	0.81
Perceived behavioral control	1.05	0.95
Luo	1.14	0.88
Kamba	1.17	0.85
Luhya	1.12	0.89
Female	1.03	0.97
Age	1.08	0.93
Middle income	1.95	0.51
High income	2.04	0.49
Exposure to business	1.21	0.82
Mean VIF	1.29	

Table 5. OLS regression results (Dependent variable = Entrepreneurial intentions).

	Model 1		Model 2		Model 3	
Female	−0.205**	[0.080]	−0.148*	[0.076]	−0.153**	[0.076]
Age	0.029*	[0.016]	0.036**	[0.015]	0.034**	[0.015]
Middle income	−0.304**	[0.134]	−0.216*	[0.126]	−0.232*	[0.125]
High income	−0.117	[0.114]	−0.089	[0.107]	−0.131	[0.108]
Exposure to business	−0.182**	[0.083]	−0.195**	[0.082]	−0.188**	[0.082]
Attitude			0.043**	[0.021]	0.041**	[0.021]
Subjective norms			−0.004	[0.003]	−0.004	[0.003]
Percieved behavioral control			0.285***	[0.041]	0.282***	[0.041]
Luo					−0.154	[0.100]
Kamba					−0.111	[0.101]
Luhya					−0.239**	[0.113]
Constant	4.105***	[0.396]	2.720***	[0.412]	2.874***	[0.417]
Pseudo LL	−451.179		−422.482		−419.534	
N	393		393		393	
DF	5		8		11	

*p < 0.10, **p < 0.05, ***p < 001

Kikuyu and Luhya tribes This result, in part, confirms our suspicions that there are ethnic differences in the level of entrepreneurial intentions.

Lastly, we wanted to test whether the effect of attitude, subjective norms and perceived behavioural control differ across groups (Hypothesis 3a, 3b and 3c, respectively). We ran a separate regression analysis for each ethnic group. The results are summarized in Table 7. From the results, it appears that the effects of the three proximal predictors are fairly uniform across the ethnic groups. Neither attitude nor subjective norms predicted entrepreneurial intentions. On the other hand, perceived behavioural control was a strong predictor of entrepreneurial intention among all

Table 6. The t-test of paired tribal groups on intentions.

	N	Mean	Mean Diff.
Kikuyu	209	4.480	0.147
Luo	76	4.333	
Kikuyu	209	4.480	0.051
Kamba	73	4.429	
Kikuyu	209	4.480	0.246**
Luhya	57	4.234	
Luo	76	4.333	−0.096
Kamba	73	4.429	
Luo	76	4.330	0.009
Luhya	57	4.234	
Kamba	73	4.429	0.195
Luhya	57	4.234	

*p < 0.10, **p < 0.05, ***p < 001

Table 7. OLS regression results (Dependent variable = Entrepreneurial intentions).

	Kikuyu		Luo		Kamba		Luhya	
	β	SD	β	SD	B	SD	β	SD
Female	−0.08	[0.11]	−0.07	[0.22]	−0.16	[0.15]	−0.51**	[0.25]
Age	0.04*	[0.02]	0.04	[0.05]	0.10**	[0.04]	0.02	[0.04]
Middle income	−0.08	[0.22]	−0.59**	[0.29]	−0.26	[0.20]	0.04	[0.36]
High income	0.06	[0.18]	−0.50*	[0.26]	−0.13	[0.20]	−0.13	[0.31]
Exposure to business	−0.28**	[0.12]	−0.19	[0.23]	0.20	[0.17]	−0.44*	[0.26]
Attitude	0.01	[0.03]	0.07	[0.05]	0.06	[0.05]	0.00	[0.07]
Subjective norms	−0.00	[0.00]	−0.01	[0.01]	−0.01	[0.01]	−0.00	[0.01]
Perceived behavioral control	0.21***	[0.06]	0.28***	[0.10]	0.39***	[0.10]	0.42***	[0.12]
Constant	3.01***	[0.60]	2.88**	[1.31]	0.76	[0.91]	2.74**	[1.052]
Pseudo LL	−209.52		−78.62		−57.66		−56.66	
N	199		71		71		52	
DF	8		8		8		8	

*$p < 0.1$, **$p < 0.05$, ***$p < 0.01$

Table 8. The Wald test of paired tribal groups on intentions.

	Kikuya vs Luo	Kikuyu vs Kamba	Kikuyu vs Luhya	Luo vs Kamba	Luo vs Luhya	Kamba vs Luhya
Attitude	1.44	0.83	0.01	0.05	1.20	0.75
Subjective norms	0.21	0.23	0.00	0.01	0.12	0.10
Percieved behavioral control	0.25	2.82*	2.00	0.75	0.74	0.04
Female	0.00	0.20	3.17*	0.11	2.01	1.89
Age	0.00	1.90	0.20	1.08	0.13	2.42
Middle income	3.29*	0.55	0.10	1.26	2.20	0.57
High income	7.17***	0.98	0.30	3.27*	1.15	0.00
Exposure to business	0.15	6.00**	0.48	2.49	0.79	6.25**

*$p < 0.10$, **$p < 0.05$, ***$p < 001$

the ethnic groups ($\beta = 0.21, p < 0.01$; $\beta = 0.28, p < 0.01$; $\beta = 0.39, p < 0.01$ and $\beta = 0.42$, $p < 0.01$ for the Kikuyu, Lou, Kamba and Luhya tribes, respectively). Interestingly, the results also hinted at the possibility of differences in the effects of the control variables. Given that apparent differences in coefficients across groups may be due to sample variability, we performed a more formal test (Wald test). The results (see Table 8) show that although the effects of the proximal predictors are fairly stable across the ethnic groups, slight differences do exist. For example, the effect of perceived behavioural control was different when comparing the Kikuyu and Kamba tribes ($\chi^2 = 2.82, p < 0.10$). Further, the Wald test confirmed that the effects of the control variables are dissimilar among the ethnic groups. The coefficient for female is significantly different for the Kikuyu and Kamba tribes ($\chi^2 = 3.17, p < 0.10$). Further, the pairwise comparison of Kikuyu and Luo show that the coefficients for middle income ($\chi^2 = 3.29, p < 0.10$) and high income ($\chi^2 = 7.17, p < 0.01$) are different. Lastly, the coefficient for exposure to business is dissimilar in two cases: between the Kikuyu and Kamba ($\chi^2 = 6.00, p < 0.05$) and Kamba and Luhya ($\chi^2 = 6.25, p < 0.05$).

DISCUSSION

The results of the study demonstrate the use of the theory of planned behaviour to measure entrepreneurial intentions in a culturally heterogeneous society, and also provide a warning regarding variations according to sub-cultural relationships. Attitude and perceived behavioural control are significant predictors of, and positively related to, entrepreneurial intent. The result is consistent with a growing number of studies which have shown attitude and perceived behavioural control as a predictors of entrepreneurial intention in the African setting (e.g., Ayuo & Kubasu, 2014; Gird & Bagraim, 2008; Malebana, 2014).

Another finding of this article is that the role of subjective norms appears insignificant, which is inconsistent with previous studies conducted in a similar setting (e.g., Ayuo & Kubasu, 2014; Kilonzo & Nyambegera, 2014). Our findings do not represent a disconfirmation of the theory of planned behaviour model, but suggest that entrepreneurial intention, in our case, is not primarily under normative control. It may be that the influence of subjective norms may be indirect, through its modification of both the attitude and perceived behavioural control constructs (Liñán & Chen, 2009). Moreover, in the opinion of Krueger et al. (2000) in the minds of subjects, social norms can be hopelessly confounded with other attitudes (attitude toward the act and perceived feasibility). The relative importance of attitude, subjective norm and perceived behavioural control in the prediction of intention, is expected to vary, depending on the behaviour in question and its context (Ajzen, 1991).

In terms of the direct effect of ethnicity on entrepreneurial intentions, studies by authors such as Mungai (2013) fail to confirm the hypothesis that there are significant differences in entrepreneurial intentions between different indigenous ethnic groups. Our research, on the other hand, demonstrates that entrepreneurial intentions vary based on ethnicity. More specifically, in our study, the Luhya and Luo tribes were less likely to have entrepreneurial intentions when compared with the Kikuyu tribe. Such findings are partially expected, given that the Kikuyu tribe has been cited as being more entrepreneurial than the others (Elkan, 1988; Mungai, 2013).

Finally, our result showed that the effects of attitude, subjective norms and perceived behavioural control appear fairly similar across ethnic groups. Hence, our result partially verifies the generalizability of the intention model (Krueger 2000). However, this result may be driven by the fact that university students may develop a culture of their own, which is different from that of their tribal grouping (Mungai, 2013). Interestingly, we also detected a slight difference in the effect of perceived behavioural control, which suggests that the antecedents to intentions may be modified by ethnic variations. Moreover, contrary to our expectations, the effect of perceived behavioural control on the intention to be entrepreneurs was stronger in the Kamba students than for the Kikuyu students. A possible explanation may lie in the fact that students from the Kikuyu tribe, in comparison with those of the Kamba tribe, expressed a more realistic perception of their control over becoming entrepreneurs asa result of having had greater exposure to business activities. They were less likely to exhibit overconfidence, which is an unrealistically positive self-evaluation (Greenwald, 1980). Research has shown that overconfidence decreases with experience (e.g., Menkhoff, Schmidt, & Brozynski, 2006). In contrast, it seems that the Kamba students are more likely to exhibit overconfidence, which replaces lack of information by overestimating ability (Salamouris, 2013).

Implications

We specifically tested the cross-ethnic generalizability of the theory of planned behavior. Our result provides further evidence for the utility of the theory of planned behaviour in predicting entrepreneurial intention in our setting. In general, the attitude and perceived behavioural control constructs appear to have the potential to explain the variance in students' entrepreneurial intention. These findings are consistent with prior research, suggesting the importance of a having a positive attitude towards entrepreneurship as well as the perception that the task is achievable through one's own effort.

While our findings seem to suggest that the use of the theory of planned behaviour is possible in culturally heterogeneous settings, the fact remains that attitude, subjective norms and perceived behavioural control explained a limited proportion of variance in the regression models. Thus, the addition of other variables to the model may improve its predictive capability. Further, our study shows that there exist differences in the entrepreneurial intentions of the ethnic groups, even as the effects of attitude, subjective and perceived behavioural control are, in general, uniform across groups. Again, this result suggests that other contextual elements may be exerting an effect on entrepreneurial intentions. In our case, for example, we see that gender, income and past exposure to entrepreneurship may account for some of the differences in intention among the tribes. Given these findings, we caution against adopting measure of intentions that rely solely on the proximal predictors. Instead, we argue that it may be necessary to consider the effect of deeper structural elements of society when undertaking intentions research. Ajzen (2014) argues that the theory of planned behaviour does not preclude the inclusion of other variables and that unless perfectly reliable and valid measures are used to measure attitude, subjective norm and perceived behavioral control, it is possible that the additional variables will b`e identified. However, like O'Keefe (2002), we caution against abstractly adding new predictors to the theory of planned behavior framework and suggest that researchers consider the five criteria proposed by Ajzen (2011) for including other explanatory variables.

In terms of culture, we detected differences in the effect of perceived behavioural control. In settings where there is substantial cultural heterogeneity (i.e. at the ethnicity and acculturation levels), ethnic aggregation may mask considerable variation in culture and values within particular subgroups. This variation, in turn, may have implications for any potential association with economic behaviour. Therefore, any study that fails to account for sub-national variations may run the risk of producing skewed results. We believe that at the very least, it is necessary to identify the appropriate level of specificity when measuring entrepreneurial intention. For instance, Mungai and Ogot (2012) suggest that in the majority of sub-Saharan countries, ethnic cultures play a more dominant role in moulding the values and perceptions of its citizens than national cultures. Therefore, an understanding of intra-societal ethnic differences may be equally or even more important than identifying national variations, especially as those interested in using entrepreneurship as a development tool attempt to provide targeted programs intended to motivate new venture creation.

On a more practical side, the research has implications for stakeholders interested in encouraging self-employment among students. As attitude and perceived behavioural control are significant predictors of intention to start a new business, it is important that stakeholders who are looking to promote entrepreneurship among students understand the factors that influence the attitude of students toward the creation of new ventures, as well as gain better insight into the conditions necessary to build perceptions of self-efficacy and controllability. Moreover, special attention should be paid to the ethnicity of the target population, given the differences between ethnic groups with regard to entrepreneurial intentions. Culturally 'tailor-made' interventions that take these differences into consideration are warranted.

Limitations and future studies

First, the use of a cross-sectional design weakens our ability to prove causality between our predictor and outcome variables; as such, a longitudinal approach would have been better suited for our study. Future research should adopt a longitudinal approach in order to prove causality as well as strengthen the explanatory power of the model. Second, we only focused on the attitude, subjective norm, and perceived behavioural control–intention relationship. While intentions are an important step in the process of pursuing entrepreneurial action, it is vital that future research moves beyond the antecedents to intentions, and examines the intention–behaviour side of the model, especially as it relates to the conditions necessary to translate intentions into action. Lastly, while it was not our aim to test all possible exogenous factors affecting entrepreneurial intention, the fact that a large portion of the variance in entrepreneurial intention remains unexplained may be a signal that other relevant exogenous variables were omitted. It would be useful to examine other salient variables that could improve the predictive power of the theory of planned behaviour, for example, social capital and self-efficacy. However, such variables must be examined taking into consideration Ajzen's criteria for including additional predictors. Additionally, given our results, it is important that future research evaluate moderators of the theory of planned behaviour relationships and identify how the theory's predictors perform under different contextual situations.

ACKNOWLEDGEMENTS

This work was supported by the Joint Doctorate Program, funded by the EACEA (Education, Audiovisual and Culture Executive Agency) of the European Commission under Grant AGTRAIN agreement number 2011 - 0019.

ORCiD

Ian K. Alexander http://orcid.org/0000-0002-7708-1393

References

Aharonovitz, G., & Nyaga, E. K. (2008). *Values and Economic Performance: Theory and some Evidence from Kenya* (Working Paper Series WP 2008-18). Washington: School of Economic Sciences, Washington State University.

Ajzen, I. (1991). The theory of planned behavior. *Organizational Behavior and Human Decision Processes*, *50*(2), 179–211. http://dx.doi.org/10.1016/0749-5978(91)90020-T

Ajzen, I. (2002). Perceived behavioral control, self-efficacy, locus of control, and the theory. *International Journal of Entrepreneurial Behaviour & Research*, 4(1), 28–50.

Aldrich, H. E., & Waldinger, R. (1990). Ethnicity and entrepreneurship. *Annual Review of Sociology*, *16*(1), 111–135. http://dx.doi.org/10.1146/annurev.so.16.080190.000551

Allison, P. (1999). *Logistic regression using the SAS system: theory and application*. Cary, NC: SAS Institute Inc.

Autio, E., Keeley, R., Klofsten, M., Parker, G., & Hay, M. (2001). Entrepreneurial intent among students in Scandinavia and in the USA. *Enterprise and Innovation Management Studies*, *2*(2), 145–160. http://dx.doi.org/10.1080/14632440110094632

Ayuo, A., & Kubasu, A. (2014). Theory of planned behaviour, contextual elements, demographic factors and entrepreneurial intentions of students in Kenya. *European Journal of Business and Management*, 6(15), 167–175.

Bandura, A. (2001). Social cognitive theory: An agentic perspective. *Annual Review of Psychology*, *52*(1), 1–26. http://dx.doi.org/10.1146/annurev.psych.52.1.1

Baumol, W. J. (1996). Entrepreneurship: Productive, unproductive, and destructive. *Journal of Business Venturing*, *11*(1), 3–22. http://dx.doi.org/10.1016/0883-9026(94)00014-X

Bhandari, N. C. (2006). Intention for entrepreneurship among students in India. *The Journal of Entrepreneurship*, *15*(2), 169–179. http://dx.doi.org/10.1177/097135570601500204

Bochner, S., & Hesketh, B. (1994). Power distance, individualism/collectivism, and job-related attitudes in a culturally diverse work group. *Journal of Cross-Cultural Psychology*, *25*(2), 233–257. http://dx.doi.org/10.1177/0022022194252005

Carr, J. C., & Sequeira, J. M. (2007). Prior family business exposure as intergenerational influence and entrepreneurial intent: A theory of planned behavior approach. *Journal of Business Research*, *60*(10), 1090–1098. http://dx.doi.org/10.1016/j.jbusres.2006.12.016

Dana, L. P. (1995). Entrepreneurship in a remote sub-Arctic community. *Entrepreneurship Theory and Practice*, 20(1), 57–72.

Davidsson, P. (1995). Culture, structure and regional levels of entrepreneurship. *Entrepreneurship & Regional Development*, 7(1), 41–62. http://dx.doi.org/10.1080/08985629500000003

De Clercq, D., Honig, B., & Martin, B. (2013). The roles of learning orientation and passion for work in the formation of entrepreneurial intention. *International Small Business Journal*, *31* (6), 652–676. http://dx.doi.org/10.1177/0266242611432360

Díaz-García, M. C., & Jiménez-Moreno, J. (2010). Entrepreneurial intention: The role of gender. *The International Entrepreneurship and Management Journal*, *6*(3), 261–283. http://dx.doi.org/10.1007/s11365-008-0103-2

Douglas, E. J., & Shepherd, D. A. (2002). Self-employment as a career choice: Attitudes, entrepreneurial intentions, and utility maximization. *Entrepreneurial Theory and Practice*, 26(3), 81–90.

Elkan, W. (1988). Entrepreneurs and entrepreneurship in Africa. *The World Bank Research Observer*, *3*(2), 171–188. http://dx.doi.org/10.1093/wbro/3.2.171

Engle, R. L., Dimitriadi, N., Gavidia, J. V., Schlaegel, C., Delanoe, S., Alvarado, I., … Wolff, B. (2010). Entrepreneurial intent: A twelve-country evaluation of Ajzen's model of planned behavior. *International Journal of Entrepreneurial Behaviour & Research*, *16*(1), 35–57. http://dx.doi.org/10.1108/13552551011020063

Foeken, D. & Owuor. S. O. 2001. *Multi-spatial livelihoods in sub-Saharan Africa: Rural farming by urban households – The case of Nakuru town*, Kenya. Mobile Africa: Changing patterns of movement in Africa and beyond 1, 125–140.

Gefen, D., Straub, D., & Boudreau, M.-C. (2000). Structural equation modeling and regression: Guidelines for research practice. *Communications of the Association for Information Systems*, 4(7), 1–70.

Gerbing, D. W., & Anderson, J. C. (1988). An updated paradigm for scale development incorporating unidimensionality and its assessment. *JMR, Journal of Marketing Research*, *25*(2), 186–192. http://dx.doi.org/10.2307/3172650

Giannetti, M., & Simonov, A. (2004). On the determinants of entrepreneurial activity: Social norms, economic environment and individual characteristics. *Swedish Economic Policy Review*, 11(2), 269–313.

Gird, A., & Bagraim, J. J. (2008). The theory of planned behaviour as predictor of entrepreneurial intent amongst final-year university students. *South African Journal of Psychology. Suid-Afrikaanse Tydskrif vir Sielkunde*, *38*(4), 711–724. http://dx.doi.org/10.1177/008124630803800410

Godin, G. & Kok, G. (1996). The theory of planned behavior: A review of its applications to health-related behaviors. *American Journal of Health Promotion*, 11(2): 87–98.

Goethner, M., Obschonka, M., Silbereisen, R. K., & Cantner, U. (2009). *Approaching the agora: Determinants of scientists' intentions to purse academic entrepreneurship* (Working Paper 2009.079). Jena, Germany: School of Business Economics, Friedrich Schiller University.

Greenwald, A. G. (1980). The totalitarian ego: Fabrication and revision of personal history. *The American Psychologist*, *35*(7), 603–618. http://dx.doi.org/10.1037/0003-066X.35.7.603

Gushue, G. V. (2006). The relationship of ethnic identity, career decision-making self-efficacy and outcome expectations among Latino/a high school students. *Journal of Vocational Behavior*, *68*(1), 85–95. http://dx.doi.org/10.1016/j.jvb.2005.03.002

Hair, J. F., Black, W. C., Babin, B. J., & Anderson, R. E. (2009). *Multivariate data analysis: A global perspective* (7th ed.). USA: Pearson.

Hairs, J. F., Anderson, R. E., Tatham, R. L., & Black, W. C. (1998). *Multivariate data analysis*. Englewood Cliffs, NJ: Printice Hall.

Hansen, J. D., Deitz, G. D., Tokman, M., Marino, L. D., & Weaver, K. M. (2011). Cross-national invariance of the entrepreneurial orientation scale. *Journal of Business Venturing*, *26*(1), 61–78. http://dx.doi.org/10.1016/j.jbusvent.2009.05.003

Haus, I., Steinmetz, H., Isidor, R., & Kabst, R. (2013). Gender effects on entrepreneurial intention: A meta-analytical structural equation model. *International Journal of Gender and Entrepreneurship, 5*(2), 130–156. http://dx.doi.org/10.1108/17566261311328828
Hirschman, C. (1982). Immigrants and minorities: Old questions for new directions in research. *The International Migration Review, 16*(2), 474–490. http://dx.doi.org/10.2307/2545107
Hofstede, G. (2001). *Culture's consequences: Comparing values, behaviors, institutions and organizations across nations.* Thousand Oaks, CA: Sage Publications.
House, R. J., Hanges, P. W., Javidan, M., Dorfman, P., & Gupta, V. (2004). *Culture, Leadership and Organizations: The GLOBE Study of 62 Societies.* Thousand Oaks, CA: Sage.
Iakovleva, T., Kolvereid, L., & Stephan, U. (2011). Entrepreneurial intentions in developing and developed countries. *Education + Training, 53*(5), 353–370. http://dx.doi.org/10.1108/00400911111147686
Izquierdo, E., & Buelens, M. (2011). Competing models of entrepreneurial intentions: The influence of entrepreneurial self-efficacy and attitudes. *International Journal of Entrepreneurship and Small Business, 13*(1), 75–91. http://dx.doi.org/10.1504/IJESB.2011.040417
Kautonen, T., Tornikoski, E. T., & Kibler, E. (2011). Entrepreneurial intentions in the third age: The impact of perceived age norms. *Small Business Economics, 37*(2), 219–234. http://dx.doi.org/10.1007/s11187-009-9238-y
Ketter, C. K., & Arfsten, M. C. (2015). Culture and entrepreneurial self-efficacy in Kenya. *International Business Research, 8*(3), 99–111. http://dx.doi.org/10.5539/ibr.v8n3p99
Kibler, E. (2013). Formation of entrepreneurial intentions in a regional context. *Entrepreneurship and Regional Development*, 25(3–4), 293–323. http://dx.doi.org/10.1080/08985626.2012.721008
Kilonzo, P. M., & Nyambegera, S. M. (2014). Determinants of entrepreneurial intention among university business students in Kenya: Lessons from Kenyatta University. *International Journal of Entrepreneurship and Small Business, 22*(2), 231–250. http://dx.doi.org/10.1504/IJESB.2014.062503
Kline, P. (2014). *An easy guide to factor analysis.* London: Routledge.
Kolvereid, L. (1996). 'Organizational employment versus self-employment: Reasons for career choice intentions. *Entrepreneurship Theory and Practice*, 20(3), 23–31.
Kothari, H. C. (2013). Impact of contextual factors on entrepreneurial intention. *International Journal of Engineering and Management Research*, 3(6), 76–82.
Kristiansen, S., & Indarti, N. (2004). Entrepreneurial intention among Indonesian and Norwegian students. *Journal of Enterprising Culture, 12*(1), 55–78. http://dx.doi.org/10.1142/S021849580400004X
Krueger, N. F., & Carsrud, A. L. (1993). Entrepreneurial intentions: Applying the theory of planned behaviour. *Entrepreneurship and Regional Development, 5*(4), 315–330. http://dx.doi.org/10.1080/08985629300000020
Krueger, N., Liñán, F., & Nabi, G. (2013). Cultural values and entrepreneurship. *Entrepreneurship and Regional Development*, 25(9–10), 703–707. http://dx.doi.org/10.1080/08985626.2013.862961
Krueger, N. F.Jr., Reilly, M. D., & Carsrud, A. L. (2000). Competing models of entrepreneurial intentions. *Journal of Business Venturing*, 15(5–6), 411–432. http://dx.doi.org/10.1016/S0883-9026(98)00033-0
Kwok, S., & Uncles, M. (2005). Sales promotion effectiveness: The impact of consumer differences at an ethnic-group level. *Journal of Product and Brand Management, 14*(3), 170–186. http://dx.doi.org/10.1108/10610420510601049
Lévesque, M., & Minniti, M. (2006). The effect of aging on entrepreneurial behavior. *Journal of Business Venturing, 21*(2), 177–194. http://dx.doi.org/10.1016/j.jbusvent.2005.04.003
LeVine, R. A., Strangman, E., & Unterberger, L. (1966). *Dreams and deeds: Achievement motivation in Nigeria.* Chicago: University of Chicago Press.
Liñán, F., & Chen, Y. W. (2009). Development and Cross-Cultural application of a specific instrument to measure entrepreneurial intentions. *Entrepreneurship Theory and Practice, 33* (3), 593–617. http://dx.doi.org/10.1111/j.1540-6520.2009.00318.x

Liñán, F., & Santos, F. J. (2007). Does social capital affect entrepreneurial intentions? *International Advances in Economic Research*, 13(4), 443–453. http://dx.doi.org/10.1007/s11294-007-9109-8

Liñán, F., Urbano, D., & Guerrero, M. (2011). Regional variations in entrepreneurial cognitions: Start-up intentions of university students in Spain. *Entrepreneurship and Regional Development*, 23(3–4), 187–215. http://dx.doi.org/10.1080/08985620903233929

Lindquist, M. J., Sol, J., & Van Praag, M. (2015). Why do entrepreneurial parents have entrepreneurial children? *Journal of Labor Economics*, 33(2), 269–296. http://dx.doi.org/10.1086/678493

Lindsay, N. J. (2005). Toward a cultural model of indigenous entrepreneurial attitude. *Journal of the Academy of Marketing Science*, 5, 1–17.

Lüthje, C., & Franke, N. (2003). The 'making' of an entrepreneur: Testing a model of entrepreneurial intent among engineering students at MIT. *R & D Management*, *33*(2), 135–147. http://dx.doi.org/10.1111/1467-9310.00288

Malebana, J. (2014). Entrepreneurial intentions of South African rural university students: A test of the theory of planned behaviour. *Journal of Economics and Behavioral Studies*, 6(2), 130–143.

Manolova, T. S., Eunni, R. V., & Gyoshev, B. S. (2008). Institutional environments for entrepreneurship: Evidence from emerging economies in Eastern Europe. *Entrepreneurship Theory and Practice*, *32*(1), 203–218. http://dx.doi.org/10.1111/j.1540-6520.2007.00222.x

Marris, P. (1968). The social barriers to African entrepreneurship. *The Journal of Development Studies*, *5*(1), 29–38. http://dx.doi.org/10.1080/00220386808421279

Mau, W. (2000). Cultural differences in career decision-making styles and self-efficacy. *Journal of Vocational Behavior*, *57*(3), 365–378. http://dx.doi.org/10.1006/jvbe.1999.1745

Menkhoff, L., Schmidt, U., & Brozynski, T. (2006). The impact of experience on risk taking, overconfidence, and herding of fund managers: Complementary survey evidence. *European Economic Review*, *50*(7), 1753–1766. http://dx.doi.org/10.1016/j.euroecorev.2005.08.001

Messick, S. (1998). Test validity: A matter of consequence. *Social Indicators Research*, *45*(1), 35–44. http://dx.doi.org/10.1023/A:1006964925094

Moriano, J. A., Gorgievski, M., Laguna, M., Stephan, U., & Zarafshani, K. (2011). A cross-cultural approach to understanding entrepreneurial intention. *Journal of Career Development*, 38 (1), 1–24.

Mueller, S. L., & Thomas, A. S. (2001). Culture and entrepreneurial potential: A nine country study of locus of control and innovativeness. *Journal of Business Venturing*, *16*(1), 51–75. http://dx.doi.org/10.1016/S0883-9026(99)00039-7

Mungai, E. N. (2013). *Socio-cultural Factors and Entrepreneurial Intentions of Undergraduate Students in Public Universities in Kenya* (Doctoral dissertation, University of Nairobi, Kenya).

Mungai, E. N., & Ogot, M. 2012. Gender, culture and entrepreneurship in Kenya. *International Business Research*, 5(5): 175–183. http://dx.doi.org/10.5539/ibr.v5n5p175

Noorderhaven, N., Thurik, R., Wennekers, S., & Stel, A. (2004). The role of dissatisfaction and per capita income in explaining self-employment across 15 European countries. *Entrepreneurship Theory and Practice*, 28(5): 447–466.

Nunnally, I. H., & Bernstein, J. C. (1994). *Psychometric theory* (3rd ed.). New York: McGraw-Hill.

O'Keefe, D.J. (2002). *Persuasion: Theory and research*. Beverly Hills, CA: Sage Publications.

Portes, A., & Rumbaut, R. G. (2006). *Immigrant America: a portrait*. California, USA: University of California Press.

Pruett, M., Shinnar, R., Toney, B., Llopis, F., & Fox, J. (2009). Explaining entrepreneurial intentions of university students: A cross-cultural study. *International Journal of Entrepreneurial Behaviour & Research*, *15*(6), 571–594. http://dx.doi.org/10.1108/13552550910995443

Salamouris, I. S. (2013). How overconfidence influences entrepreneurship. *Journal of Innovation and Entrepreneurship*, 2(8), 1–6. http://dx.doi.org/10.1186/2192-5372-2-8

Schlaegel, C., He, X., & Engle, R. L. (2013). The direct and indirect influences of national culture on entrepreneurial intentions: A fourteen nation study. *International Journal of Management*, 30(2), 597–609.

Sudarkasa, N. (1982). Sex roles, education, and development in Africa. *Anthropology & Education Quarterly*, *13*(3), 279–288. http://dx.doi.org/10.1525/aeq.1982.13.3.05×0987y
Urban, B., Van Vuuren, J. J., & Owen, R. H. (2008). Anticedents to entrepreneurial intentions: Testing for measurement invariance for cultural values, attitudes and self-efficacy beliefs across ethnic groups. *SA Journal of Human Resource Management*, *6*(1), 1–9. http://dx.doi.org/10.4102/sajhrm.v6i1.132
Valdez, M. E., & Richardson, J. (2013). Institutional determinants of macro-level entrepreneurship. *Entrepreneurship Theory and Practice*, *37*(5), 1149–1175. http://dx.doi.org/10.1111/etap.12000
Walker, G. J., Courneya, K. S., & Deng, J. (2006). Ethnicity, gender, and the Theory of Planned Behavior: The case of playing the lottery. *Journal of Leisure Research*, 38, 224–248.
Wilson, F., Kickul, J., & Marlino, D. (2007). Gender, entrepreneurial Self-Efficacy, and entrepreneurial career intentions: Implications for entrepreneurship Education1. *Entrepreneurship Theory and Practice*, *31*(3), 387–406. http://dx.doi.org/10.1111/j.1540-6520.2007.00179.x
Wilson, F., Marlino, D., & Kickul, J. (2004). Our entrepreneurial future: Examining the diverse attitudes and motivations of teens across gender and ethnic identity. *Journal of Developmental Entrepreneurship*, 9(3), 177–197.
Zhao, H., Seibert, S. E., & Hills, G. E. (2005). The mediating role of self-efficacy in the development of entrepreneurial intentions. *The Journal of Applied Psychology*, *90*(6), 1265–1272. http://dx.doi.org/10.1037/0021-9010.90.6.1265

ENTREPRENEURIAL OPPORTUNITIES AND POVERTY IN SUB-SAHARAN AFRICA: A REVIEW & AGENDA FOR THE FUTURE

Jacob A. L. Vermeire and Garry D. Bruton

Entrepreneurship, with its focus on opportunities, is often seen as one of the cornerstones of poverty alleviation in sub-Saharan Africa (SSA). However, evidence for the positive impact of entrepreneurship programs on poverty is mixed and now widely debated. Therefore, scholars have called for a better theoretical understanding of opportunities in SSA in the face of severe resource constraints that characterize the region. In this paper, we aim to shed further light on this issue and outline an agenda for future research. To this end, we first review the current literature on opportunities (discovered and created) and poverty (income-based and capabilities-based). We next employ four case examples of poor entrepreneurs in SSA that challenge assumptions from Western entrepreneurship theories and illustrate what could be fruitful avenues for future research on entrepreneurial opportunities and poverty in SSA.

INTRODUCTION

Scholars view opportunity as a core element of entrepreneurship (Venkataraman, 1997). Despite the scholarly interest that opportunities have received (e.g. Busenitz, Plummer, Klotz, Shahzad, & Rhoads, 2014; Davidsson, 2015), our understanding remains largely limited to those opportunities that can be created or discovered in developed market economies. Researchers have started to argue that entrepreneurship theory from developed economies are impacted by boundary conditions in developing economies that will, in turn, affect our understanding of the overall theory (Reid, Roumpi, & O'Leary-Kelly, 2015; West, Bamford, & Marsden, 2008). This could particularly be the case for entrepreneurial opportunity since the lack of access to capital and established institutions in settings of extreme poverty in many developing economies can preclude the poor from pursuing entrepreneurship in the same manner that is understood in mature economies (Bradley, McMullen, Artz, & Simiyu, 2012). In this paper we will examine what is understood about opportunities (discovered and created) in mature economies and then consider the boundary conditions of poverty and its implications for entrepreneurship. We will focus specifically on opportunities and poverty in the setting of sub-Saharan Africa (SSA) in order to contextualize this understanding. We will ground the development of a research agenda for SSA through case examples from the region.

Sub-Saharan Africa today is widely seen as the "last frontier" of the global economy and a centre of great entrepreneurial opportunity (Economist, 2013; Moghalu, 2014). The setting of abundant natural resources, for example minerals (KPMG, 2013), a highly motivated population, plus an absence of established firms to provide jobs is driving entrepreneurship among the youth in SSA (Kew, 2014). The result is that it is widely argued by scholars and others that part of the solution to the high level of poverty in SSA is entrepreneurship (Herrington & Kelley, 2012; Khavul, Bruton, & Wood, 2009). The World Bank highlights that 389 million people in SSA, which is 43% of the total population, currently live below the international poverty line of US$1.90 a day, the highest concentration of extreme poor in the world (Beegle, Christiaensen, Dabalen, & Gaddis, 2016). Thus, SSA offers a good setting to build an understanding of how opportunity discovery and creation changes in a setting that is characterized by severe constraints, meeting the call for more attention to the impact of such contextual elements on the entrepreneurial process (Webb, Tihanyi, Ireland, & Sirmon, 2009). Additionally, an examination of entrepreneurial opportunities in this setting responds to the call to build further understanding of how entrepreneurship can contribute to the alleviation of poverty (Bruton, Ketchen, & Ireland, 2013; Kodithuwakku & Rosa, 2002).

In summary, this research contributes to the existing literature in three important ways. First, it makes a theoretical contribution to the understanding of how severe resource constraints impact the boundary conditions of the concept of entrepreneurial opportunity. Second, and in turn, it contributes to a greater understanding of how entrepreneurship can help to solve the issue of poverty. We will, in particular, expand this understanding of entrepreneurship as a solution to poverty in light of the severely limited institutional development of the market economy that characterizes SSA in general. Finally, we contribute to the understanding of entrepreneurship and poverty in SSA. To date, the understanding of SSA in general remains very limited in scholarly journals, particularly in the domain of entrepreneurship (George, Corbishley, Khayesi, Haas, & Tihanyi, 2016). This article will help to fill that void, specifically in consideration of the domain of entrepreneurship.

THEORETICAL BACKGROUND

Entrepreneurial Opportunities

Before we can move to build an understanding of how severe resource constraints in settings of poverty can impact entrepreneurial opportunities, we first must briefly examine the current literature on the concept of opportunity. There are two dominant views of entrepreneurial opportunities, both set in Western research traditions. These two views of opportunities, the discovery perspective and the creation perspective, have different philosophical underpinnings and make different predictions about how opportunities come into existence and how they are exploited (Alvarez & Barney, 2010).

The discovery perspective on opportunities is the oldest view of opportunities and has largely dominated the field of entrepreneurship over the last century. The roots of the discovery view trace back to the "enlightenment" period in the 18th century that was led by now famous Western philosophers such as Locke and Berkeley (Russell, 1946). These philosophers advanced the belief that a theoretical statement can only be meaningful if its elements can be verified through empirical observation (Brown, 1970). This view is also at the heart of critical realism, which now forms the cornerstone of scholarly work on discovery opportunities (McMullen & Shepherd, 2006). For example, in examining the assumptions made about the nature of discovery opportunities, its embeddedness in critical realism becomes clear (Alvarez & Barney, 2010). According to the discovery perspective, opportunities are objective entities that are "out there", ready to be recognized and potentially exploited by entrepreneurs (e.g. Kirzner, 1973; Schumpeter, 1934; Shane & Venkataraman, 2000). Opportunities in the discovery view exist independently from the perceptions and/or actions of economic actors, thus entrepreneurs do not have to form opportunities themselves (Shane, 2000). It is commonly agreed that discovery opportunities are formed through "exogenous shocks", i.e. unexpected events that can be the consequence of sudden changes in technology, politics, and socio-demographics, among other factors (Davidsson, 2015; Shane, 2003). Because discovery opportunities are believed to emerge independently from human actors, this also makes them "objective" and "real" (Alvarez & Barney, 2010). Hence, even when nobody discovers a certain opportunity, it is assumed that this opportunity will still exist. Because of the assumed independency between entrepreneur and opportunity, a substantial amount of time can expire between the moment that the opportunity emerges and the moment that an entrepreneurial individual discovers the opportunity. To explain why some individuals are more capable of discovering opportunities before others do, a historically large group of researchers have attempted to demonstrate systematic individual-level differences between entrepreneurs and other groups of economic actors (e.g. managers) (Gartner, 1989).

A competing, but more recent, view of opportunity discovery is the view of opportunities as created. In contrast to the strong separation of opportunity and entrepreneur in the discovery view, the creation perspective on opportunities takes up a very different position that is strongly rooted in evolutionary realism (Alvarez, Barney, & Anderson, 2013). Whereas discovery opportunities were said to reflect objective realities, creation opportunities begin as subjective social constructions. According to the creation perspective, the formation of an opportunities is a path-dependent processes resulting in unique and subjective opportunities that could "not exist until entrepreneurs create them through a process of enactment" (Alvarez, et al., 2013: 307). Enactment here means that social constructions are shaped and moulded as individual seek to create an opportunity by testing their ideas within their idiosyncratic social contexts (Weick, 1979). Unlike discovery opportunities, those economic actors that create opportunities do not have to be constantly on the outlook out for shocks or disruptive changes to start their entrepreneurial journey. To create an opportunity, economic actors rather start with drawing on the resources that are available to them, trying to turn them into opportunities that have the potential to generate future economic wealth (Baker & Nelson, 2005; Sarasvathy, 2001). If a person does not know from the beginning what the opportunity (s)he wants to create will be like in the end, (s) he cannot really use objective historical information or make historical comparisons. As a result, too much focus on pre-existing knowledge about markets and industries can even hinder an individual in creating an opportunity (March, 1991; Mosakowski, 1997). Instead, to create an opportunity, an individual who initially only has a vague idea must act and seek feedback from potential markets to nurture the idea and to shape it further until an opportunity is "enacted" (Weick, 1979). Thus, while the discovery of opportunities requires entrepreneurs to learn as much as possible about existing opportunities, the primary aim of an individual who creates an opportunity should be to question and constantly test the held beliefs about what could be an opportunity for him or her. In the creation perspective, it is generally argued that entrepreneurs are not a special "breed" with specific characteristics and traits, yet opportunity creation scholars leave the option open that initially small psychological differences can become more outspoken as a consequence of engaging in an opportunity process (Aldrich & Ruef, 2006).

The foundations of the two views of opportunity (discovery and creation) lead to very different positions in the analysis of opportunities and entrepreneurship (Alvarez & Barney, 2007; Alvarez, et al., 2013). Currently, no one view dominates the analysis by scholars. Thus, as we consider opportunities in severe resource constraints we must take into account both views.

Severe Resource Constraints & Poverty

Just as there are various views on opportunities, there are also various views on what is meant by scholars when they discuss severe resource constraints in poverty settings. The United Nations has established the eradication of poverty as a Millennium Development Goal (MDG) which Colquitt and George (2011) refer to as the grandest challenge that academics should aim to address in their scholarly work. Like with all grand challenges, poverty is a much-debated problem with multiple explanations of it and solutions to it (e.g. Haugen & Boutros, 2015; Moyo, 2010). There are two main streams of scholarship in the conceptualization of poverty (Alkire & Santos, 2014), which we label here as the income-based view and the capabilities-based view. We will briefly review these two streams of thought on poverty before considering how the severe resource constraints from poverty can impact the analysis of entrepreneurial opportunities, since how we define poverty will affect our analysis.

A dominant group of scholars and policymakers hold to an objective, monetary perspective of poverty (Sen, 2006). In this view, who is poor and who is not poor is based on one's income (or purchasing power over commodities) and whether or not this income is under or above a fixed "poverty line". To use poverty lines in absolute terms as the total number of people in poverty, one can typically derive such data from national account statistics which are available for most countries and tend to be updated yearly (Dhongde & Minoiu, 2013). However, if one wants to say something about the income distribution of people in a certain region (i.e. inequality), and thus use poverty lines in relative terms, there is no alternative than to use nationally representative household surveys (Chen & Ravallion, 2007). Individuals, households or regions that fall under a certain poverty line are believed to have too little money to buy even the most basic necessities to survive.

One criticism of this approach to poverty is that appropriate poverty lines differ between countries (because some goods are absolute necessities in some countries, but not in others) and there can be differences among regions in countries (e.g. urban versus rural (Kates & Dasgupta, 2007)). This recognition has led Chen and Ravallion to argue that there should also be a globally lower bound because of "the cost of a nutritionally adequate diet (and even of social needs) cannot fall to zero"

(2010: 1578). Despite the argument of Chen and Ravallion (2010), the $2.00 a day benchmark, which marks the median poverty line for developing countries (Chen & Ravallion, 2010), is the most widely accepted global poverty line to date (Collins, Morduch, Rutherford, & Ruthven, 2009). However, the accepted cut off value evolves over time and among different groups of scholars with poverty lines ranging between $1.00 and $2.50 per day (Dhongde & Minoiu, 2013; Ravallion, Datt, & van de Walle, 1991).

Despite the widespread use of the absolute level of poverty, the validity and usefulness of income-based poverty lines for measuring global poverty is widely debated (Dhongde & Minoiu, 2013). This has resulted in a drive to a subjective, non-monetary view advanced by Nobel Prize winner Amartya Sen, a view we label as capability based (Nussbaum, 2006). Sen questioned the purpose of development and argued that the aim should be generally to increase peoples' quality of life and personal freedom (Sen, 1999). Therefore, the focus should be on improving poor peoples' "capabilities to function", which include capabilities related to health, education and general living standards that allows a person to meet a minimum level of functioning and to be part of a community without shame (Sen, 2006). This social dimension is also key to understanding the relative character of income in conceptualizing poverty, i.e. that a person is deprived compared with the wealth of others in his or her social environment (Smith, 1776). What an improved capability to function for a person means depends on what a person values in life and this varies among individuals from different ages, geographical regions, etc. (Alkire & Santos, 2014). This also explains, for example, why many poor – to the surprise of outsiders – spend so "little" of their limited money on good nutrition at the expense of things that make their lives less boring (such as a television) or that affects the quality of their social lives (e.g. expensive wedding or funeral arrangements) (Banerjee & Duflo, 2011). But money is not just a means to an end, and thus the extent to which people with the same income-level can satisfy their goals in life vary greatly. In sum, poverty in this subjective, non-monetary perspective refers to the failure to meet a set of basic capabilities, which is highly related to, but not the same as, lowness of income (Alkire & Santos, 2014). Recently, this approach to understanding poverty has also been reflected in the Multidimensional Poverty Index that was released by the UN's Human Development Report Office (UNDP, 2010).

Entrepreneurship as a Solution to Poverty

Extreme poverty remains a core problem for 836 million people in the world (United Nations, 2015). For decades, policymakers and researchers have looked for solutions to alleviate poverty, yet no clear answers have come forward (e.g. Banerjee & Duflo, 2011; Verhelst, 1986). The result is that it has been argued that a new approach to poverty is needed in order to eradicate poverty. This is especially true for SSA, as over a trillion U.S. dollars has been provided in aid to the region over the last 50 years (Lupton, 2011); yet, SSA has the highest percentage of poor of all developing regions (Alkire & Santos, 2014) and is the only region in the world that has not shown a decrease in terms of poverty over time (Kates & Dasgupta, 2007).

The solutions to poverty that has been principally pursued is the systematic financial aid from developed economies to governments and organizations in developing economies. While accounts of such aid programs date back to the late 19th century, the belief in capital investments as a means for economic development (and hence poverty reduction) spurred the successful implementation of the Marshall Plan following World War II (Moyo, 2010). The Marshall Plan pumped over $100 billion current U.S. dollars (then US$13 billion) to help a war-torn Europe recover to its previous level of economic development (Hogan, 2002). For more than half a century now, the World Bank has continued to follow the path of financial aid as a solution to poverty that faces regions around the world. In 2015 alone, The World Bank spent $60 billion on loans, grants, equity investments and guarantees to help address poverty; $15 billion in 2015 was transferred to countries and private businesses in SSA, turning the region into the largest recipient of World Bank aid (The World Bank, 2015). While some have lauded foreign financial aid (e.g. Sachs, 2006), others have raised concerns about the focus of current efforts (e.g. Haugen & Boutros, 2015), and still others have even questioned the positive impact on poverty alleviation, particularly in the case of Africa (e.g. Easterly, 2006; Moyo, 2010).

A new alternative to large government aid programs that has gained traction to address the problem of poverty in SSA is the promotion of entrepreneurship (George, Corbishley, Khayesi, Haas, & Tihanyi, 2016; Khavul, 2010). Entrepreneurship is viewed as a solution for poverty for a number of reasons. First, new businesses contribute to the development of an economy and have a long-term impact on the society as a whole through the employment they bring about (Ahlstrom, 2010; Naudé, 2010), a relationship that is also maintained in SSA (Goedhuys & Sleuwaegen, 2009). It has been recognized that without encouragement, new domestic businesses often remain micro-businesses (Mead & Liedholm, 1998). Also, micro-business owners in SSA rarely hire enough employees to grow into medium-sized businesses (Biggs & Oppenheim, 1986; Tybout, 2000). Thus, programs to promote entrepreneurship in SSA that focus on people and businesses that have growth potential and can create paid employment for others have the potential to create far greater welfare consequences. For instance, a case study of a World Bank supported firm in SSA showed that five indirect jobs were created for every direct job supported by the firm (Kumar & Abdo, 2012). Such employment multiplier effects are important, especially since incomes received by the employed tend to be shared among household members that have no jobs (Klasen & Woolard, 2009). Secondly, the movement to focus on entrepreneurship is driven by the fact that aid that goes to developing countries in SSA is primarily earmarked for public aid projects, but is also often diverted into non-productive purposes, including personal wealth accumulation (Moyo, 2010). Indeed, corruption in SSA is "widespread and deeply rooted as a social and cultural phenomenon that hinders public welfare and social development" (George, et al., 2016: 384). In part, this explains why the trillion dollars spent over the last half century has generated so little impact on poverty. Finally, this movement to entrepreneurship is also driven by the fact that it is philosophically appealing for entrepreneurship to help solve poverty in the region since then the solution is locally generated, with those effected by poverty driving their own destiny, instead of coming from the excesses of wealthy donor countries that they have decided to share with the poor. This view is in contrast to viewing "the bottom of the pyramid" as a largely untapped market for multinational firms (Prahalad, 2004). Rather than just a market for others, it is argued by those who focus on entrepreneurship that the poor are more than customers; they are the means themselves to alleviate poverty (cf. Karnani, 2007).

Entrepreneurship as a solution to poverty has been part of the driving force in the growth of the microlending industry. While the concept of microlending has existed for centuries, in recent years there has been a massive growth in the industry which seeks to lift people out of poverty through the provision of small, unsecured business loans to encourage new venture growth (Khavul, 2010; Yunus, 1998). It is now estimated that by 2014, microlending had reached 211 million people worldwide (Reed et al., 2015). Yet there have been serious questions raised as to whether traditional microcredit programs are in fact creating the desired effect and generating businesses that allow their owners and others to exit poverty. This due to the fact that very few borrowers from microfinance institutions (MFIs) actually form businesses that expand beyond self-employment, which brings into question whether the microloans are even generating entrepreneurial businesses (Banerjee & Duflo, 2011; Bruton, Ahlstrom, & Si, 2015). This lack of success is pushing scholars to look for a deeper understanding of how entrepreneurship works in the settings of extreme poverty. Until there is a deeper theoretical understanding, such as through the work in this paper, there will not be progress made in practice of using entrepreneurship as a solution to help solve the problem of poverty.

It has been recognized that opportunity is contingent upon the specific economic, social and institutional setting in which entrepreneurs find themselves (Mair, Marti, & Ventresca, 2012; Weiss & Montgomery, 2005). Thus, the setting of severe resource constraints that dominate SSA will shape how the opportunity is viewed and pursued. Consequently, we next turn to a systematic assessment of the literature to see how poverty in SSA stretches or modifies our theoretical understanding of the concept of entrepreneurial opportunities.

LITERATURE REVIEW

To build a foundation for understanding opportunities and poverty in SSA, we looked initially to the reviews of the broad topic of entrepreneurial opportunities, specifically the set of 210 articles published between 2000 and 2014 that Davidsson (2015) had recently reviewed. Davidsson had examined leading journals in the field of management, entrepreneurship, and psychology[1] to identify these 210 articles. Following the same procedure as Davidsson (2015), we examined not only those 210 articles, but also relevant papers that were published in these top-tier academic outlets in 2015.[2] This process generated an additional 21 articles published in 2015 that were relevant for our review. The result was a final set of 231 articles on entrepreneurial opportunities for the period 2000–2015.

However, our focus here is on opportunity in settings of severe poverty. Thus, in a subsequent step, we then sought to extract all potentially relevant articles on entrepreneurial opportunities and poverty. To this end, we first searched for the word "poverty" in the bodies of the 231 publications and then examined each article that appeared in our search results to see whether the use of poverty was related to entrepreneurship. This resulted in an initial list of 19 articles. To identify additional articles that did not include poverty, yet could have relevance, we ran additional searches with five terms that are often related to poverty in the literature: pyramid (cf. bottom-of-the-pyramid or base of the pyramid), necessity (cf. necessity entrepreneurship), developing countries, informal (cf. informal firms), and microfinance. This resulted in the identification of an additional 13 articles. It is important to note however that there was very large variation in the 32 articles in terms of how much the authors focused on entrepreneurial opportunities and poverty. For instance, the number of times that one or more of our search terms appeared in the body of the text ranged between 1 and 197. Further examination of these differences led us to drop six articles that were neither directly nor indirectly concerned with poverty, bringing our final set of articles on entrepreneurial opportunities and poverty to 26 (Appendix A lists these 26 articles). Among these 26 only two publications focused specifically on SSA (i.e. Bradley, et al., 2012; Khavul, et al., 2009). Both articles are empirical contributions that extend the boundaries of established entrepreneurship theories by examining opportunities among resource-constrained entrepreneurs in Kenya and/or Uganda. More specifically, Bradley et al. (2012) demonstrated that poor entrepreneurs need more than capital alone to increase their firms' performance; they also need to focus on specific types of innovation that can work in economically developing regions (but would not necessarily work in mature economies). Khavul et al. (2009) showed that family ties of poor entrepreneurs can also hamper (not only facilitate) the exploitation of opportunities.

The set of 26 articles can be categorized into four main categories based on the article's focal field: entrepreneurship and poverty (three articles), sustainable entrepreneurship (15 papers), macro-level entrepreneurship (four articles), and finally four other articles that do not fit into a clear category. Looking deeper at these sets of articles, the three publications on poverty highlight that entrepreneurship in contexts of poverty has the potential to expand the boundaries of Western-based theories (Khavul, et al., 2009). It is agreed that simply promoting opportunity discovery will not bring much change to the lives of the entrepreneur, if they discover and exploit replicative opportunities that are known to everyone (Alvarez & Barney, 2014; Bradley, et al., 2012). Consequently, the authors shed light on the different types of opportunities that can be discovered and created in poverty settings, and their potential for helping to solve poverty.

The largest set of articles are labeled as sustainable entrepreneurship. These articles focus not specifically on the poor, but rather on richer entrepreneurs and firms that aim to serve the poor, leaving many of the particulars about entrepreneurship in poverty unexamined. This body of literature often examines the "triple bottom line", this is seeking to make an economic, social and environmental impact (Kuckertz & Wagner, 2010). As the authors develop theoretical contributions to the field of sustainable entrepreneurship, they only touch on poverty in a general sense (Dean & McMullen, 2007). We concur with the view that there might be systemic linkages between environmental, economic, and social problems which would indicate that there is a connection between poverty and sustainability. Yet, we argue that there is also a need for more poverty-focused research among scholars in the field of sustainable entrepreneurship, since the relationship between poverty and sustainability does not address the depth of the issue of poverty.

Finally, examining the eight remaining papers, linkages that are drawn between entrepreneurship and poverty are more indirect (e.g. Sequeira, Carr, & Rasheed, 2009). The four macro-level papers principally focus on necessity-motivated entrepreneurship and hint that poor entrepreneurs are dealing with different institutional forces than those in wealthier countries (Stenholm, Acs, & Wuebker, 2013; Thai & Turkina, 2014; Valdez & Richardson, 2013). Similarly, in the four uncategorized articles, it is suggested that informal entrepreneurship (in developing regions this often means entrepreneurship by the poor) is characterized by a different institutional setting and a different process of opportunity origination and exploitation compared with formal entrepreneurship (Bhagavatula, Elfring, van Tilburg, & Van de Bunt, 2010; Short, Ketchen, Shook, & Ireland, 2010; Webb, et al., 2009).

The review of the 26 articles demonstrates that the discovery perspective is by far the most widely used. Although only a few articles in our review explicitly examined entrepreneurial opportunities and poverty, for most of the articles it was possible to deduce which perspective (discovery or creation) the authors had taken in the development of their papers. It should be noted, however, that for 21 of these papers no explicit attention was paid to explaining why they had chosen the perspective (discovery or creation) they had.[3] Nonetheless, there are five articles where both discovery and creation were explicitly recognized and embraced (Alvarez & Barney, 2014; Bradley, et al., 2012; Corner & Ho, 2010; Short, et al., 2010; Webb, Kistruck, Ireland, & Ketchen, 2010). These five articles make clear that both perspectives can lead to substantially different theorizing, and enable a fuller understanding of entrepreneurship and poverty.

DEVELOPMENT OF A FUTURE AGENDA

Building on the existing literature we review above, we want to develop greater insight into entrepreneurship and poverty in SSA. Specifically, we bring together the different perspectives around opportunity (creation and discovery) and poverty (income and capability) into a 2 by 2 framework, as shown in Figure 1. To guide the development of this framework with its 4 different cells, we ground the theoretical propositions with four specific cases from SSA.

Cases are useful to shed light on new and complex topic areas (Eisenhardt & Graebner, 2007) such as opportunity discovery and creation among the poor in SSA. This is particularly so since cases allow one to make interpretations about the data that would not be possible without a deep understanding of the social context (cf. Glaser & Strauss, 1967). In keeping with poverty as a relative concept, we chose to collect data among the poor in South Africa, which is reported as the most unequal country in SSA and even the world (Beegle, et al., 2016). To build our cases, we first partnered up with a microfinance institution (MFI) that considers poverty alleviation through entrepreneurship of paramount importance (GiveWell, 2012; M-CRIL, 2012; The Small Enterprise Foundation, 2015). As we were seeking to shed light on how different perspectives on entrepreneurial opportunities were related to increases in income and capabilities, we purposefully sampled (Corbin & Strauss, 2015) among successful microfinance clients, which could be identified as those taking (very) high business loans. At the time of our data collection (2015), all four entrepreneurs in our cases were borrowers from the same MFI, living in the

		Entrepreneurial opportunities	
		Discovery view	***Creation view***
Poverty	***Income-based view***	1	2
	Capabilities-based view	3	4

Figure 1. A 2 × 2 Framework on Entrepreneurial Opportunities and Poverty.

Table 1. Case Characteristics and Data Points.

Case #	Name[1]	Gender	MFI loan[2,3]	Business activities	Inter-views	Field visits[4]	Pictures
1	Eva	Female	50,000 ZAR	Window sills Small shop Tavern	1	1	16
2	Millicent	Female	25,000 ZAR	Baking Hot food	1	3	11
3	Patric	Male	30,000 ZAR	Small shop	1	1	7
4	Nonhle	Female	7,000 ZAR	Traditional beads Traditional alcohol Live cattle	2	4	11

[1]To maintain the participants' anonymity and privacy, fictitious names are used. [2]Average business loan disbursed by the MFI was |ZAR 2,912 (The Small Enterprise Foundation, 2015). [3] When converted at the 2015-year average of 1.00 US Dollar (USD) = 12.77 South African Rand (ZAR), loans were: USD 3,915.00; |USD 1,957.00 USD; |USD 2,349.00 and USD 548.00 for cases #1, 2, 3 and 4 respectively (http://www.usforex.com/forex-tools/historical-rate-tools/historical-exchange-rates). [4]Visits to do face-to-face interviews are also counted.

same region around Tzaneen, a small town in the heart of Limpopo. This province in the northern part of the country borders Botswana, Zimbabwe and Mozambique and has the highest level of poverty in South Africa (Statistics South Africa, 2016). For a brief overview of the characteristics of the four entrepreneurs and the number of data points collected throughout the year, see Table 1.

These four cases help us to illustrate and generate future theory and research on opportunity and poor entrepreneurs in SSA. The following section, which discusses the four cells of our frameworks, follows a consistent pattern. We first discuss what occurs in a cell and how this can help to build our understanding of opportunity in settings of poverty. Thereafter, we discuss the case that fits with this cell. Finally, we discuss how this case provides fresh insight into entrepreneurial opportunity in a setting of poverty.

Opportunity Discovery and Income-based Poverty (Cell 1)

The most conservative approach to studying entrepreneurship in poverty contexts of SSA is the one where the dominant views of opportunity and poverty are employed, specifically the discovery perspective on opportunities and the income-based view on poverty. Given the traditional focus of entrepreneurship scholars on the "discovery and exploitation of profitable opportunities" (Shane & Venkataraman, 2000: 217), there is a natural fit with the income-based perspective on poverty. Thus, if entrepreneurs seek opportunity exploitation for financial gain, it seems reasonable to expect that poverty can be solved when an individual successfully recognizes an opportunity and the result could lift the entrepreneur above the financial level of poverty (Figure 1, Cell 1).

Looking more deeply at this cell through our case, it is true that the poor are mainly motivated to pursue entrepreneurial opportunities to generate an income. Yet data from the Global Entrepreneurship Monitor consistently shows that the institutional environment that characterizes poverty-struck regions favors replicative, rather than high-impact types of entrepreneurship (Stenholm, et al., 2013; Thai & Turkina, 2014; Valdez & Richardson, 2013). Alvarez and Barney (2014) argue that most opportunities that the poor discover are replication opportunities that are hardly profitable upon exploitation and need few resources or abilities. Thus, while most opportunities discovered by poor entrepreneurs can generate enough income to sustain the person, such undifferentiated firms are very unlikely to result in the economic change that everybody is hoping for (Bradley, et al., 2012).

When entrepreneur #1 (Eva), a poor mother of seven children started her first business, the selling of self-made window sills, she also "knew that the small business *she* had [...] was not bringing enough money". Consequently, she "tried to do a lot of things to bring money in" the household, "*she* didn't care the kind of job *she* did, all *she* needed was money". Thus, to generate an income, Eva added a clothes-business, then a small shop and now she successfully runs a registered tavern as well.

Indeed, entrepreneurial success in poverty settings seems rarely to be the result of the discovery of singular opportunities. Unlike the popularized and heroic stories of entrepreneurs who stuck to one idea and now employ the whole village, we see from our case that increasing income through the discovery of opportunities requires a sequential exploitation of sometimes highly diverse business opportunities (Khavul, et al., 2009). While diversification is well described in strategy and for large firms (Palich, Cardinal, & Miller, 2000), it is largely uncovered in the context of entrepreneurship. In addition, the extent to which such processes differ from serial entrepreneurship, which focuses on those entrepreneurs who start multiple businesses over time (Wright, Robbie, & Ennew, 1997), remains an open question to date.

Opportunity Creation and Income-based Poverty (Cell 2)

An individual who creates an opportunity cannot, like in an opportunity discovery process, choose the opportunity that could maximize his (her) future profits as the specifics of creation opportunities are per definition unknown at the start of the origination process (Sarasvathy, 2001). However, similar to opportunity discovery, scholars have argued that the motivation to engage in an opportunity creation process remains the formation and exploitation of a profitable opportunity (e.g. Baker & Nelson, 2005; Fisher, 2012). Thus, opportunity creation is consistent with efforts to promote entrepreneurship as a tool for alleviating income-based poverty (Figure 1, Cell 2).

While creating opportunities in poverty settings can indeed lead to significant financial returns that raise someone above the level of poverty (Bradley, et al., 2012), trying to raise income through opportunity creation is extremely risky for the poor. This is because the pool of resources that poor entrepreneurs have at hand (e.g. money, time) is often shared between life domains, implying that the use of limited resources for business can severely affect resource allocation to the household as well. Indeed, Webb, Pryor and Kellermanns (2015) recently pointed to the strong family embeddedness of micro-enterprises in developing countries. Thus, investing in the business without knowing the potential returns can have serious consequences when the entrepreneur, or his (her) family, is confronted with unexpected negative events such as health-emergencies, hunger or theft (Collins, et al., 2009). More than once, scholars have pointed out that exactly such unpredictable shocks explain a large portion of the closings among (female-headed) new ventures in developing regions (e.g. Banerjee & Duflo, 2011; Mead & Liedholm, 1998).

Entrepreneurial case #2, Millicent, illustrates this cell. She started her business because "*she* did not like the idea of asking *her* husband for money [...] and with no money in the house *she* had to do something". Over time, Millicent created a highly profitable and sustainable business (baking and a kitchen for hot food) through observing "every little thing that happened" in the village. Millicent introduced herself to us as a member of the Transformation Church and it became clear that her religious beliefs also helped her to persist in attempts to maintain and even grow her business. For example, while sharing the story of how her delivery van got stolen one night, she stressed the role of God to explain how everything turned out to be fine in the end: "Around 2am I sang and praised. I had no idea why but it was the spirit of the Lord that was within me. So we reported the matter at the police station and we ended up getting a new car [...]. So that did not stop me from selling the following day – this all happened in the year 2000."

This story highlights the need for a deeper understanding by scholars of religious values and beliefs in overcoming challenges that characterize opportunity creation. Overall, scholarly work on the relationship between religion and entrepreneurship has remained very limited (Audretsch, Boente, & Tamvada, 2013). This is in part because religion is seen as too distinct from organizations that are primarily focused on profit (Tracey, 2012). However, religion is deeply rooted in SSA and permeates the everyday (working) lives of many individuals (Ellis & ter Haar, 1998; Paris, 1995). Responding to the call for more research at the intersection of religion and economic activities in Africa (Walsh, 2015), Reid, Roumpi and O'Leary-Kelly (2015) found some evidence of female entrepreneurs in Ghana who invoked spirituality particularly to cope with (business) challenges and in making future projections. Future research among poor entrepreneurs in SSA would be particularly enlightening in the context of opportunity creation, as not knowing what the future opportunity will look like (Alvarez & Barney, 2007) gives people very little to hold on to.

Opportunity Discovery and Capabilities-based Poverty (Cell 3)

The consideration of capability development rather than simply focusing purely on a level of income highlights the issue of the meaning of money (e.g. Furnham, 2014; Mitchell & Mickel, 1999; Zelizer, 1989). Linking the meaning of money and the capabilities-based view on poverty, the aspiration for a better education, health or living standard generally requires those in poverty to increase income. Hence, it is reasonable to expect that capabilities-based poverty can be tackled through the profits that result from the discovery of opportunities (Figure 1, Cell 3).

However, there is also a potential problem in that poor entrepreneurs generally lack the resources to discover and exploit substantially profitable opportunities. Especially when profits are small, poor entrepreneurs are faced with the issue of time as a key challenging factor to invest in their capabilities (e.g. through savings) and fight themselves a way out of poverty. Savings are important, as improving education, health and living conditions requires long-term investments and are capital intensive. Thai and Turkina (2014) also point out that economic development goes hand in hand with future-oriented behavior such as future investments and delayed gratification. However, dealing with long-term plans is difficult in extreme poverty because people in such contexts tend to be focused on present scarcity (Mani, Mullainathan, Shafir, & Zhao, 2013), leading to a neglect of future issues (Shah, Mullainathan, & Shafir, 2012). Overall, the view that the poor do not care about the future, and have an "innate inclination toward short-sighted behaviour" has been widely accepted (Banerjee & Duflo, 2011: 185). Nevertheless, research among poor entrepreneurs has uncovered significant variation in people's future time orientation and firm performance (Bruton, Khavul, & Chavez, 2011; Kodithuwakku & Rosa, 2002).

Entrepreneur #3, Patric, is our case for this cell. Patric is a man who started a "spaza" shop, which is a shop run from home and the most prominent type of small retail business in South Africa (Ligthelm, 2005). Similar business opportunities are thus easy to observe, discover and replicate. However, unlike most other spaza shop-owners, Patric managed to grow his spaza shop to a point where he could employ people. He also opened a second shop in a neighboring village and, as he says, he even has "more plans to grow myself and the business". According to the microfinance loan officer, Patric is successful as he invests in his future – an action not typically followed by others in poverty. Patric also donates "to less privileged, especially when they face problems" with socially important (and expensive) events or when parents ask for financial assistance so that they can send their children to school. Thus, Patric is focusing on building capabilities and pursuing activities other than just monetary return. However, the fact that his store is typical of so many others shows that he is pursuing opportunity discovery rather than creation.

This case example calls for further investigation into how a focus on the future can be promoted among entrepreneurs in poverty, especially since there seems to be positive spill-over effects for the capabilities of other poor members in the community. In this light, we also note that current empirical research on sustainable entrepreneurship and poverty is very much focused on Western-based firms (e.g. Gras & Mendoza-Abarca, 2014; Muñoz & Dimov, 2015; Renko, 2013). If deep knowledge about the social environment is necessary to discover sustainable entrepreneurial opportunities (Patzelt & Shepherd, 2011), we see great potential for future theory building with sustainable entrepreneurs who experience poverty themselves. SSA could be a particularly interesting context for such research, since the region is known for its strong social pressure to share resources and to support members of the community (Mangaliso, 2001).

Opportunity Creation and Capabilities-based Poverty (Cell 4)

Although the creation view on opportunities has less supporters than the discovery perspective (Arend, Sarooghi, & Burkemper, 2015), the debate between opportunity creation and opportunity discovery is mainly a philosophical debate and most authors will view both origination processes as equally valuable and even complementary in practice (Reymen, Andries, Berends, Mauer, Stephan, van Burg 2015; Sarasvathy, 2001). However, as creation opportunities lay the foundations for new markets, they are often viewed as the opportunities that have greater impact over the long haul (Baker & Nelson, 2005). Thus, from a theoretical point of view, poor entrepreneurs who create opportunities will be able to generate more profits over the long term and thus have increased chances to increase their capabilities to function (Figure 1, Cell 4).

Bradley et al. (2012) also demonstrated that opportunity creation among micro-entrepreneurs in Kenya was positively related to firm performance (and hence poverty). However, counter to what could be expected in mature economies, the authors also found that in creating opportunities, doing things only somewhat differently (e.g. trying another way to attract more customers) and not doing something completely new, had a positive impact. Indeed, given the extreme resource constraints that the poor face, and the consequences for what they can afford to lose (Alvarez & Barney, 2014), the lion's share of the opportunities created by poor entrepreneurs are more likely to bring modest changes to the markets and result in less sustainable opportunities than theoretically expected.

Entrepreneur #4 (Nonhle) has experienced a path as argued by cell #4. Nonhle relentlessly tried to grow her business by continuously seeking to differentiate her business from that of others. For example, after one of the interviews, she suggested that the first author buy bead collars from her and sell them in Belgium (his home country). Nonhle's past entrepreneurial actions also led her to substantially increase her living standard (e.g. housing conditions) and with the money she made she could even send her son to law school. However, her village had become less and less conducive for doing business over the last years. She also saw her income decrease, forcing her to lower her living standards as her poverty increased. As a consequence, she saw no further use of engaging in opportunity creation: "I don't really know what went wrong [...] I have been working very hard all my life so I am tired. I am tired and I don't know what to do anymore".

An important question that emerges from this case study relates to the psychological effects of failure in opportunity creation, as it can severely affect one's motivation to fight poverty. Similarly, Banerjee and Duflo note that "A sense of stability may be necessary for people to take the long view. It is possible that people who don't envision substantial improvements in their future quality of life opt to stop trying and therefore end up staying where they are" (2011: 229). Compared to discovery opportunities, failing in a creation process might be a heavier burden to carry. It is possible that bearing uncertainty (inherent to creation) is mentally more exhausting than bearing risk (inherent to discovery). In addition, because creating opportunities is a very idiosyncratic process, a person might feel more emotionally connected to the outcomes (cf. Cardon, Zietsma, Saparito, Matherne, & Davis, 2005) and thus suffer more from its failure.

DISCUSSION

Poverty alleviation remains one of the biggest challenges for SSA. Economic growth is traditionally conceived as a cornerstone of poverty alleviation, and particularly the promotion of entrepreneurship has been advanced as a key tool to make it happen. However, the impact of many pro-poor entrepreneurship programs that have been carried out over the last decades (e.g. microlending) has been limited. Moreover, our literature review has pointed out that entrepreneurship and poverty in SSA is a topic that has only received scant scholarly attention. In this paper we have tried to fill this gap.

To gain a more in-depth understanding that can guide future research we have reviewed the existing literature on opportunities and poverty and used four case examples from SSA to substantiate new theoretical questions. In the development of this article, we have systematically used the different views on opportunities (discovered and created) and poverty (based on income or capabilities). Although these are fundamentally different lenses, only a handful of scholars have currently recognized the potential implications of picking one perspective over another in studying entrepreneurship and poverty in SSA. As our illustrative cases suggest, many questions remain to be answered as one examines opportunity formation and poverty from a psychological (individual-level) perspective (cf. Frese, 2000). Looking at opportunity discovery, Cell 1 hints that to increase income in poverty, entrepreneurs need to walk different business paths over time, a finding that calls for longitudinal research designs that look beyond entrepreneurship as a single-venture effort. Cell 3 is illustrative of the poor who engage in entrepreneurship not only to grow themselves, but also the people within their community. While such stories are easily found in anecdotal accounts, academics have largely focused on outsiders in affluent countries, while ignoring those sustainable entrepreneurs that are actually experiencing poverty from the inside. Looking at opportunity creation, Cell 2 raises the question of how religious beliefs help entrepreneurs to cope with the uncertainties when creating opportunities to raise income. Cell 4 shows that failing to create opportunities that increase capabilities can be detrimental to entrepreneurs' motivation and even pull them back into poverty, an issue that calls for a greater awareness of the "ups and downs" in opportunity formation.

All in all, we hope that our work has opened some new windows for scholars to examine entrepreneurship and poverty in their future research. We believe that SSA provides scholars with great contexts for studying entrepreneurship, and that such research is needed to inform those individuals and organizations in their relentless efforts to fight poverty.

ACKNOWLEDGEMENTS

This work was supported by the Intercollegiate Center for Management Science and Vlerick Business School. We thank the Small Enterprise Foundation (SEF) for facilitating the data collection among their clients, the clients who participated in this study, Mathobela Shai for all research assistance, and Miguel Meuleman for his overall support of the entrepreneurship research in SSA.

NOTES

1. The list of journals that were scrutinized here include (in alphabetical order): Academy of Management Journal; Academy of Management Review; Entrepreneurship Theory and Practice; Administrative Science Quarterly; Journal of Applied Psychology; Journal of Business Venturing; Journal of Management Studies; Journal of Management; Journal of Organizational Behavior; Management Science; Organization Science; Organization Studies, Organizational Behavior and Human Decision Processes; Personnel Psychology; Strategic Entrepreneurship Journal; and Strategic Management Journal
2. We searched for articles with opportunit* in the title, keywords or abstract ("opportunit" followed by the truncation "*" broadened our search to both opportunity and opportunities). Both authors of this article then examined independently each publication to ensure its

eligibility for this review (e.g. publications that were excluded included those that referred to research opportunities, learning opportunities, etc.).

3. Scholars should question whether taking another perspective (discovery or creation) may have affected the results found or assumptions made.

REFERENCES

Ahlstrom, D. (2010). Innovation and growth: How business contributes to society. *The Academy of Management Perspectives*, *24*(3), 11–24. http://dx.doi.org/10.5465/AMP.2010.52842948

Aldrich, H. E., & Ruef, M. (2006). *Organizations evolving* (2nd ed.). Thousand Oaks, CA: Sage.

Alkire, S., & Santos, M. E. (2014). Measuring acute poverty in the developing world: Robustness and scope of the multidimensional poverty index. *World Development*, *59*, 251–274. http://dx.doi.org/10.1016/j.worlddev.2014.01.026

Allison, T. H., Davis, B. C., Short, J. C., & Webb, J. W. (2015). Crowdfunding in a prosocial microlending environment: Examining the role of intrinsic versus extrinsic cues. *Entrepreneurship Theory and Practice*, *39*(1), 53–73. http://dx.doi.org/10.1111/etap.12108

Alvarez, S. A., & Barney, J. B. (2007). Discovery and creation: Alternative theories of entrepreneurial action. *Strategic Entrepreneurship Journal*, *1*(1-2), 11–26. http://dx.doi.org/10.1002/sej.4

Alvarez, S. A., & Barney, J. B. (2010). Entrepreneurship and epistemology: The philosophical underpinnings of the study of entrepreneurial opportunities. *The Academy of Management Annals*, *4*(1), 557–583. http://dx.doi.org/10.1080/19416520.2010.495521

Alvarez, S. A., & Barney, J. B. (2014). Entrepreneurial opportunities and poverty alleviation. *Entrepreneurship Theory and Practice*, *38*(1), 159–184. http://dx.doi.org/10.1111/etap.12078

Alvarez, S. A., Barney, J. B., & Anderson, P. (2013). Forming and exploiting opportunities: The implications of discovery and creation processes for entrepreneurial and organizational research. *Organization Science*, *24*(1), 301–317. http://dx.doi.org/10.1287/orsc.1110.0727

Arend, R. J., Sarooghi, H., & Burkemper, A. (2015). Effectuaion as ineffectual? Applying the 3E theory-assessment framework to a proposed new theory of entrepreneurship. *Academy of Management Review*, *40*(4), 630–651. http://dx.doi.org/10.5465/amr.2014.0455

Audretsch, D. B., Bönte, W., & Tamvada, J. P. (2013). Religion, social class, and entrepreneurial choice. *Journal of Business Venturing*, *28*(6), 774–789. http://dx.doi.org/10.1016/j.jbusvent.2013.06.002

Baker, T., & Nelson, R. E. (2005). Creating something from nothing: Resource construction through entrepreneurial bricolage. *Administrative Science Quarterly, 50*(3), 329–366. http://dx.doi.org/10.2189/asqu.2005.50.3.329
Banerjee, A. V., & Duflo, E. (2011). *Poor economics: A radical rethinking of the way to fight global poverty.* New York: Public Affairs.
Beegle, K., Christiaensen, L., Dabalen, A., & Gaddis, I. (2016). *Poverty in a rising Africa.* Washington, DC: The World Bank. http://dx.doi.org/10.1596/978-1-4648-0723-7
Bhagavatula, S., Elfring, T., van Tilburg, A., & van de Bunt, G. G. (2010). How social and human capital influence opportunity recognition and resource mobilization in India's handloom industry. *Journal of Business Venturing, 25*(3), 245–260. http://dx.doi.org/10.1016/j.jbusvent.2008.10.006
Biggs, T., & Oppenheim, J. 1986. *What drives the size distribution of firms in developing countries?* Employment and Enterprise Analysis Discussion Paper (6). Cambridge, MA: HIID.
Bradley, S. W., McMullen, J. S., Artz, K., & Simiyu, E. M. (2012). Capital is not enough: Innovation in developing economies. *Journal of Management Studies, 49*(4), 684–717. http://dx.doi.org/10.1111/j.1467-6486.2012.01043.x
Brown, H. I. (1970). *Perception, theory and commitment.* Chicago, IL: Precedent Publishing.
Bruton, G. D., Ahlstrom, D., & Si, S. (2015). Entrepreneurship, poverty, and Asia: Moving beyond subsistence entrepreneurship. *Asia Pacific Journal of Management, 32*(1), 1–22. http://dx.doi.org/10.1007/s10490-014-9404-x
Bruton, G. D., Ketchen, D. J.Jr., & Ireland, R. D. (2013). Entrepreneurship as a solution to poverty. *Journal of Business Venturing, 28*(6), 683–689. http://dx.doi.org/10.1016/j.jbusvent.2013.05.002
Bruton, G. D., Khavul, S., & Chavez, H. (2011). Microlending in emerging economies: Building a new line of inquiry from the ground up. *Journal of International Business Studies, 42*(5), 718–739. http://dx.doi.org/10.1057/jibs.2010.58
Busenitz, L. W., Plummer, L. A., Klotz, A. C., Shahzad, A., & Rhoads, K. (2014). Entrepreneurship research (1985-2009) and the emergence of opportunities. *Entrepreneurship Theory and Practice, 38*(5), 981–1000. http://dx.doi.org/10.1111/etap.12120
Cardon, M. S., Zietsma, C., Saparito, P., Matherne, B. P., & Davis, C. (2005). A tale of passion: New insights into entrepreneurship from a parenthood metaphor. *Journal of Business Venturing, 20*(1), 23–45. http://dx.doi.org/10.1016/j.jbusvent.2004.01.002
Chen, S., & Ravallion, M. (2007). Absolute poverty measures for the developing world, 1981–2004. *Proceedings of the National Academy of Sciences of the United States of America, 104* (43), 16757–16762. http://dx.doi.org/10.1073/pnas.0702930104
Chen, S., & Ravallion, M. (2010). The developing world is poorer than we thought, but no less successful in the fight against poverty. *The Quarterly Journal of Economics, 125*(4), 1577–1625. http://dx.doi.org/10.1162/qjec.2010.125.4.1577
Cohen, B., & Winn, M. I. (2007). Market imperfections, opportunity and sustainable entrepreneurship. *Journal of Business Venturing, 22*(1), 29–49. http://dx.doi.org/10.1016/j.jbusvent.2004.12.001
Collins, D., Morduch, J., Rutherford, S., & Ruthven, O. (2009). *Portfolios of the poor: how the world's poor live on $2 a day.* Princeton: Princeton University Press.
Colquitt, J. A., & George, G. (2011). Publishing in AMJ—Part 1: Topic choice. *Academy of Management Journal, 54*(3), 432–435. http://dx.doi.org/10.5465/AMJ.2011.61965960
Corbin, J., & Strauss, A. (2015). *Basics of qualitative research: Techniques and procedures for developing grounded theory.* Thousand Oaks, CA: Sage.
Corner, P. D., & Ho, M. (2010). How opportunities develop in social entrepreneurship. *Entrepreneurship Theory and Practice, 34*(4), 635–659. http://dx.doi.org/10.1111/j.1540-6520.2010.00382.x
Davidsson, P. (2015). Entrepreneurial opportunities and the entrepreneurship nexus: A re-conceptualization. *Journal of Business Venturing, 30*(5), 674–695. http://dx.doi.org/10.1016/j.jbusvent.2015.01.002
Dean, T. J., & McMullen, J. S. (2007). Toward a theory of sustainable entrepreneurship: Reducing environmental degradation through entrepreneurial action. *Journal of Business Venturing, 22*(1), 50–76. http://dx.doi.org/10.1016/j.jbusvent.2005.09.003

Dhongde, S., & Minoiu, C. (2013). Global poverty estimates: A sensitivity analysis. *World Development*, *44*, 1–13. http://dx.doi.org/10.1016/j.worlddev.2012.12.010
Easterly, W. (2006). *The white man's burden: Why the West's efforts to aid the rest have done so much ill and so little good.* New York: Penguin Press.
Economist. 2013, April 6. *Investing in Africa: The hottest frontier.* Retrieved from http://www.economist.com/news/finance-and-economics/21575769-strategies-putting-money-work-fast-growing-continent-hottest
Eisenhardt, K. M., & Graebner, M. E. (2007). Theory building from cases: Opportunities and challenges. *Academy of Management Journal*, *50*(1), 25–32. http://dx.doi.org/10.5465/AMJ.2007.24160888
Ellis, S., & ter Haar, G. (1998). Religion and politics in sub-Saharan Africa. *The Journal of Modern African Studies*, *36*(2), 175–201. http://dx.doi.org/10.1017/S0022278X9800278X
Fisher, G. (2012). Effectuation, causation, and bricolage: A behavioral comparison of emerging theories in entrepreneurship research. *Entrepreneurship Theory and Practice*, *36*(5), 1019–1051. http://dx.doi.org/10.1111/j.1540-6520.2012.00537.x
Frese, M. (2000). *Success and failure of microbusiness owners in Africa: A psychological approach.* Westport, CT: Praeger Pub Text.
Furnham, A. (2014). *The new psychology of money.* East Sussex: Routledge.
Gartner, W. B. (1989). "Who is an entrepreneur?" is the wrong question. *Entrepreneurship Theory and Practice*, *13*(4), 47–68.
George, G., Corbishley, C., Khayesi, J. N. O., Haas, M. R., & Tihanyi, L. (2016). Bringing Africa in: Promising directions for management research. *Academy of Management Journal*, *59*(2), 377–393. http://dx.doi.org/10.5465/amj.2016.4002
GiveWell. 2012. *Small Enterprise Foundation (SEF).* Retrieved from http://www.givewell.org/international/charities/Small-Enterprise-Foundation
Glaser, B., & Strauss, A. (1967). *The discovery of grounded theory.* Chicago: Aldine.
Goedhuys, M., & Sleuwaegen, L. (2010). High-growth entrepreneurial firms in Africa: A quantile regression approach. *Small Business Economics*, *34*(1), 31–51. http://dx.doi.org/10.1007/s11187-009-9193-7
Gras, D., & Mendoza-Abarca, K. I. (2014). Risky business? The survival implications of exploiting commercial opportunities by nonprofits. *Journal of Business Venturing*, *29*(3), 392–404. http://dx.doi.org/10.1016/j.jbusvent.2013.05.003
Haugen, G. A., & Boutros, V. (2015). *The locust effect: Why the end of poverty requires the end of violence.* New York: Oxford University Press.
Herrington, M., & Kelley, D. (2012). African entrepreneurship: Sub-Saharan regional report. *Global Entrepreneurship Monitor.* Cape Town: The Graduate School of Business, University of Cape Town.
Hockerts, K., & Wüstenhagen, R. (2010). Greening Goliaths versus emerging Davids – Theorizing about the role of incumbents and new entrants in sustainable entrepreneurship. *Journal of Business Venturing*, *25*(5), 481–492. http://dx.doi.org/10.1016/j.jbusvent.2009.07.005
Hogan, M. J. (2002). *The Marshall Plan: America, Britain and the Reconstruction of Western Europe, 1947–1952.* Cambridge: Cambridge University Press.
Karnani, A. (2007). The mirage of marketing to the bottom of the pyramid: How the private sector can help alleviate poverty. *California Management Review*, *49*(4), 90–111. http://dx.doi.org/10.2307/41166407
Kates, R. W., & Dasgupta, P. (2007). African poverty: A grand challenge for sustainability science. *Proceedings of the National Academy of Sciences of the United States of America*, *104*(43), 16747–16750. http://dx.doi.org/10.1073/pnas.0708566104
Kew, J. (2014). Africa's young entrepreneurs: Unlocking the potential for a brighter future. *Global Entrepreneurship Monitor.* Cape Town: The Graduate School of Business, University of Cape Town.
Khavul, S. (2010). Microfinance: Creating opportunities for the poor? *The Academy of Management Perspectives*, *24*(3), 58–72. http://dx.doi.org/10.5465/AMP.2010.52842951
Khavul, S., Bruton, G. D., & Wood, E. (2009). Informal family business in Africa. *Entrepreneurship Theory and Practice*, *33*(6), 1219–1238. http://dx.doi.org/10.1111/j.1540-6520.2009.00342.x
Kirzner, I. M. (1973). *Competition and entrepreneurship.* Chicago: University of Chicago press.

Klasen, S., & Woolard, I. (2009). Surviving unemployment without state Support: Unemployment and household formation in South Africa. *Journal of African Economies, 18*(1), 1–51. http://dx.doi.org/10.1093/jae/ejn007
Kodithuwakku, S. S., & Rosa, P. (2002). The entrepreneurial process and economic success in a constrained environment. *Journal of Business Venturing, 17*(5), 431–465. http://dx.doi.org/10.1016/S0883-9026(01)00074-X
KPMG. (2013). *Mining in Africa towards 2020*. Johannesburg, South Africa: KPMG.
Kuckertz, A., & Wagner, M. (2010). The influence of sustainability orientation on entrepreneurial intentions — Investigating the role of business experience. *Journal of Business Venturing, 25*(5), 524–539. http://dx.doi.org/10.1016/j.jbusvent.2009.09.001
Kumar, R., & Abdo, H. (2012). *Indirect Job Creation Among IFC Clients: Findings from micro case studies in MAS.* Washington DC: International Finance Corporation, World Bank Group.
Kwon, S. W., & Arenius, P. (2010). Nations of entrepreneurs: A social capital perspective. *Journal of Business Venturing, 25*(3), 315–330. http://dx.doi.org/10.1016/j.jbusvent.2008.10.008
Ligthelm, A. A. (2005). Informal retailing through home-based micro-enterprises: The role of spaza shops. *Development Southern Africa, 22*(2), 199–214. http://dx.doi.org/10.1080/03768350500163030
Lupton, R. D. (2011). *Toxic charity: How churches and charities hurt those they help (and how to reverse it)*. New York: Harper Collins.
M-CRIL. (2012). *The Small Enterprise Foundation: Social rating*. Retrieved from http://www.sef.co.za/files/2013-03-07%20-%20SEF%20Social%20Rating%202012.pdf.
Mair, J., Marti, I., & Ventresca, M. J. (2012). Building inclusive markets in rural Bangladesh: How intermediaries work institutional voids. *Academy of Management Journal, 55*(4), 819–
Mangaliso, M. (2001). Building competitive advantage from Ubuntu: Management lessons from South Africa. *The Academy of Management Executive, 15*(3), 23–33. http://dx.doi.org/10.5465/AME.2001.5229453
Mani, A., Mullainathan, S., Shafir, E., & Zhao, J. (2013). Poverty impedes cognitive function. *Science, 341*(6149), 976–980. http://dx.doi.org/10.1126/science.1238041
March, J. G. (1991). Exploration and exploitation in organizational learning. *Organization Science, 2*(1), 71–87. http://dx.doi.org/10.1287/orsc.2.1.71
McMullen, J. S., & Shepherd, D. A. (2006). Entrepreneurial action and the role of uncertainty in the theory of the entrepreneur. *Academy of Management Review, 31*(1), 132–152. http://dx.doi.org/10.5465/AMR.2006.19379628
Mead, D. C., & Liedholm, C. (1998). The dynamics of micro and small enterprises in developing countries. *World Development, 26*(1), 61–74. http://dx.doi.org/10.1016/S0305-750X(97)10010-9
Mitchell, T. R., & Mickel, A. E. (1999). The meaning of money: An individual-difference perspective. *Academy of Management Review, 24*(3), 568–578.
Moghalu, K. C. (2014). *Emerging Africa: How the global economy's 'last frontier' can prosper and matter.* London: Penguin Books.
Mosakowski, E. (1997). Strategy making under causal ambiguity: Conceptual issues and empirical evidence. *Organization Science, 8*(4), 414–442. http://dx.doi.org/10.1287/orsc.8.4.414
Moyo, D. (2010). *Dead aid: Why aid is not working and how there is a better way for Africa.* London: Penguin Books.
Muñoz, P., & Dimov, D. (2015). The call of the whole in understanding the development of sustainable ventures. *Journal of Business Venturing, 30*(4), 632–654. http://dx.doi.org/10.1016/j.jbusvent.2014.07.012
Naudé, W. (2010). Entrepreneurship, developing countries, and development economics: New approaches and insights. *Small Business Economics, 34*(1), 1–12. http://dx.doi.org/10.1007/s11187-009-9198-2
Nussbaum, M. C. (2006). Poverty and Human Functioning: Capabilities as Fundamental Entitlements. In D. B. Grusky, S. M. R. Kanbur & A. K. Sen (Eds.), *Poverty and Inequality*: 47–75. Stanford, California: Stanford University Press.

Palich, L. E., Cardinal, L. B., & Miller, C. C. (2000). Curvilinearity in the diversification-performance linkage: An examination of over three decades of research. *Strategic Management Journal, 21*(2), 155–174. http://dx.doi.org/10.1002/(SICI)1097-0266(200002)21:2<155::AID-SMJ82>3.0.CO;2-2

Paris, P. J. (1995). *The spirituality of African peoples: The search for a common moral discourse.* Minneapolis, MN: Fortress Press.

Patzelt, H., & Shepherd, D. A. (2011). Recognizing opportunities for sustainable development. *Entrepreneurship Theory and Practice, 35*(4), 631–652. http://dx.doi.org/10.1111/j.1540-6520.2010.00386.x

Prahalad, C. K. (2004). *Fortune at the bottom of the pyramid: Eradicating poverty through profits.* Upper Saddle River, NJ: Wharton School Publishing.

Ravallion, M., Datt, G., & van de Walle, D. (1991). Quantifying absolute poverty in the developing world. *Review of Income and Wealth, 37*(4), 345–361. http://dx.doi.org/10.1111/j.1475-4991.1991.tb00378.x

Reed, L. R., Rao, D. S. K., Rivera, C., Gailly, S., Sanchez, X., Rogers, S., ... (2015). *Mapping pathways out of poverty: The state of the microcredit summit campaign report, 2015.* Washington, DC: Microcredit Summit Campaign.

Reid, M., Roumpi, D., & O'Leary-Kelly, A. M. (2015). Spirited women: The role of spirituality in the work lives of female entrepreneurs in Ghana. *Africa Journal of Management, 1*(3), 264–283. http://dx.doi.org/10.1080/23322373.2015.1062710

Renko, M. (2013). Early challenges of nascent social entrepreneurs. *Entrepreneurship Theory and Practice, 37*(5), 1045–1069. http://dx.doi.org/10.1111/j.1540-6520.2012.00522.x

Reymen, I. M. M. J., Andries, P., Berends, H., Mauer, R., Stephan, U., & van Burg, E. (2015). Understanding dynamics of strategic decision making in venture creation: A process study of effectuation and causation. *Strategic Entrepreneurship Journal, 9*(4), 351–379. http://dx.doi.org/10.1002/sej.1201

Russell, B. (1946). *A history of Western philosophy.* New York: Simon & Schuster.

Sachs, J. D. (2006). *The end of poverty: Economic possibilities for our time.* New York: Penguin Press.

Sarasvathy, S. D. (2001). Causation and effectuation: Toward a theoretical shift from economic inevitability to entrepreneurial contingency. *Academy of Management Review, 26*(2), 243–263.

Schumpeter, J. A. (1934). *The theory of economic development: An inquiry into profits, capital, credit, interest, and the business cycle.* Cambridge, MA: Harvard University Press.

Sen, A. K. (1999). *Development as Freedom.* New York: Knopf.

Sen, A. K. (2006). Conceptualizing and Measuring Poverty. In D. B. Grusky, S. M. R. Kanbur & A. K. Sen (Eds.), *Poverty and Inequality*: 30–46. Stanford, California: Stanford University Press.

Sequeira, J. M., Carr, J. C., & Rasheed, A. A. (2009). Transnational entrepreneurship: Determinants of firm type and owner attributions of success. *Entrepreneurship Theory and Practice, 33*(5), 1023–1044. http://dx.doi.org/10.1111/j.1540-6520.2009.00333.x

Shah, A. K., Mullainathan, S., & Shafir, E. (2012). Some consequences of having too little. *Science, 338*(6107), 682–685. http://dx.doi.org/10.1126/science.1222426

Shane, S. (2000). Prior knowledge and the discovery of entrepreneurial opportunities. *Organization Science, 11*(4), 448–469. http://dx.doi.org/10.1287/orsc.11.4.448.14602

Shane, S. (2003). *A general theory of entrepreneurship: The individual-opportunity nexus.* Northampton, Massachusetts: Edward Elgar Publishing. http://dx.doi.org/10.4337/9781781007990

Shane, S., & Venkataraman, S. (2000). The promise of entrepreneurship as a field of research. *Academy of Management Review, 25*(1), 217–226.

Shepherd, D. A., & Patzelt, H. (2011). The new field of sustainable entrepreneurship: Studying entrepreneurial action linking 'what is to be sustained' with 'what is to be developed'. *Entrepreneurship Theory and Practice, 35*(1), 137–163. http://dx.doi.org/10.1111/j.1540-6520.2010.00426.x

Short, J. C., Ketchen, D. J., Shook, C. L., & Ireland, R. D. (2010). The concept of "opportunity" in entrepreneurship research: Past accomplishments and future challenges. *Journal of Management, 36*(1), 40–65. http://dx.doi.org/10.1177/0149206309342746

Smith, A. (1976). 1776. *An inquiry into the nature and causes of the wealth of nations.* In R. H. Campbell & A. S. Skinner (Eds), Oxford: Clarendon.
Statistics South Africa. 2016. *Statistics by theme: Living conditions.* Retrieved from http://www.statssa.gov.za/?page_id=739&id=1
Stenholm, P., Acs, Z. J., & Wuebker, R. (2013). Exploring country-level institutional arrangements on the rate and type of entrepreneurial activity. *Journal of Business Venturing, 28*(1), 176–193. http://dx.doi.org/10.1016/j.jbusvent.2011.11.002
Sun, S. L., & Im, J. (2015). Cutting microfinance interest rates: An opportunity co-creation perspective. *Entrepreneurship Theory and Practice, 39*(1), 101–128. http://dx.doi.org/10.1111/etap.12119
Thai, M. T. T., & Turkina, E. (2014). Macro-level determinants of formal entrepreneurship versus informal entrepreneurship. *Journal of Business Venturing, 29*(4), 490–510. http://dx.doi.org/10.1016/j.jbusvent.2013.07.005
The Small Enterprise Foundation. 2015. *2015 Annual Report.* Retrieved from http://www.sef.co.za/files/SEF_AFS_2015.pdf
The World Bank. (2015). *Annual Report 2015.* Washington, DC: The World Bank.
Tracey, P. (2012). Religion and organization: A critical review of current trends and future Directions. *The Academy of Management Annals, 6*(1), 87–134. http://dx.doi.org/10.1080/19416520.2012.660761
Tybout, J. R. (2000). Manufacturing firms in developing countries: How well do they do, and why? *Journal of Economic Literature, 38*(1), 11–44. http://dx.doi.org/10.1257/jel.38.1.11
UNDP. (2010). *The real wealth of nations. Pathways to human development.* New York: UNDP.
United Nations. (2015). *The millenium development goals report 2015.* New York: United Nations.
Valdez, M. E., & Richardson, J. (2013). Institutional determinants of macro-level entrepreneurship. *Entrepreneurship Theory and Practice, 37*(5), 1149–1175. http://dx.doi.org/10.1111/etap.12000
Venkataraman, S. (1997). The distinctive domain of entrepreneurship research: An editor's perspective. *Advances in Entrepreneurship, Firm Emergence, and Growth, 3*, 119–138. Retrieved from https://www.researchgate.net/publication/228316384_The_Distinctive_Domain_of_Entrepreneurship_Research
Verhelst, T. (1986). *Het recht anders te zijn (The right to be different).* Antwerpen: Unistad Uitgaven.
Walsh, J. P. (2015). Organizations and management scholarship in and for Africa...and the world. *The Academy of Management Perspectives, 29*(1), 1–6. http://dx.doi.org/10.5465/amp.2015.0019
Webb, J. W., Kistruck, G. M., Ireland, R. D., & Ketchen, J. D. J., Jr. (2010). The entrepreneurship process in base of the pyramid markets: The case of multinational enterprise/nongovernment organization alliances. *Entrepreneurship Theory and Practice, 34*(3), 555–581. http://dx.doi.org/10.1111/j.1540-6520.2009.00349.x
Webb, J. W., Pryor, C. G., & Kellermanns, F. W. (2015). Household enterprise in base-of-the-pyramid markets: The influence of institutions and family embeddedness. *Africa Journal of Management, 1*(2), 115–136. http://dx.doi.org/10.1080/23322373.2015.1024089
Webb, J. W., Tihanyi, L., Ireland, R. D., & Sirmon, D. G. (2009). You say illegal, I say legitimate: Entrepreneurship in the informal economy. *Academy of Management Review, 34*(3), 492–510. http://dx.doi.org/10.5465/AMR.2009.40632826
Weick, K. E. (1979). *The social psychology of organizing.* Reading, MA: Addison-Wesley.
Weiss, J., & Montgomery, H. (2005). Great expectations: Microfinance and poverty reduction in Asia and Latin America. *Oxford Development Studies, 33*(3-4), 391–416. http://dx.doi.org/10.1080/13600810500199210
West, G. P.III, Bamford, C. E., & Marsden, J. W. (2008). Contrasting entrepreneurial economic development in emerging Latin American economies: Applications and extensions of resource-based theory. *Entrepreneurship Theory and Practice, 32*(1), 15–36. http://dx.doi.org/10.1111/j.1540-6520.2007.00214.x
Wright, M., Robbie, K., & Ennew, C. (1997). Venture capitalists and serial entrepreneurs. *Journal of Business Venturing, 12*(3), 227–249. http://dx.doi.org/10.1016/S0883-9026(96)06115-0

Yunus, M. (1998). *Banker to the poor: The autobiography of Muhammad Yunus, founder of the Grameen Bank*. London: Aurum.
Zahra, S. A., Gedajlovic, E., Neubaum, D. O., & Shulman, J. M. (2009). A typology of social entrepreneurs: Motives, search processes and ethical challenges. *Journal of Business Venturing*, *24*(5), 519–532. http://dx.doi.org/10.1016/j.jbusvent.2008.04.007
Zahra, S. A., Newey, L. R., & Li, Y. (2014). On the frontiers: The implications of social entrepreneurship for international entrepreneurship. *Entrepreneurship Theory and Practice*, *38*(1), 137–158. http://dx.doi.org/10.1111/etap.12061
Zelizer, V. A. (1989). The social meaning of money: "Special monies. *American Journal of Sociology*, *95*(2), 342–377. http://dx.doi.org/10.1086/229272

APPENDIX A

Articles about Opportunities and Poverty

Authors (Year)	Journal[1]	Type (Methods)	Adopted Field
Allison, Davis, Short & Webb (2015)	ETP	Empirical (Quantitative)	Sustainable entrepreneurship
Cohen & Winn (2007)	JBV	Conceptual	Sustainable entrepreneurship
Corner & Ho (2010)	ETP	Empirical (Qualitative)	Sustainable entrepreneurship
Dean & McMullen (2007)	JBV	Conceptual	Sustainable entrepreneurship
Gras & Mendoza-Abarca (2014)	JBV	Empirical (Quantitative)	Sustainable entrepreneurship
Hockerts & Wüstenhagen (2010)	JBV	Conceptual	Sustainable entrepreneurship
Kuckertz & Wagner (2010)	JBV	Empirical (Quantitative)	Sustainable entrepreneurship
Muñoz & Dimov (2015)	JBV	Empirical (Quantitative)	Sustainable entrepreneurship
Patzelt & Shepherd (2011)	ETP	Conceptual	Sustainable entrepreneurship
Renko (2013)	ETP	Empirical (Quantitative)	Sustainable entrepreneurship
Shepherd & Patzelt (2011)	ETP	Conceptual	Sustainable entrepreneurship
Sun & Im (2015)	ETP	Empirical (Quantitative)	Sustainable entrepreneurship
Webb, Kistruck, Ireland & Ketchen (2010)	ETP	Conceptual	Sustainable entrepreneurship
Zahra, Gedajlovic, Neubaum, Shulman (2009)	JBV	Conceptual	Sustainable entrepreneurship
Zahra, Newey & Li (2014)	ETP	Conceptual	Sustainable entrepreneurship
Bhagavatula, Elfring, van Tilburg, van de Bunt (2010)	JBV	Empirical (Quantitative + Qualitative)	Micro-entrepreneurship

(Continued)

Appendix A. Continued.

Authors (Year)	Journal[1]	Type (Methods)	Adopted Field
Sequeira, Carr & Rasheed (2009)	ETP	Empirical (Quantitative)	Immigrant Entrepreneurship
Short, Ketchen, Shook & Ireland (2010)	JOM	Conceptual	N/R
Webb, Tihanyi, Ireland & Sirmon (2009)	AMR	Conceptual	Informal Entrepreneurship
Alvarez & Barney (2014)	ETP	Conceptual	Entrepreneurship in Poverty
Bradley, McMullen, Artz & Simiyu (2012)	JMS	Empirical (Quantitative)	Entrepreneurship in Poverty
Khavul, Bruton & Wood (2009)	ETP	Empirical (Qualitative)	Entrepreneurship in Poverty
Kwon & Arenius (2010)	JBV	Empirical (Quantitative)	Macro-level Entrepreneurship
Stenholm, Acs & Wuebker (2013)	JBV	Empirical (Quantitative)	Macro-level Entrepreneurship
Thai & Turkina (2014)	JBV	Empirical (Quantitative)	Macro-level Entrepreneurship
Valdez & Richardson (2013)	ETP	Empirical (Quantitative)	Macro-level Entrepreneurship

[1]AMR = Academy of Management Review; ETP = Entrepreneurship Theory & Practice; JBV = Journal of Business Venturing; JMS = Journal of Management Studies; JOM = Journal of Management

LEAVING A SOCIAL VENTURE: SOCIAL ENTREPRENEURIAL EXIT AMONG THE MAASAI IN NORTHERN TANZANIA

Alexander Tetteh Kwasi Nuer, Miguel Rivera-Santos, Carlos Rufín and Gert Van Dijk

Arguing that the exit of social ventures is likely to follow specific patterns, due the uniqueness of a social entrepreneur's goals, the social venture's emphasis on the provision of public goods, and its relationship to stakeholders, we conduct a qualitative analysis of the entrepreneurial exit of a Dutch social venture in Northern Tanzania. Our analysis suggests that the choice of exit and the potential exit routes are indeed specific to social ventures, as the original social goals of the venture influence the decision to exit and its implementation. Specifically, we find that the goal of leaving a sustainable venture after the exit and the preference for the transfer of ownership to local community members was paramount for the social entrepreneur. Our results also highlight the difficulties associated with the unique role of stakeholders in social ventures, due to different perceptions and interests about the meaning and implementation of entrepreneurial exit.

INTRODUCTION

Although the entrepreneurship literature has traditionally focused on the notion of entrepreneurial opportunity, on the characteristics of individual entrepreneurs, and on the determinants of the emergence of new ventures in their market, social, and global contexts (Ács & Audretsch, 2006), some scholars have argued that it is also crucial to pay attention to entrepreneurial exit, i.e. the entrepreneur's decision to leave and/or terminate his/her venture. Because entrepreneurial exit can be a signal of high performance as much as low performance (Wennberg, Wiklund, DeTienne, & Cardon, 2010), understanding both the determinants of the choice to exit and the exit route chosen by the entrepreneur is key to understanding the very nature of success in an entrepreneurial venture. The fact that entrepreneurs can significantly increase their personal wealth through the sale of their venture (Certo, Covin, Daily, & Dalton, 2001) further reinforces the importance of understanding exit as a key dimension of an entrepreneurial strategy.

While this recent research stream has started to shed more light on exit strategies of for-profit entrepreneurs, significantly less is known about the specific exit strategies of social venture entrepreneurs (SVEs) (Sarason & Hanley, 2015). Yet, there are reasons to believe that exits in for-profit and social ventures may follow different patterns. First, because the overall objectives of social ventures are different, focusing at least partially on social and environmental issues (Dacin, Dacin, & Tracey, 2011; Kievit, 2012; Pless, 2012; van Dijk, 2011), the objectives of the SVE's exit are likely to also be different, since the entrepreneur's personal wealth is typically not his/her ultimate goal in the venture, with important potential implications for his/her exit decision. Second, the focus on social and environmental goals characteristic of social ventures is typically associated with a greater accountability to, and a greater involvement of, stakeholders (Austin, Stevenson, & Wei-Skillern, 2006; Rivera-Santos, Holt, Littlewood, & Kolk, 2015). This characteristic relationship between the social entrepreneur and the venture's stakeholders is likely to have implications for exit decision, as stakeholders may wish to influence the decision. Finally, because the output created by social ventures typically combines private and public goods (Rivera-Santos & Rufín, 2011), the extent to which private gains can be extracted from the venture's activity is lesser than in for-profit ventures (Weisbrod, 1975), also with likely implications for the type of exit preferred by social entrepreneurs. Overall, exploring the specificities of exit decisions in the context of social ventures thus seems particularly important, as it helps relax several implicit assumptions in the literature on entrepreneurial exit.

With the goal of addressing this important gap in the literature, we seek to answer, with this study, the following question: *What are the specificities of exit strategies in the context of social ventures?* Using a qualitative case-based approach, we analyze the case of a Dutch social venture, active in the dairy sector, deciding to exit a social venture started among five Maasai communities located in Northern Tanzania. Our findings suggest that entrepreneurial exit in the context of social ventures differs from traditional for-profit exits, in that it can be associated with the continuation of the venture in a way that the entrepreneur considers appropriate, rather than profits or personal wealth for the entrepreneur, leading to increased levels of complexity. This complexity is associated with constraints in the choice of exit routes and with the criteria for the selection of the new owners, reflecting the goal of ensuring that the ongoing venture keeps its social emphasis. Our findings further uncover the specific importance of stakeholders in social venture exit decisions, not unique to, but particularly important in, the Base of the Pyramid context, as different interests and different perceptions regarding the very notion of ownership and control create an additional level of complexity in the exit decision.

Our contributions are threefold. First, we contribute to the entrepreneurship literature by relaxing the key implicit assumption that the entrepreneur will pursue profitability and personal wealth. As our findings suggest, this implicit assumption has important implications, especially for the entrepreneur's choice of exit routes, which are influenced by the broader goals of social ventures, beyond profitability. Second, our study highlights the particular importance of stakeholders' perceptions and interests for entrepreneurial exit in the context of social ventures. Our data analysis shows significant differences across stakeholders regarding the meaning of an exit and its modalities, making the implementation of an exit strategy challenging. Finally, we contribute to the Base of the Pyramid literature by highlighting the implications of co-existing institutions on entrepreneurial exit. Specifically, we find that different conceptions of ownership and control among the Maasai impacted the implementation of the exit routes chosen by the SVE.

This paper is structured as follows. After a review of what we know about entrepreneurial exit in the context of social ventures, we introduce the case we analyze in this study and describe our methodology. We then present our findings, before discussing their contribution to our understanding of entrepreneurial exit and their implication for future research.

ENTREPRENEURIAL EXIT AND SOCIAL VENTURES

A recent stream of entrepreneurship scholars has argued for the importance of understanding the entrepreneur's decision to exit his/her venture or his/her choices in terms of exit routes as a key element of entrepreneurial strategies (DeTienne & Cardon, 2012; Wennberg et al., 2010), even though very little attention has been paid to the potential specificities of exit in the context of social ventures (Sarason & Hanley, 2015). To be able to understand these potential specificities, it is thus important to first understand both the characteristics of entrepreneurial exits in the context of for-profit ventures and the characteristics of social ventures.

Entrepreneurial Exit

Entrepreneurial exit can be defined a situation in which at least one of the entrepreneurs that started a venture exits the firm he/she helped found (DeTienne & Wennberg, 2015). It can be a sign of both good and poor performance, reflecting situations in which the entrepreneur exits to "harvest" the value of the venture or in situations of distress, and can take two basic forms: liquidation and sale (Wennberg et al., 2010). Both forms cover a variety of exit routes, which can be defined as the mode chosen for the exit, and can include a variety of degrees of loss of control associated with the exit, as an entrepreneur can exit a venture but be involved in the venture in a different capacity. Exit can be planned ahead, even as early as the creation of the venture, for instance in cases in which the entrepreneur plans for another entity, be it an individual or a group of individuals, to own and take over the venture for continuation after his/her exit (van Dijk, 2011).

Several exit routes have been identified in the literature, although the literature suggests that the main distinction among routes lies between liquidation and sale (Gimeno, Folta, Cooper, & Woo, 1997; Wennberg et al., 2010). Liquidation refers to situations in which the ownership of the venture is not transferred to a new entity (van Dijk, 2011) and the venture itself ceases its activities. Although liquidation is often associated with entrepreneurial failure, since it signals that neither the entrepreneur nor a potential investor is willing to invest further in the venture (Acs & Audretsch, 2010), it can also be a signal of performance if the liquidation of the venture increases the entrepreneur's wealth (DeTienne & Wennberg, 2015; Wennberg et al., 2010).

The sale of the venture, i.e., the transfer of ownership and control from the entrepreneur to another entity, like a liquidation, can be a signal of performance as much as a signal of failure (Wennberg et al., 2010). Importantly, a sale can be associated with different degrees of loss of ownership and control by the entrepreneur, as an exit does not necessarily mean that the entrepreneur ends his/her relationship with the venture. At one end of the continuum, the sale of a venture can be associated with a complete exit, in which the entrepreneur loses all control over his/her venture. But the sale can also be associated with a partial exits, in which the entrepreneur relinquishes part of the control but continues being involved in the venture through a different capacity, such as management or as a member of the board (Boeker & Karichalil, 2002). At the other end of the continuum, the founder of the original venture can stay on and continue leading the venture with the new acquirer's agreement, at least temporarily (Capron & Mitchell, 2010).

A venture can be sold to, or acquired by, another entity, be it an individual or another organization, such as an investor or another company (Boeker & Karichalil, 2002; DeTienne & Cardon, 2012; Wiersema & Liebeskind, 1995). Outright sale as an exit route is typically chosen when an entrepreneur becomes disinterested in the mission of his/her venture, encounters difficulties in the market place, or does not have enough resources, such as financial or managerial capability, to continue investing in the venture (Boeker & Karichalil, 2002; DeTienne & Cardon, 2012), although similar patterns can also lead to undesired acquisitions, for instance through leveraged buyouts (Wiersema & Liebeskind, 1995). A venture can also merge with another organization through a Merger and Acquisition (M&A), when resources and capabilities of the two organizations are complementary (Capron & Mitchell, 2010). A venture, however, does not necessarily need to be sold to, or merged with, an external organization. Instead, it can, for instance, be acquired by its own management though a management buyout (MBO) (Scholes, Wright, Westhead, & Bruining, 2010; Wright, Hoskisson, Busenitz, & Dial, 2000), in situations in which knowledge embedded in current employees is considered particularly important for the venture. Finally, the venture can be sold via an initial public offering (IPO), through which at least part of the venture's equity is transferred to shareholders. Often considered the preferred entrepreneurial exit strategy, especially for early investors (Levis & Vismara, 2013; Wang & Sim, 2001), it is typically chosen when a venture needs significant financial resources to grow and can be associated with the entrepreneur staying involved in the venture, even though studies suggest that such founder-CEOs may not be associated with long-term performance (Wasserman, 2003).

The literature on entrepreneurial exit thus highlights that the determinants of an entrepreneur's decision to exit are varied and could be associated with both success and failure; that there is a variety of exit routes, which reflect the characteristics of the venture at the time of the exit decision; and that entrepreneurial exit is not necessarily associated with a complete loss of ownership and control over the venture, as the entrepreneur may, in certain cases, stay involved in the venture in a different capacity.

Social Entrepreneurship

In parallel, the literature on social entrepreneurship has highlighted the specificities of entrepreneurial ventures that combine profitability, social, and environmental goals, typically trying to solve problems that are too complex to be solved with a profit motive only (van Dijk, 2011). While authors agree that the combination of different goals is the key characteristic of social ventures, there is an ongoing debate regarding the precise definition of the concept (Cho, 2006; Doherty, Haugh, & Lyon, 2014; Parkinson & Howorth, 2008; Rivera-Santos et al., 2015). Some authors have emphasized the entrepreneur's self-perception as a social entrepreneur as a key difference between social and for-profit entrepreneurship (Mair, Battilana, & Cardenas, 2012a; Meyskens, Robb-Post, Stamp, Carsrud, & Reynolds, 2010; Santos, 2012), whereas others have considered that the definitional difficulty lies in the empirical variety of social ventures, leading to the development of typologies as a way to define social entrepreneurship (Dacin, Dacin, & Matear, 2010; Mair et al., 2012a; Zahra, Gedajlovic, Neubaum, & Shulman, 2009). For the purpose of this study, we follow the literature and define social ventures as entrepreneurial ventures combining profit, social, and/or environmental goals.

This combination of goals is important, since emphasis of social ventures on alleviating social and/or environmental issues means that the output of their activity does not only involve private goods, from which profit can be extracted, but also public goods (Weisbrod, 1975). The particular emphasis on type of output makes social ventures akin to non-profits (Anheier & Ben-Ner, 2003), explaining why both types of organization emerge in activities that private firms find too unprofitable to supply (Doh & Teegen, 2003; Santos, 2012). A public good is defined as a good whose benefits can extend to people who do not engage in it, meaning that it is nonexcludable, and whose benefits are not diminished by the fact that other people engage in it, meaning that it is nonrival (Weisbrod, 1975). A typical example of public good is unpolluted air, which benefits anybody who breathes it, even if that person did not engage in environmental efforts, and whose benefit is not diminished by additional people breathing it. Because solving problems associated with public goods is particularly complex, some authors argue that social ventures can be characterized by their focus on solving 'wicked' problems (Kievit, 2012; van Dijk, 2011).

The fact that social ventures engage, at least partially, in the production of public goods has important implications for the social venture entrepreneur. Because public goods are nonrival and nonexcludable, their production cannot lead to profits, which explains why firms typically do not focus on activities associated with public goods (Rivera-Santos & Rufín, 2011). Although, contrasting with non-profits (Anheier & Ben-Ner, 2003; Doh & Teegen, 2003), social ventures do not exclusively engage in the production of public goods, the fact that an important part of their activity focuses on public goods means that social ventures cannot typically lead to profitability levels comparable to for-profit ventures (Dacin et al., 2011; Harjula, 2007; Santos, 2012). As a result, the goal of social venture entrepreneurs is typically more associated with the completion of the social mission of the venture rather than profitability or private wealth (Emerson, 2003; van Dijk, 2011).

Beyond the goal of the SVE, the importance of public goods in the activities of a social venture also has implications for the ownership and control of the venture. The fact that private profits are more difficult to achieve in social ventures typically leads to relying on different types of investors, who accept lower financial returns, and makes some ownership forms, such as shareholder ownership, particularly challenging (King, 2008). In other terms, financing and ownership patterns in social ventures typically differ from ownership patterns in for-profit ventures, as some sources of capital are not available to social entrepreneurs (Scofield, 2011). The emphasis on public goods does not only impact the SVE's relation to providers of capital, though, as research suggests that it is also associated with a greater involvement of other stakeholders in the activities of the social venture (Rivera-Santos et al., 2015). Paralleling the particular importance of stakeholders for non-profits (Peterson, 2010) or for corporate social responsibility initiatives (Fransen, 2012), stakeholders that are impacted by the social or environmental goals of a given social venture are typically more involved in the social venture's activity. In their study of social entrepreneurship in Africa, Rivera-

Santos et al. (2015), for instance, found that community members are more involved in the decision making of social ventures than in the decision making of for-profit ventures. Similarly, Webb, Kistruck, Ireland, and Ketchen (2010) found that stakeholders play a particularly important role in the governance of social ventures at the Base of the Pyramid, while Haugh (2007) explored how communities can help create social ventures to solve some of their public good problems.

Overall, the literature of social entrepreneurship and social ventures thus suggests that the social ventures' emphasis on the provision of public goods has important implications for the way they operate, for the profile of their founders, for their ownership and financing structures, and for their relationship to stakeholders. These specificities are likely to have important implications for entrepreneurial exit in the context of social ventures, since they seem to be at odds with some of the implicit assumptions underlying the entrepreneurial exit literature, in particular in terms of the goals of the entrepreneur and the possible exit routes. In the following section, we introduce the case study through which we empirically explore the specificities of entrepreneurial exit in social ventures.

METHODOLOGY

Research context

For this in-depth case study, we collected data on a venture started by the SVE Stichting Het Groene Woudt (SHGW), a Dutch non-profit established in 2005 that uses a social venturing business model to engage in community economic development (SHGW, 2012). Reflecting our definition of a social venture, SHFW's goals emphasize social returns, but also require financial returns, at least in the long term. In this particular context, the social venture set up milk factories, called *engitengs* in the Maa language, in five Maasai communities in Northern Tanzania (Terrat, Naberera, Orkesumet, Same and Longido).

At the time of the data collection, SHGW, after establishing the social venture and the *engitengs*, providing the necessary infrastructure, such as water, electricity and machinery, and setting up the elements of a sustainable business model, was exploring what it viewed as the last step of the model. i.e., the exit after completion of its mission. The case of SHGW among the Maasai in Northern Tanzania thus constitutes an ideal setting to study the specificities of entrepreneurial exit in the context of social ventures.

With the goal of transferring the ownership and control of the ventures to the local communities, SHGW had proposed to set up a social enterprise development fund (SEDF) that would cover the financial means of exit. In terms of finances, the SV investor wanted a gradual exit from the established business. The SEDF was expected to function as an intermediary vehicle which would reach out to non-traditional investors, such as communities that were interested in impact investments. The fund was to act as a local resource mobilization strategy through partnerships with local corporate organizations such as banks, private foundations, multinational corporations and multilateral donors with limited resources. The SEDF was to be governed by a board of directors (BOD) and managed by a fund manager who had expertise in banking. The BOD was responsible for decision-making concerning social enterprises prepared by the entrepreneur with support from the fund manager. Members of the BODs of different mother companies were to ensure the sound financial and operational management of businesses they worked for. The SVE was responsible for providing the financial and other support that the SEDF and individual established businesses may require.

Data Collection

Two study trips to the five communities and to the city of Arusha were conducted in October 2011 and June 2012, corresponding with a dry and a rainy season, respectively. In parallel, directors and management of the Dutch non-profit, SHGW, were interviewed between October 2010 and December 2013 in The Netherlands. The qualitative study protocol for the data collection in Tanzania was based on Malterud (2001) and Twumasi (2001), because their methods are specifically designed for qualitative data collection in rural communities from the developing world.

Data collection consisted of open-ended and semi-structured interviews; focus groups with community members, suppliers, and staff of the factories and the community-based organization; participant observation; and secondary data from the non-profit, the communities, the government, and internet searches. Follow-up phone interviews and emails with respondents were made when clarifications were needed.

Respondents were identified from desktop studies and from suggestions made by the local staff of the Dutch non-profit (SHGW), the milk factory management organization (DOSI), a local community-based organization present in the five communities (IOPA), staff of the milk factories, and various community members. The respondents were either contacted by local informants or directly by the lead author, both before and during the field visits. The goal of the research was described to the respondents prior to the interviews and focus groups, and they all accepted to participate in the study on that basis. No remuneration or gifts were involved.

The main participants for this study were community members, including traditional leaders; local government wardens from the communities; management and staff of the factory units, or *engiteng* in the Maa language; management and staff of the community-based organization (IOPA); management and staff of the milk factory management organization (DOSI); district coordinating heads or their representatives; individual Maasai who are revered or influential within the communities; and suppliers of milk, mostly female. About 50% of the study participants were present during both field visits, which allowed for the validation of earlier responses in the second trip. On the non-profit side, respondents included all the directors, and interviews and discussions were held in The Netherlands.

The interviews included both open-ended and semi-structured interviews, lasting about 50 minutes each, and organized around themes and questions that were pretested with four Tanzanian PhD students studying in The Netherlands at the time of this research (Malterud, 2001; Silverman, 2006). A total of 30 interviews were conducted. All interviews were fully recorded, when the respondent consented. Out of the 30 interviews, three were not recorded, one with a manager of the local CBO and two with elders from the communities. In addition to the recordings, extensive notes and pictures were taken for all interviews. Open-ended interviews started with traditional greetings in the case of community members and normal greetings otherwise, followed by the presentation of the research. Themes covered in these interviews included: ownership; conflict resolution; the setting up of the milk factories; challenges and issues related to the milk factories; exit strategies and sustainability of the factories; and some personal information about the respondent. For the purpose of the present study, we focus on the discussions of exit among the different parties involved, but our methodology thus gives us the opportunity to put this theme in the broader context of the social venture. Semi-structured interviews were reserved for traditional leaders, elected local government wardens, management and directors of the various organizations, in order to collect more precise data on their own experiences, but covered the same themes as open-ended interviews. The majority of the interviews were conducted in English, although some were conducted in the Maa language through two research assistants fluent in both English and Maa.

Similarly, focus group discussions brought together representatives of the various organizations, community members and traditional leaders, in each community, and lasted for about 50 minutes. All focus group discussions were recorded, with the consent of the participants, complemented by extensive notes and pictures. A total of 10 focus groups were conducted, five during the trip in the dry season, and five during the trip in the rainy season. After traditional greetings, the lead author started discussions around the different themes, allowing for a flexible flow of the discussion between the lead author and the focus group participants. The focus group discussions were conducted in the Maa language through two research assistants fluent in both English and Maa.

Data Coding

Data collected were transcribed and coded by means of ATLAS.ti software. Following the software's procedure, quotations from accessible documents, interviews and discussions were linked to the themes prior to the software-based analysis. Data generated by the software were then linked back to categories of respondents. This approach allowed the researcher to map categories of respondents with their perceived experience. The results of this analysis are presented in the following section.

FINDINGS

Results generated from the analyzed data revealed that exit is – at the superficial level – seen to be synonymous with 'transfer of ownership' in the understanding of all parties involved. However, further analysis of what exit 'means' revealed more complex definitions within the context of a particular stakeholder's understanding. Primary and secondary data analyzed from the perspective of the SVE defined exit to entail transfer of equity and assets. Data analyzed from the perspectives of directors, management and staff of the social venture and the NGO, however, showed a mixture of definitions. For example, whilst some directors and members of management saw exit as 'handing over' a project initiative, others defined exit to mean the transfer of equity as related to traditional business models. Respondents in communities, referred to as 'local stakeholders' in this study, had varied perceptions of the definition of exit. These types of respondents understood exit to mean 'handing over property or inheritance to the next of kin'. The meaning of exit was, therefore, contextualized in the case of this particular social venture to mean handing the social venture over to the communities without necessarily considering equity transfer or acquisition. A common definition identified among these respondents was that the social venture was seen as a project established with the intention of being handed over to the communities in which it had been established. Exit was, therefore, interpreted within and between respondents' understanding of the local parlance. As an example, most respondents had perceived exit to connote inheritance of a property left behind by a parent or and elder within their locality. It is thus important, in order to provide a better understanding of the complex reality of entrepreneurial exit in this context, to delve deeper into the different findings corresponding to the different aspects of exit: the definition(s) of exit among the various involved parties; the exit routes; the interpretations of, and conditions, for exit; and the perceptions of identified exit routes and strategies.

Definitions of Exit

Exit emerged from the analyzed data to essentially mean 'transfer of ownership' to all respondents, though different attachments to and forms, interpretations and understandings of the concept were identified by different respondents. From local stakeholders' point of view, the meaning of exit centers around 'leaving' the social venture business for new owners, in this context the communities, to take over. Due to the difficulty in defining business and entrepreneurial exit in the Maa language, the lead author had to rely on related words and phrases to contextualize the research question regarding exit. In local Maa parlance, exit connotes 'to leave something behind', 'to go away', 'to die' or 'death'. From the data analyzed, it emerged that exit, as understood from a Maasai background, is synonymous with a father or an elder leaving an inheritance to family members. Traditionally, an elder or father who becomes inactive or weak due to old age or ill health is likely to hand over family property or business, such as cattle and land, to the next of kin. The death of such a person will automatically lead to the distribution or re-distribution of properties to sons (and, to some extent, daughters).

The following emerged from a conversation with one of the board chairmen of the social venture:

> '*If the father dies, the factory will not die because there is a mother, and there is another thing that can make it sustainable. If you are a grown-up in the family and if you know you can get direction from your father and that we can now go back to the NGO and know the ways we can survive. Now the* engiteng *is growing from the NGO and it shows we can survive …* ' [Comment from a board chairman at the e*ngiteng* in Terrat, 2012]

Further, the SVE leaving (exiting) the business venture connotes that the Social Venture Entrepreneur will have to train local staff and build local capacity, as well as provide a high breed of cattle before they transfer their equity. Another definition of exit also connotes death of the founder, after which the social venture will be handed over to the communities and beneficiaries. A focus group discussion analyzed is summarized in the statements below.

> '*… If you say you want to leave, and you let the community know you are going, then you need to prepare them to know. And if the community is trained for about 5 years, and the 5 years will help them a lot … because, they don't really know if it [the factory] belongs to them, then later on when they know, they have to plan for the factory … if the NGO wants to go.*' [Comment by a community leader during a focus group discussion in Orkesumet, 2012]

'... *In this sense, if the investors will like to go, there are so many things to do; that is, to improve purchasing, now they should improve the cattle, they should help with those type of cattle that can produce a lot of milk ... for the factory ...*' [Comment by a management committee member during focus a group discussion at Longido, 2012]

'... *If the social venture dies, and we know beforehand, then we can have some strategies in place. If this is not there, then it will be difficult to run the factory. The company cannot continue if the factory is not there ... If the social venture is not there then we cannot work. The social venture should have a strategy in place and it should be explained to us. This is not there now.*' [Comment by a community leader during a focus group discussion in Orkesumet, 2011]

In contrast, the SVE defined its own exit strategies from the social venture as follows:

'*By establishing a SEDF or joining an existing financial institution which can function as a SEDF in Kenya or Tanzania, the SVE can start exiting from the established social venture. This can be done by ceding part ownership in the social businesses towards a SEDF. Since the SVE will not be the only participant in the SEDF, it will help the SVE to slowly exit the social businesses as sole financer, while minimizing financial risks for the social businesses ...*' [the SVE, 2009]

This definition of exit by the SV investor highlights the importance of financial return envisioned by the SVE. This is, however, different from the types of definition other respondents gave.

Exit Routes

To understand the dynamics associated with exit routes in the context of this venture, we compared the documents issued by the SVW describing the exit route with the information provided by respondents. The results are presented in Figures 1 and 2.

As shown in Figure 1, the SVE had proposed cooperative, employee-owned, divestiture, communal ownership and an investment fund creation as possible exit routes through which they were likely to transfer ownership of the business venture. These

'When making the initial investment: one should already have a preferred Transfer of Ownership model in mind, in order to structure the venture directly and involve the right parties. Structuring goes beyond legal form and financing, but also involves governance and organization. Given the entrepreneurial nature of the ventures and the dynamic environment, the actual exit can be different from initially envisioned.

Various transfer of ownership models are possible and one can also think of hybrid forms. The main models are listed below.

Cooperative (e.g. farmer owned)
Employee owned company facilitated via a 'employee stock ownership plan'
Divestment to local entrepreneur(s)
Communal ownership via a trust or other body
Investment fund providing equity, like a 'Social Enterprise Development Fund'.

Figure 1. Exit routes as defined by the SVE.

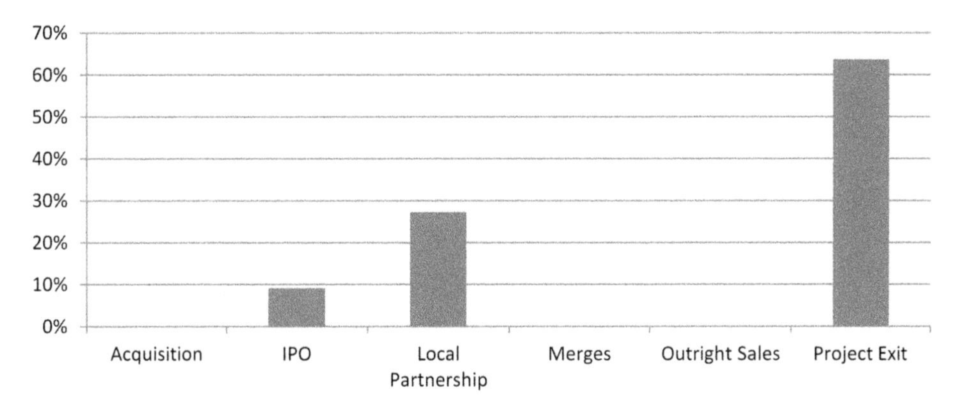

Figure 2. Exit routes identified by respondents

proposed routes were then contrasted with the routes extracted from the data from respondents. The exit routes identified from the interviews, focus group discussions and documents analyzed were aggregated with the use of ATLAS.ti software in Figure 2.

The project-based exit route, i.e., the exit through the withdrawal of the founder ensuring that the project is sustainable after the exit, was ranked highest by respondents (70%). This was followed by local partnership (26%) and IPO (9%). Acquisition, mergers and outright sales in the context of the social venture and the *engitengs* were not mentioned by respondents. The three highest-ranked exit routes, i.e. project-based exit, local partnership and IPO, were further analyzed based on the respondents' preferences, and are reported in Figure 3.

Exit routes identified (Figure 2) and preferred (Figure 3) show that the project route of exit dominates the list of exit routes in terms of identification and preference. That is, 100% of local stakeholder, 60% of directors and management and 33% of the NGO respondents touched on the project-based exit criteria or route. Sixty-seven per cent of the NGO respondents preferred a local partnership route of exit. Twenty per cent of directors and management supported such a preference as well. Local stakeholders did not mention local partnership as an exit route during informal interviews and focus group discussions. IPO was only mentioned by 20% of directors and management as a preferred exit strategy.

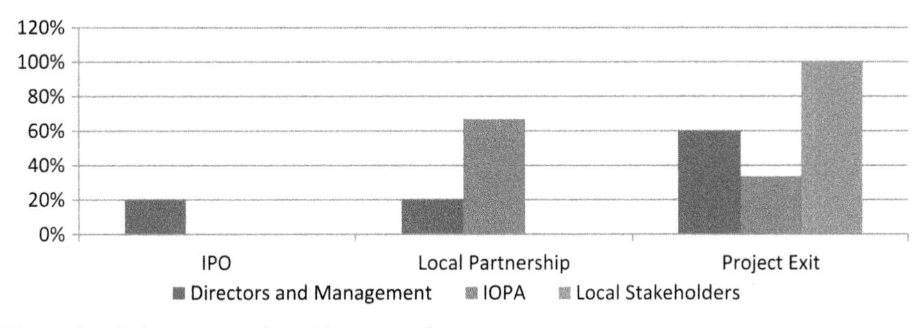

Figure 3. Exit routes preferred by respondents

Interpretations of and Conditions for Exit

Since the definitions and routes of exit were not explicitly justified or explained by respondents in the interviews and discussions that were the basis of Figures 2 and 3, a conversation analysis was conducted to extract quotations from the available data. The aim was to understand why respondents identified certain exit routes over others.

Directors, management and staff of the social venture and the NGO, and local stakeholders revealed that there was no exit strategy in place at the time the social venture and the *engitengs* were established. Data extracted from these respondents again revealed that the offloading of shares by the SVE could be a good strategy. These respondents, however, mentioned inadequacy and unavailability of information for such an exit strategy to translate it into a working strategy with which to meet the primary objectives for setting up the social venture. Respondents, therefore, suggested the SVE would have to develop an ownership structure that incorporates local and individual ownership perspectives. The quote below summarizes this form of interpretation.

> '... *Share offloading could be good but people do not know. People are not informed and they do not know the shareholding structure. [Knowing] this could be healthy and lead to a sense of ownership. The NGO should have a bigger share to sustain it, local individuals should be considered ... individuals are not good and could create a problem ... The SVE should do something that if they go, they should be proud of what they have done ... The* engitengs *should not die ...*' [Comment by a director of the social venture]

Furthermore, exit was interpreted as project-based and, to a larger extent, as an NGO-donor-related transfer of the social venture to the communities and targeted population within operational areas of the social venture. The respondents used the word 'project' in most of the discussions and informal interviews conducted among directors, staff, management of the NGO and the *engitengs*. A similar term was prevalent among community respondents and staff of the *engitengs*. Exit for the social venture was, therefore, interpreted to mean that the SVE would leave behind the social venture to the communities and beneficiaries. The project-based interpretation of exit is captured in the quotations below.

> '... *The leaders are not against the project but now, they don't have a big say. The business must teach the people who have no idea of an exit strategy because it will take a lot of time to send the idea to the people. The question of ownership is not in the minds of the people ...*' [Comment by a manager of the social venture during an informal interview, 2012]

> '... *The community in future may be able to run the factory. Now the main power lies with the board of directors of the social venture. The board of directors is not on paper ... exit should have conditions set by the SVE. Running the factories is expensive; maintenance and production are expensive ...*' [Comment by a director of the social venture, 2011]

Perception of Identified Exit Routes

Respondents justified their answers by stating that the SVE's aim and objective were not vividly expressed to all stakeholders when the social venture was initiated. Respondents revealed that multiple roles had been given to the SVE in setting up and running the social venture, and, therefore, different perceptions of the venture had arisen among them. Local stakeholders, for instance, mentioned that for the SVE and the NGO, sustainability of the social venture was questionable and, as such, neutrality of decisions for the social venture in general, and in the context of exit, should involve internal and external stakeholders. An anonymous respondent categorically mentioned that the local communities are not just clients of the SVE; rather, they are important stakeholders and, therefore, decision-making on exit should emanate from both the SVE and the NGO, and community stakeholders.

Almost all responses from the five communities and a number of directors, management and staff also revealed the perception that women should play a larger part in deciding what form of exit was to be taken by the SVE. A perceived exit decision that seemed to have emerged from the entire discussions centered around local partnership and the project-based exit route. A call to re-visit the concept and mission of the social venture was highlighted in the statement below:

> '*... We should redesign the exit of the social business ... I see the sustainability to be something natural to both internal and external stakeholders. And all the intended people are all stakeholders. There is a lot of ignorance when it comes to development and it is based on the belief and faith we do have about development. When the institution is there, for me, then I am not a client but a stakeholder, and if we are actively involved it will be a uniform client-oriented exit. We should all believe and have faith in the business ...* ' [Comment by a director of the social venture during an informal interview, 2012]

Respondents mentioned that the social venture was established within a precarious and informal environment. It was also revealed that ignorance of local stakeholders regarding what type of venture the social venture was categorized as, had played a part in what they perceived as the most important exit strategy that SVE should follow. A call for the clarification of the type of business venture the social venture was, was echoed by almost all respondents interviewed. A member of the directors of the social venture was of the opinion, as quoted below, that the different perceptions that stakeholders hold had to be harmonized.

> '*... It will also bring different opinions because people are asking when the exit was since from the beginning they never heard of it. I think through the participation community, like trying to pay people so that they can use resources effectively. There should be a long time for preparation and when the project exit, those people who are not Tanzanians should also exit ...* ' [Interview with a management member of the social venture, 2012]

The above quotation presents an interesting revelation that shows that the SVE had not made explicit what exit route or criteria they had planned to its management and local stakeholders. Based on the above responses, further enquiries were made regarding actions and steps that respondents would wish the SVE and the NGO to take in order to ensure that they exited per their mission for establishing the social venture.

Social capacity-building activities for communities, suppliers and all stakeholders emerged as an important step proposed for the SVE and the NGO to engage in. Training of potential local manpower to manage the social venture was further suggested based on the high level of illiteracy that prevails within the Maasai communities. Identification and recruitment of local entrepreneurs and eminent people from the communities to serve in decision-making and governance portfolios were suggested as a further step that social entrepreneurs should adopt. Personalities such as local entrepreneurs and eminent people from the communities, it was suggested, could become future investors when the time for exit by the SVE drew nearer. Another step to be considered was a suggestion to involve women, the primary intended beneficiaries of the NGO, to become board members and active decision-makers. Finally, the respondents suggested the establishment of an association to work in concert with the social venture and the NGO. The quote below supports steps suggested by respondents.

> '… *the things to be considered; they must identify the number of people who are ready to work; they must allow local investors to invest* … ' [Comment during a focus group discussion in Terrat, 2012]

From the financial perspective, respondents mentioned that the social venture would have to help set up local markets for end products manufactured at the factory. A timeline of approximately five years was further suggested by local respondents as ideal for the SVE to consider staying on before they exited from the established social venture. The identification of local investors as important owners emerged again as an important step that ought to be taken by the SVE in order to ensure that ownership of the social venture was transferred to local persons who would keep to the mission for establishing the social venture. Minority shareholding occasioned by the Initial Public Offer (IPO) emerged as another form of exit suggested to the SVE. Equity transfer of the NGO, mostly, emerged from the directors and management of the social venture who seemed to be well-informed on the future prospects of the social venture established (this was mentioned by three out of the social venture's four directors). In this context, respondents again suggested a timeline of between five and fifteen years over which to fully transfer ownership of the social venture. According to the respondents, such a period would create the enabling environment for them to understand the whole concept of social venture investments. A director of the social venture expressed such a feeling in the statement below.

> '… *Ask yourself, do we really want people to enter our company? You actually get shocked but at the moment the company starts making money you look at the profits. At 5 years, it is better to start with minority shareholdings and gradually it will increase* … ' [Comment by a director of the social venture, 2012]

The general manager of the social venture revealed similar sentiments and opinions in the statement presented below.

> '… *usually the company or organization starts by setting a time frame, but usually it takes 5 years before people will realize what they are doing. Who decides when to exit and at what time to exit?*' [Interview with a general manager of the social venture, 2012]

The executive director of the social venture, who also served as a director of the NGO and a respected Maasai community leader, mentioned the following as the most preferred exit steps for the SVE.

> '… *build the local attention and resources to those basics, enable communities to understand the notion of change* … *it requires time, about ten to fifteen years. It requires a*

whole generation, even the government doesn't get it, and it is not only the local people who don't understand the concept … consistencies need to be there …' [Interview with the executive director of the NGO, 2012]

Our findings thus suggest that both the exit decision taken and the exit route chosen by SHGW were significantly more complex than expected, mostly as a result of the constraints set by the social goals of the SVE and due to differing perceptions and preferences by key stakeholders. In the following section, we conclude by discussing the implications of this study for our understanding of entrepreneurial exit in the context of social ventures.

DISCUSSION AND CONCLUSION

In this study, our goal was to explore the specificities of entrepreneurial exit in the context of social ventures. Arguing that the exit of social ventures is likely to follow specific patterns, due the uniqueness of a social entrepreneur's goals, the social venture's emphasis on the provision of public goods, and its relationship to stakeholders, we conducted a qualitative analysis of the entrepreneurial exit of a Dutch social venture in Northern Tanzania. Our analysis suggests that the choice of exit and the potential exit routes are indeed specific to social ventures, as the original social goals of the venture influence the decision to exit and its implementation. Specifically, we find that the goal of leaving a sustainable venture after the exit and the preference for the transfer of ownership to local community members was paramount for the social entrepreneur. Our results also highlight the difficulties associated with the unique role of stakeholders in social ventures, due to different perceptions and interests about the meaning and implementation of entrepreneurial exit.

Our findings provide three main contributions to the literature. First, we contribute to the entrepreneurship literature, specifically the stream of research focusing on entrepreneurial exit, by relaxing the key implicit assumption that the entrepreneur will pursue profitability and personal wealth. As our findings suggest, relaxing this implicit assumption has important implications, as it influences not only the choice of exit but also the exit route. It influences the choice of exit because the social entrepreneur will pursue his/her original goals in the exit as he/she did in the venture, thus constraining the choice of exit (DeTienne & Cardon, 2012; Wennberg et al., 2010). It similarly influences the choice of exit route, as some routes, such as IPOs or M&As, for instance, are likely to be challenging, if not impossible, due to the nature of social enterprises. These insights open interesting avenues for future research. In particular, the fact that a social entrepreneur is likely to wish to ensure that the venture continues its original social mission after he/she leaves indicates that he/she may wish to keep some level of control after the exit, suggesting the possibility that partial exits may be more prevalent among social ventures than among for-profit ventures (Boeker & Karichalil, 2002; Capron & Mitchell, 2010). A quantitative study of the entrepreneurial exit routes in social ventures, especially in terms of the extent to which the entrepreneur actually surrenders control, would provide fascinating insights into our understanding of exit choices.

Second, our study underscores the particular role that stakeholders play in social ventures. Previous studies have found evidence of the importance of stakeholders in social ventures as they are active (Haugh, 2007; Rivera-Santos et al., 2015; Webb et al., 2010), but our results show that stakeholders also play an important role in the SVE's exit. Specifically, we find that different stakeholders have different understandings of the meaning of the exit and different preferences in terms of exit routes, which has very important implications, especially when the exit involves the transfer of ownership and control to the stakeholders. The additional challenge created by the influence of stakeholders is specific to social ventures, and is thus likely to be associated with different patterns in the decision-making processes leading to an entrepreneurial exit. This finding also opens avenues for future research, as an analysis of the differential influence of specific stakeholders on the exit decision is likely to provide important insights into our understanding of social ventures in their context. Members of the community served by the social venture, for instance, may have different interests in the venture's exit from donors, management, or members of other communities, leading to potential tensions in the exit decision that are specific to social ventures.

Our findings also contribute to the Base of the Pyramid literature by highlighting the implications of co-existing institutions on entrepreneurial exit. Scholars have highlighted the importance of understanding the implications of co-existing and potentially conflicting institutions at the Base of the Pyramid, defined as markets in which consumers barely have sufficient resources for day-to-day living (Viswanathan, Sridharan, & Ritchie, 2010), for business and social ventures (Kistruck, Beamish, Qureshi, & Sutter, 2013; Kistruck, Sutter, Lount, & Smith, 2013; Kolk, Rivera-Santos, & Rufín, 2014; Mair, Martí, & Ventresca, 2012b; Parmigiani & Rivera-Santos, 2015; Rivera-Santos, Rufín, & Kolk, 2012; Rufín & Rivera-Santos, 2013; Webb et al., 2010). Our findings underscore the challenges associated with co-existing institutions in the context of entrepreneurial exit, as the very notion of ownership and ownership transfer differed significantly between members of the Maasai community and the Dutch organization, creating specific challenges for the implementation of the exit. This insight highlights the need to further investigate the implications of co-existing institutions not only for the creation of business and social ventures at the Base of the Pyramid, which has been the focus of research so far, but also for their ongoing activity and exit, which we are only now beginning to understand.

Finally, this study also has implications for social entrepreneurs not only as they prepare to exit their activity, but also as they prepare to start a venture. Indeed, our findings show that it is crucial for SVEs to be aware of the specific dynamics and constraints of entrepreneurial exit in the context of social ventures. In particular, our study suggests that being aware of the constraints in terms of exit routes, and including stakeholders early on to ensure that there is no misunderstanding regarding the meaning and implementation of exit, is likely to significantly reduce the tensions associated with exit. Similarly, SVEs active at the Base of the Pyramid should recognize that local, community-based institutions may have different rules associated with ownership and business transactions, which need to be incorporated into exit strategies.

As any academic endeavor, this study has limitations. While the qualitative approach of this research allows for a fine-grained understanding of phenomena, it also has implications for generalizability. Our study focuses on one Dutch organization active in the dairy sector among the Maasai in Northern Tanzania, leading to specificities in the social venture that are likely to impact the perceptions of entrepreneurial exit and exit routes, at least to some extent. Similar studies with different social and/or environmental ventures, in different industries, and among different communities could therefore complement and fine-tune our findings. Second, as is often the case with qualitative studies in relatively isolated settings, the author collecting the data collaborated with speakers of kiSwahili and of the Maa language, which may have influenced the dynamic of the interviews, in spite of the precautions taken to ensure that the translations of the interviews were correct. These challenges are common to studies in ethnically diverse areas, especially at the Base of the Pyramid.

Our goal with this study was to start exploring the understudied phenomenon of entrepreneurial exit in the context of social ventures. Our findings suggest that, due to the specificities of social ventures, both the exit decision and the exit routes seem to follow different patterns from those studied in for-profit ventures. We hope that this research will entice other researchers to pursue this fascinating line of research, especially in an African setting, which seems particularly well-suited to this type of study.

References

Acs, Z. J., & Audretsch, D. B. (Eds.) (2010). *Handbook of Entrepreneurship Research. An Interdisciplinary Survey and Introduction* (2nd ed.). New York, NY: Springer. http://dx.doi.org/10.1007/978-1-4419-1191-9

Ács, Z. J., & Audretsch, D. B. (Eds.) (2006). *Handbook of entrepreneurship research: An interdisciplinary survey and introduction*. New York, NY: Springer Science & Business Media.

Anheier, H. K., & Ben-Ner, A. (2003). *The Study of the Nonprofit Enterprise. Theories and Approaches*. New York, NY: Kluwer Academic/Plenum Publishers.

Austin, J., Stevenson, H., & Wei-Skillern, J. (2006). Social and commercial entrepreneurship: Same, different, or both? *Entrepreneurship Theory and Practice, 30*(1), 1–22. http://dx.doi.org/10.1111/j.1540-6520.2006.00107.x

Boeker, W., & Karichalil, R. (2002). Entrepreneurial transitions: Factors influencing founder departure. *Academy of Management Journal, 45*(4), 818–826. http://dx.doi.org/10.2307/3069314

Capron, L., & Mitchell, W. (2010). Finding the right path. *Harvard Business Review, 88*(7-8), 102–107.

Certo, S. T., Covin, J. G., Daily, C. M., & Dalton, D. R. (2001). Wealth and the effects of founder management among IPO-stage new ventures. *Strategic Management Journal, 22*(6-7), 641–658. http://dx.doi.org/10.1002/smj.182

Cho, A. H. (2006). Politics, values and social entrepreneurship: A critical appraisal. In J. Mair, J. Robinson, & K. Hockerts (Eds.), *Social Entrepreneurship* (pp. 34–56). Basingstoke: Palgrave Macmillan. http://dx.doi.org/10.1057/9780230625655_4

Dacin, M. T., Dacin, P. A., & Tracey, P. (2011). Social entrepreneurship: A critique and future directions. *Organization Science, 22*(5), 1203–1213. http://dx.doi.org/10.1287/orsc.1100.0620

Dacin, P. A., Dacin, M. T., & Matear, M. (2010). Social entrepreneurship: Why we don't need a new theory and how we move forward from here. *The Academy of Management Perspectives, 24*(3), 37–56. http://dx.doi.org/10.5465/AMP.2010.52842950

DeTienne, D. R., & Cardon, M. S. (2012). Impact of founder experience on exit intentions. *Small Business Economics, 38*(4), 351–374. http://dx.doi.org/10.1007/s11187-010-9284-5

DeTienne, D. R., & Wennberg, K. (2015). *Research Handbook of Entrepreneurial Exit*. Northampton, MA: Edward Elgar Publishing. http://dx.doi.org/10.4337/9781782546979

Doh, J. P., & Teegen, H. (2003). *Globalization and NGOs: Transforming Business, Government, and Society*. Wesport, CT: Praeger.

Doherty, B., Haugh, H., & Lyon, F. (2014). Social enterprises as hybrid organizations: A review and research agenda. *International Journal of Management Reviews, 16*(4), 417–436. http://dx.doi.org/10.1111/ijmr.12028

Emerson, J. (2003). Where money meets mission. *Stanford Social Innovation Review, 1*(2), 38–47.

Fransen, L. (2012). Multi-stakeholder governance and voluntary programme interactions: Legitimation politics in the institutional design of Corporate Social Responsibility. *Socio-economic Review, 10*(1), 163–192. http://dx.doi.org/10.1093/ser/mwr029

Gimeno, J., Folta, T. B., Cooper, A. C., & Woo, C. Y. (1997). Survival of the fittest? Entrepreneurial human capital and the persistence of underperforming firms. *Administrative Science Quarterly, 42*(4), 750–783. http://dx.doi.org/10.2307/2393656

Harjula, L. (2007). Tensions between venture capitalists' and business-social entrepreneurs' goals. *Greener Management International, 51*, 79–87.

Haugh, H. (2007). Community-led social venture creation. *Entrepreneurship Theory and Practice, 31*(2), 161–182. http://dx.doi.org/10.1111/j.1540-6520.2007.00168.x

Kievit, H. (2012). *Social venturing entrepreneurship: een plaatsbepaling*. Breukelen, Nederland: Nyenrode Business Universiteit.

King, B. L. (2008). *Social Venture Capital. Encyclopedia of Alternative Investments*. Boca Raton, Florida: CRC Press.

Kistruck, G. M., Beamish, P. W., Qureshi, I., & Sutter, C. J. (2013a). Social intermediation in base-of-the-pyramid markets. *Journal of Management Studies, 50*(1), 31–66. http://dx.doi.org/10.1111/j.1467-6486.2012.01076.x

Kistruck, G. M., Sutter, C. J., Lount, R. B., & Smith, B. R. (2013b). Mitigating principal-agent problems in base-of-the-pyramid markets: An identity spillover perspective. *Academy of Management Journal, 56*(3), 659–682. http://dx.doi.org/10.5465/amj.2011.0336

Kolk, A., Rivera-Santos, M., & Rufín, C. (2014). Reviewing a decade of research on the "base/bottom of the pyramid" (BOP) concept. *Business & Society, 53*(3), 338–377. http://dx.doi.org/10.1177/0007650312474928

Levis, M., & Vismara, S. (2013). *Handbook of research on IPOs*. Northampton, MA: Edward Elgar Publishing. http://dx.doi.org/10.4337/9781781955376.

Mair, J., Battilana, J., & Cardenas, J. (2012a). Organizing for society: A typology of social entrepreneuring models. *Journal of Business Ethics, 111*(3), 353–373. http://dx.doi.org/10.1007/s10551-012-1414-3

Mair, J., Martí, I., & Ventresca, M. (2012b). Building inclusive markets in rural Bangladesh: How intermediaries work institutional voids. *Academy of Management Journal, 55*(4), 819–850. http://dx.doi.org/10.5465/amj.2010.0627

Malterud, K. (2001). Qualitative research: Standards, challenges, and guidelines. *Lancet, 358* (9280), 483–488. http://dx.doi.org/10.1016/S0140-6736(01)05627-6

Meyskens, M., Robb-Post, C., Stamp, J. A., Carsrud, A. L., & Reynolds, P. D. (2010). Social ventures from a Resource-Based Perspective: An exploratory study assessing global Ashoka Fellows. *Entrepreneurship Theory and Practice, 34*(4), 661–680. http://dx.doi.org/10.1111/j.1540-6520.2010.00389.x

Parkinson, C., & Howorth, C. (2008). The language of social entrepreneurs. *Entrepreneurship and Regional Development, 20*(3), 285–309. http://dx.doi.org/10.1080/08985620701800507

Parmigiani, A., & Rivera-Santos, M. (2015). Sourcing for the base of the pyramid: Constructing supply chains to address voids in subsistence markets. *Journal of Operations Management, 33-34*(1), 60–70. http://dx.doi.org/10.1016/j.jom.2014.10.007

Peterson, D. K. (2010). Agency perspectives on Ngo governance. *Journal of Management Research, 2*(2), 1–11. http://dx.doi.org/10.5296/jmr.v2i2.294

Pless, N. M. (2012). Social entrepreneurship in theory and practice – An introduction. *Journal of Business Ethics, 111*(3), 317–320. http://dx.doi.org/10.1007/s10551-012-1533-x

Rivera-Santos, M., & Rufín, C. (2011). Odd couples: Understanding the governance of Firm-NGO alliances. *Journal of Business Ethics, 94*(S1), 55–70. http://dx.doi.org/10.1007/s10551-011-0779-z

Rivera-Santos, M., Rufín, C., & Kolk, A. (2012). Bridging the institutional divide: Partnerships in subsistence markets. *Journal of Business Research, 65*(12), 1721–1727. http://dx.doi.org/10.1016/j.jbusres.2012.02.013

Rivera-Santos, M., Holt, D., Littlewood, D., & Kolk, A. (2015). Social entrepreneurship in sub-Saharan Africa. *The Academy of Management Perspectives, 29*(1), 72–91. http://dx.doi.org/10.5465/amp.2013.0128

Rufín, C. & Rivera-Santos, M. (2013). Cross-sector governance: From institutions to partnerships, and back to institutions. In A. Crane & M. M. Seitanidi (Eds.), *Social Partnerships and Responsible Business: A Research Handbook* (pp. 125–142). London: Routledge.

Santos, F. (2012). A positive theory of social entrepreneurship. *Journal of Business Ethics, 111* (3), 335–351. http://dx.doi.org/10.1007/s10551-012-1413-4

Sarason, Y. & Hanley, G. (2015). 10. Social ventures: exploring entrepreneurial exit strategies with a structuration lens. In D. R. DeTienne & K. Wennberg (Eds.), *Research Handbook of Entrepreneurial Exit* (pp. 214–226). Cheltenham: Edward Elgar Publishing.

Scholes, L., Wright, M., Westhead, P., & Bruining, H. (2010). Strategic changes in family firms post management buyout: Ownership and governance issues. *International Small Business Journal*, *28*(5), 505–521. http://dx.doi.org/10.1177/0266242610370390

Scofield, R. (2011). *The Social Entrepreneur's Handbook: How to Start, Build, and Run a Business That Improves the World*. New York, NY: McGraw Hill Professional.

SHGW. (2012). *Stichting Het Groene Woudt – Annual report*. Driebergen-Rijsenburg, Netherlands: SHGW.

Silverman, D. (2006). *Interpreting qualitative data*. (3rd Ed). London: Thousand Oaks.

Twumasi, P. A. (2001). *Social Research in Rural Communities* (2nd ed.). Accra: Ghana Universities Press.

van Dijk, G. (2011). Social Venturing and Cooperative Entrepreneurship-Motives for Entry and Institutions for Exit in Developing Countries. In F. van der Velden (Ed.), *New Approaches to Development Cooperation*. Utrecht, The Netherlands: Context, International Cooperation.

Viswanathan, M., Sridharan, S., & Ritchie, R. (2010). Understanding consumption and entrepreneurship in subsistence marketplaces. *Journal of Business Research*, *63*(6), 570–581. http://dx.doi.org/10.1016/j.jbusres.2009.02.023

Wang, C. K., & Sim, V. Y. (2001). Exit strategies of venture capital-backed companies in Singapore. *Venture Capital: An International Journal of Entrepreneurial Finance*, *3*(4), 337–358. http://dx.doi.org/10.1080/13691060110060664

Wasserman, N. (2003). Founder-CEO succession and the paradox of entrepreneurial success. *Organization Science*, *14*(2), 149–172. http://dx.doi.org/10.1287/orsc.14.2.149.14995

Webb, J. W., Kistruck, G. M., Ireland, R. D., & Ketchen, D. J. J., Jr. (2010). The Entrepreneurship process in base of the pyramid markets: The case of multinational enterprise/nongovernment organization alliances. *Entrepreneurship Theory and Practice*, *34*(3), 555–581. http://dx.doi.org/10.1111/j.1540-6520.2009.00349.x

Weisbrod, B. A. (1975). Toward a theory of the voluntary nonprofit sector in a three-sector economy. In E. Phelps (Ed.), *Altruism, morality, and economic theory* (pp. 171–196). New York: Russell Sage Foundation.

Wennberg, K., Wiklund, J., DeTienne, D. R., & Cardon, M. S. (2010). Reconceptualizing entrepreneurial exit: Divergent exit routes and their drivers. *Journal of Business Venturing*, *25*(4), 361–375. http://dx.doi.org/10.1016/j.jbusvent.2009.01.001

Wiersema, M. F., & Liebeskind, J. P. (1995). The effects of leveraged buyouts on corporate growth and diversification in large firms. *Strategic Management Journal*, *16*(6), 447–460. http://dx.doi.org/10.1002/smj.4250160604

Wright, M., Hoskisson, R. E., Busenitz, L. W., & Dial, J. (2000). Entrepreneurial growth through privatization: The upside of management buyouts. *Academy of Management Review*, *25*(3), 591–601.

Zahra, S. A., Gedajlovic, E., Neubaum, D. O., & Shulman, J. M. (2009). A typology of social entrepreneurs: Motives, search processes and ethical challenges. *Journal of Business Venturing*, *24*(5), 519–532. http://dx.doi.org/10.1016/j.jbusvent.2008.04.007

NETWORK BRICOLAGE AS THE RECONCILIATION OF INDIGENOUS AND TRANSPLANTED INSTITUTIONS IN AFRICA

Kevin McKague and Christine Oliver

ABSTRACT

This paper argues that *network bricolage* can play an important role in reconciling informal indigenous institutions rooted in African history with formal institutions mostly transplanted from outside. Drawing on the literature on bricolage, social entrepreneurship, networks and institutional entrepreneurship, and illustrated with an example, we define network bricolage as a process that involves interest alignment and a relational governance structure among network actors. Our analysis distinguishes network bricolage from organizational-level bricolage and develops a theory to explain it. A greater understanding of network bricolage has important implications for the theory and practice of entrepreneurship in Africa, including the need to understand the deeper ontological and epistemological assumptions that underpin informal and formal institutions.

ENTREPRENEURSHIP IN AFRICA

Based on a comprehensive study of entrepreneurship and management in Africa, Dia (1994) argued that the most important and persistent challenge in sub-Saharan Africa is reconciling local African institutions and practices with formal institutions and practices adopted from elsewhere. The central crisis for entrepreneurs and managers in Africa, he argued, is "due to a structural and functional disconnect between informal, indigenous institutions rooted in the region's history and culture and formal institutions mostly transplanted from outside" (Dia, 1994: 1). Formal regulatory, normative and cultural-cognitive institutions (Scott, 2008) not rooted in African culture (tax legislation and formal insurance policies, for example) tend to suffer from lack of legitimacy and effectiveness in creating incentives and shaping entrepreneurial behavior. In contrast, indigenous African institutions rooted in local rules, norms and culture (such as extended family and communal support systems) often enjoy greater legitimacy, adherence and respect, as they have a stronger connection to the identities of individuals and organizations. However, despite the strengths of local institutions, they can also have limitations, including discrimination based on gender, family connection, and age, for example. What is needed is neither formalization of informal institutions or informalization of formal institutions, but a reconciliation and "convergent synergy … between adaptive formal institutions and renovated indigenous institutions" (Dia, 1994: 2).

This view is consistent with institutional theory, which examines the influence of widely held social belief systems on individuals and organizations within a community, society or institutional field (Scott, 2008). Institutions are the "socially constructed, historical patterns of material practices, assumptions, values, beliefs, and rules by which individuals produce and reproduce their material subsistence, organize time and space, and provide meaning to their social reality" (Thornton & Ocasio, 1999: 804). Institutional theory analyzes the dynamics and interactions of multiple institutional systems of meaning that shape individual and organizational behavior (Friedland & Alford, 1991) including how two different institutional orders can become integrated. This view of the core challenge for entrepreneurial and management theory development in Africa is also consistent with the work of Zoogah and colleagues (Zoogah, 2008; Zoogah, & Nkomo, 2013; Zoogah, Peng & Woldu, 2015) who argues the need to understand how the two most important aspects of the African context – traditional and modern institutions – influence entrepreneurial and organizational behavior.

The idea of institutional reconciliation and convergence is also reflected in the French expression "*enracinement et ouverture*" coined by former Senegalese President, Leopold Senghor (1964). It suggests that to function effectively, African institutions have to be both rooted (*enracinees*) in local history and open (*outvertes*) to outside influences. When formal and informal institutions can be reconciled, build on each other and converge, entrepreneurs can be more likely to achieve their objectives, including strengthened economic, social and environmental performance. Our central question is therefore: *How can we understand the process of institutional reconciliation from the perspective of entrepreneurship in Africa?*

To answer this question, we draw on the literature on social entrepreneurship in subsistence markets, bricolage, networks, and institutional theory. Drawing on insights from this literature, this paper explains how we can understand the process of institutional reconciliation in Africa as *network bricolage*. Throughout the paper, we use the example of Honey Care Africa, an East African for-profit social enterprise operating in Kenya, Tanzania and South Sudan, to illustrate the concept. This example is not intended to serve as data for the paper, but rather is offered as an illustrative case to help in understanding the theoretical arguments presented.

Based on the literature, we identify three core processes of bricolage that operate at both the organizational and network levels of analysis to reconcile institutions in Africa: using resources at hand, combing existing resources for new purposes, and negotiating actions and meanings in context. Uniquely, we also distinguish two core process of bricolage that operate primarily at the network level of analysis: interest alignment and relational governance among network members. We also discern four norms of network governance that we propose are likely to facilitate effective network bricolage: transparency, trust-based ties, representation and distributed power. We argue that network bricolage is a process that allows entrepreneurs ways to address the key challenge of reconciling indigenous and transplanted institutions in Africa.

This paper begins with a review of the literature on social entrepreneurship in subsistence markets, bricolage, networks and institutional theory. We then introduce a theory of network bricolage to explain the process and outcomes of establishing and governing effective entrepreneurial approaches to social enterprise development and draw on the Honey Care Africa example to illustrate our theoretical arguments. The paper concludes with a discussion of implications for theory and practice.

SOCIAL ENTREPRENEURSHIP IN SUBSISTENCE MARKETS

To glean the most relevant insights from the entrepreneurship literature, we turned to theory and research on a particularly relevant specialized field: social entrepreneurship in subsistence markets. We define social entrepreneurship as approaches to social and ecological value creation that are financially self-sustaining, provide direct benefit to low-income individuals, and have the potential to reach significant scale (Kubzansky, Cooper, & Barbary, 2011; McMullen, 2011; Mendoza & Thelen, 2008). Social entrepreneurship "creates new models for the provision of products and services that cater directly to basic human needs that remain unsatisfied by current economic or social institutions" (Seelos & Mair, 2005: 243–244). Examples of social enterprises in Africa include Living Goods (Gupta & Perepu, 2010), One Acre Fund (Sherman & Donnelly, 2011) Kidogo, Sanergy (Auerbach, 2016), Farm Shop, mKopa (Miller, 2012), Tiviski Dairy, Bridge International Academies (Rangan & Lee, 2010), Technoserve (Karnani & McKague, 2014), Honey Care Africa (Jiwa, 2007);and Fan Milk (Jones-Christensen et al., 2010). Social entrepreneurs create social enterprises to address issues such as poverty alleviation, improved healthcare, education or sanitation in slums, improved agricultural productivity and incomes for smallholder farmers, or increased access to clean electricity. These enterprises engage in production, trade and other revenue generating activities to increase financial self-reliance and allow for scaling of their social impact through leveraging market forces (Di Domenico, Haugh & Tracey, 2010; Mair & Marti, 2009).

For the purposes of this paper, we define the literature on subsistence markets to include a variety of streams in the entrepreneurship and management literature, which focuses on low-income market contexts where indigenous informal institutions are likely to be present with formal institutions. When we refer to literature on subsistence marketplaces, we include the bottom- or base-of-the-pyramid (BoP) approach (Kolk, Rivera-Santos & Rufín, 2013; London, 2016; London, & Anupindi, 2012; Prahalad, 2005; Sprague, 2008), community-based enterprise (Peredo & Chrisman, 2006), approaches that focus on cross-sector partnerships for poverty alleviation (Gradl, Krämer, & Amadigi, 2010; Hamann & Boulogne, 2008; Kolk & Lenfant, 2012), sustainable local enterprise networks (Wheeler, McKague, Thompson, Davies, Medalye, & Prada, 2005), social entrepreneurship (Rivera-Santos, Holt, Littlewood, & Kolk, 2015; Thumbadoo & Wilson, 2007; Webb, Kistruck, Ireland & Ketchen, 2010), inclusive markets (Mendoza & Thelen, 2008), social business (Yunus, Moingeon, & Lehmann-Ortega, 2010) and the literature on subsistence marketplaces itself (Viswanathan & Rosa, 2010; Rosa & Viswanathan, 2007). Taken together, this literature all addresses, in some form or another, enterprise in subsistence market contexts in low-income economies where informal institutions are likely to be present together with formal institutions.

We intentionally chose the literature on social enterprises in subsistence markets due to its potential to offer insights into the process of institutional reconciliation in Africa. Social enterprises often intentionally position themselves in the marketplace to address coordination failures and fill institutional voids in communities and contexts with limited access to services and resources (Di Domenico, Haugh & Tracey, 2010; Peredo & Chrisman, 2006). Coordination failures occur when neither private sector actors, market forces (Stiglitz, 2009) nor governments (Hall, 2010) provide the institutional rules and norms to reduce transaction costs, facilitate information flow and align incentives for market production and trade (Datta-Chaudhuri, 1990). In developed economies, economically and socially productive activity is coordinated by the market mechanism together with effective government regulatory institutions (North, 1990). However, in many least developed country contexts, coordination failures by markets and government lead to institutional voids (Mair & Marti, 2009; Mair, Marti, & Ventresca, 2012). In the context of social enterprises working in subsistence marketplaces, an institutional void is "a situation where absent and /or weak institution arrangement prevent those excluded by poverty from participating in market activities" (Mair & Marti, 2009: 494).

Institutional "voids" were originally described in the mainstream management literature on doing business in emerging markets because Western managers perceived an absence of formal market institutions and intermediaries (such as functioning credit markets or systems or legal contract enforcement, for example) (Khanna & Palepu, 2005). However, in light of Dia's (1994) key framing of the central issue for entrepreneurs and managers in Africa noted above, and a more recent nuanced view of how social enterprises work with institutions in subsistence markets (Mair, Marti, & Ventresca, 2012), we can understand social enterprises in low-income markets as working to reconcile local and transplanted institutions. In contexts where formal government regulatory institutions are missing, research has found that social enterprises and other market-based organizations rely on informal institutions governed by deeply embedded relationships and networks (London & Hart, 2004; Rivera-Santos & Rufín, 2010). Institutional voids may not have strong formal institutions, but rather than viewing them only in terms of voids, they can be understood as opportunity spaces (Mair, Marti, & Ganly, 2007). Furthermore, instead of seeing institutional voids only as opportunities for entering a market with a new product, service or organization (Hart, 2005), they can also be understood as the space where formal and informal institutions can be acknowledged, understood, integrated and reconciled. In the mainstream entrepreneurship literature, underlying formal and modern regulatory, normative and cultural institutions that facilitate market exchange are taken for granted and do not sufficiently address the key issue of institutional reconciliation that is the central challenge for entrepreneurs in Africa. The solution to a weak or missing modern, formal market institutions is not greater imposition of formal institutions, but more nuanced negotiation and reconciliation between formal and informal institutions. Traditional formal sector entrepreneurs and firms operate primarily under the formal, modern institutional norms for doing business. For the purposes of our theory development, insights from mainstream firms in Africa are less relevant than social enterprises in subsistence markets as a source of possible insight. A focus on findings from the social entrepreneurship literature in subsistence markets therefore has unique potential to help entrepreneurs understand the fundamental issues they face to achieve their objectives.

Networks

Subsistence markets – which we defined as low-income contexts where informal and formal institutions are substantively present – have features that are distinct from traditional, formal market contexts in developed contexts (Hart & London, 2005; Milstein, London and Hart, 2007). Subsistence markets are contexts where formal property rights and other formal market institutions are weak or non-existent (De Soto, 2000), transaction costs are high (McKague and Oliver, 2012), information is unavailable (McKague, Zietsma, & Oliver 2015), capital is less accessible (Ansari, Munir & Gregg, 2012), and organizational environments are unstable and uncertain (Reficco & Márquez, 2012).

Because the institutional context of subsistence markets contains elements of both formal and informal markets and a variety of market and non-market stakeholders that are embedded in different normative and cultural/cognitive institutions (Scott, 2008), the literature has identified that networks play an important role in social enterprise development (Hart & London, 2005; Riverra-Santos & Rufín, 2010; Wheeler et al., 2005). In their work on multinational enterprises entering base-of-the-pyramid markets, Hart and London (2005: 30) found that multinational companies need to "become indigenous to the places in which they operate" and develop "native capabilities" that respect local culture so that they "become truly embedded in the local context." Although much literature focuses on partnerships between two organizations (often multinational companies partnering with non-governmental organizations or local communities), greater attention is needed at the network level of analysis.

Network theory focuses on understanding the content, structure and governance of the multiple interrelationships among three or more organizations informally collaborating together (Birley, 1985; Hoang & Antoncic, 2003). In their study of networks in subsistence markets, Rivera-Santos & Rufín (2010) identified several characteristics of what social enterprise networks in subsistence markets look like. They found that, compared with traditional business networks in developed markets, social enterprise networks in subsistence markets were "likely to be less centralized, wider in scope, less dense overall (but also containing high-density clusterings), and contain more structural holes; network ties are more commonly direct and informal, are actualized more frequently, and involve a multiplicity of domains of interaction among network members; the diversity of network members is greater" (Rivera-Santos & Rufín, 2010: 136). This review of the literature on network content, structure and governance is helpful to understand the process of reconciling formal and informal institutions by social enterprises in subsistence marketplaces.

Networks consisting of a variety of market actors (e.g. social enterprises, companies, small- and medium-sized enterprises, micro-entrepreneurs) and non-market actors (government, non-governmental organizations, universities, chiefs) in subsistence marketplaces are used to addressing coordination failures and institutional voids. One way this is achieved is through establishing a high density of network ties that facilitates the flow of information (Rivera-Santos & Rufín, 2010). This, in turn, can reduce transaction costs and build trust in a self-reinforcing virtuous cycle. Because institutional voids in subsistence markets often lack "suppliers, customers, technologies, product requirements, service demands, distribution channels" (Milstein, London & Hart, 2007: 90) and other formal market infrastructure and intermediaries, networks with a broad diversity of members can be utilized to solve problems and internalize missing parts of the value creation (access to credit, for example) and value distribution process (norms ensuring fair weighing of farmer's produce, for example). In more developed markets, access to credit would be facilitated by the private sector and standards of weights and measures would be regulated and enforced by the government. In subsistence markets, network members are coordinated and incentivized to fill gaps in the value chain and reconcile formal and informal market rules and norms.

Networks in subsistence markets are characterized by a greater prevalence of structural holes than networks in wealthy, developed markets (Rivera-Santos & Rufín, 2010). In imperfect markets, organizations and individuals often lack access to complete or accurate information. Organizations able to position themselves to control the flow of information between two networks act as "brokers" to bridge information between "structural holes" (Burt, 1995). In subsistence markets, social entrepreneurs often use their knowledge of a wide range of stakeholders to position themselves as a broker of resources and information across structural holes in a network (Rivera-Santos & Rufín, 2010). Although networks in subsistence markets take resources, effort, and time to be established, once they are developed and well governed, they can be an effective structure to solve coordination failures and fill institutional voids through facilitating exchange of resources and information among network members. This capability gives the network and the brokering organization (often a social entrepreneur) increased capabilities in bridging and reconciling indigenous and transplanted institutions.

Bricolage

The limited work on bricolage in the management literature to date has confined its focus to the individual level of analysis (Weick, 1998) and organization level of analysis (Baker & Nelson, 2005; Garud & Karnøe, 2003; Rao, Morin, & Durand, 2005) with little attention yet focused on the network level of analysis. The concept of bricolage in the management literature has its theoretical origins in the work of Levi-Strauss (1966: 17) who referred to bricolage as a particular way that human beings relate to their environment which includes making do "with whatever is at hand." Bricolage is an action-oriented process of improvisation in which a bricoleur – one who engages in bricolage – "creates something out of nothing" to generate new solutions to existing problems. Levi-Strauss contrasted bricolage with another way that people can relate to their environment, which he labeled 'engineering', which requires expert planning, analytic thinking, and rationally identifying objectives and the specific resources by which the objectives would be achieved (Stinchfield, Nelson & Wood, 2013). Levi-Strauss developed the ideal types of the bricoleur and the engineer as a way to distinguish these two different human ways of being without necessarily ranking them (Boxenbaum & Rouleau, 2011). The bricoleur understands the world according to direct and intimate experience with the complex non-linear environment (which Halme and Lindeman (2009) suggest are characteristics of subsistence marketplaces). This differs from the engineer's approach to knowledge generation based on reductionism and the scientific method. Although studies in anthropology have examined individuals as "bricoleurs who tinker, borrow, improvise, experiment and recombine existing elements (Douglas, 1986)" (Rao et al., 2005: 971), the application of bricolage to management studies has been limited and recent. Among the first to do so were Baker and Nelson (2005: 330) whose study of a sample of small resource-constrained firms showed that bricolage as a process of making do with and recombining elements at hand explained the firms' entrepreneurial success in rendering unique products and services and creating self-perpetuating value. According to Baker and Nelson (2005), core to the process of bricolage is a bias toward action, a refusal to accept historical limitations in the firm's environment, an improvisational approach to combining existing resources for new purposes, and the use of existing resources as a platform for entrepreneurial success. Garud and Karnøe's (2003) study of bricolage in the Danish wind turbine industry, for example, showed how Danish engineers scoured scrap dealers for materials and used existing resources for new purposes to grow their business.

Social enterprises utilize dense multi-stakeholder networks in subsistence markets to address coordination failures and bridge institutional voids. Drawing on network theory to inform our understanding of reconciling local indigenous informal institutions with transplanted formal institutions is therefore likely to be helpful to our development of a theory of network bricolage.

Although Baker, Miner, and Eesley (2003) have previously discussed a process of using pre-existing contact networks as network bricolage, their study was based on new computer training and consulting firms in the Research Triangle area of North Carolina with their use of 'network' denoting an entrepreneur's existing rolodex of contacts or new contacts made through 'networking' events. Their findings, therefore, emerge from experiences in knowledge intensive industries in a context where entrepreneurs have access to significant local stocks of human, financial, and other sources of capital and assume a narrower concept of inter-organizational relational networks.

Institutional Entrepreneurship

The literature on institutional entrepreneurship examines those conditions under which novel initiatives are able to emerge in institutionalized settings (Dacin, Goodstein, & Scott, 2002). We follow Garud, Jain, and Kumaraswamy's (2002: 196–197) definition of institutional entrepreneurs as actors who "create a whole new system of meaning that ties the functioning of disparate sets of institutions together ... Assuming the role of champions, they energize efforts toward collective action and devise strategies for establishing stable sequences of interaction with other organizations to create entirely new industries and associated institutions." Rao, Monin and Durand (2005: 987) argue that "although neo-institutionalists agree that culture is a tool kit and that actors engage in bricolage, there is little research on how actors creatively tinker with techniques from rival categories infused with competing logics."

Social entrepreneurs in subsistence markets in Africa possess the potential to identify synergistic interests and objectives among different members of their networks that can be organized into novel self-perpetuating sources of value creation. Consistent with Maguire, Hardy, and Lawrence's (2004: 658) study of institutional entrepreneurship in an "underorganized domain", we characterize social entrepreneurship as institutional entrepreneurship whose success depends upon "the way in which institutional entrepreneurs connect their change projects to the activities and interests of other actors in a field." When social enterprise approaches to poverty alleviation in

Africa, for example, operate at a collaborative network level, these approaches have the potential to generate cooperation, overcome coordination failures, align interests across multiple actors to mobilize constituencies, and access resources (Rao, Morrill, & Zald, 2000).

Although Wijen and Ansari (2007) described a process of collective institutional entrepreneurship; Tracey, Phillips and Jarvis (2011) described bridging institutional entrepreneurship, and Montgomery, Dacin and Dacin (2012) described a process of collective social entrepreneurship, all of the constructs and theories discussed were based on non-African contexts where resources were significant and local stocks of human, financial and other sources of capital were available and functioning market institutions were taken for granted.

The Nature of Indigenous and Transplanted Institutions in Africa

Dia (1994) identified the reconciliation of indigenous and transplanted institutions as the most important issue for African entrepreneurs and our review of the literature provided greater insight into the nature and differences between these institutional belief systems. Here we have employed Weber's (1997) analytical tool of ideal types to help us understand the differences as suggested by the literature. Ideal types are abstract, hypothetical constructs which identify elements common to most, but not all, cases of a given phenomenon. Ideal types can be useful for understanding and describing social phenomena. In the real world, phenomena (such as indigenous and transplanted institutions) may be situated somewhere between the two ideal types. We have labeled our two ideal types *bricolage* and *engineering* following the terms used by Levi-Strauss (1966) to compare and contrast two different ways that human beings can understand and relate to their environment – see Table 1.

The differences between bricolage and engineering approaches to problem solving, value creation and coordination are rooted in different ontological and epistemological assumptions about the world, the nature of reality and knowledge. The engineering approach is underpinned by a positivist ontology. Our ontology is our assumption about the nature of reality. A positivist ontology assumes that an objective reality exists beyond individual perception and that this reality can be discovered and analyzed and that solutions to problems can be specified before they are solved. Within a positivist ontology, cause-effect relationships can be isolated from their context, measured and observed, thus making the local context and the complexity of interrelationships less important. In contrast, an interpretivist ontology assumes that reality is subjective and derived from human perception and meaning systems. With an interpretivist ontology, solutions to problems require searching for opportunities within the existing context to move toward incremental improvements or 'good-enough' solutions. An in-depth understanding of local resources and institutions is important along with experimentation and tight information feedback loops to learn whether particular solution ideas are working or not. The bricoleur understands the world according to direct and intimate experience with the complex environment. This differs from the engineer's approach to knowledge generation based on reductionism and the scientific method.

In the entrepreneurship and management literature, bricolage "remains extremely underdeveloped" (Baker, Miner and Eesley, 2003: 270) while the positivist paradigm predominates (Morgan, 1980). This may be the case because management, including

Table 1. Bricolage vs Engineering.

	Bricolage	Engineering
Levi-Strauss, 1966	Mythical worldview: Belief in responding intuitively to situations as they arise	Scientific worldview: Belief in the superiority of rationality and scientific reasoning
Easterly, 2006	Searching	Planning
Baker et al. 2003	Improvisation	Design-execution
Scribner, 1986	Practical thinking: Leading to day-to-day opportunistic behavior	Theoretical thinking: Leading to analysis and abstraction
Ontology	Interpretivist	Positivist
Epistemology	The world is a complex, chaotic, interconnected system	The world can be reduced to orderly, independent component parts
Metaphors	Jazz music, detective	Architectural blueprint, scientist
Assumptions about the external environment	Rapidly changing, unpredictable and ambiguous	Stable, predictable and measurable
Orientation toward resource-seeking	Resourcefulness: Focus on possible creative uses of available resources	Specification: Identify and source specialized resources designed for the job
Assumptions about learning and knowledge	Do-it-yourself: Knowledge generated from interaction with context on the ground	Specialist: Solutions designed by expert based on pre-existing knowledge
Assumptions about errors and mistakes	Welcome: Seen as essential for learning what will work and what won't	Seen as failure of the plan: To be avoided by sufficient specification of materials, design and execution ahead of time
Assumptions about the future	Future is unknowable and uncertain: Complex inter-relationship of variables	Future is knowable and predictable: Follows predictable cause-effect relationships
Assumptions about solutions to problems	Emergent: Must be discovered by experimentation, interacting and learning from the local context	Rational: Solutions pre-exist and can be known ahead of time by subject experts
Logics	Exploratory Intuitive Fluid Subjective Inductive Uncertain Nonlinear Action-oriented Relative Workable	Analytic Logical Measurable Objective Deductive Certain Linear Analysis-oriented Absolute Efficient

management in Africa, is assumed to be a predominantly rational (if bounded) activity (Simon, 1991). Under this assumption, managers are expected to articulate a strategy and allocate resources to meet stated objectives (Fisher, 2012). This rational positivism with its focus on stability and uncertainty reduction has been at the heart of the management literature since its inception (Taylor, 1911/2004) and has been reinforced by the industrial organization paradigm (Porter, 1981).

Over the last three to four decades, however, the entrepreneurship and management literature has increasingly moved beyond its core assumption of rationality (Stinchfield, Nelson and Wood, 2013). Increasingly, an alternative view has also been articulated that recognizes that resources, opportunities, institutions and meanings can be understood as socially constructed rather than objectively constituted (Fisher, 2012; Sarasvathy, 2001; Scott, 2008). If rational assumptions are incomplete, the role of social construction, social norms, relationships and networks becomes more important. Examining management in Africa in the complex context of social entrepreneurship in subsistence markets around institutional voids helps surface the need for greater attention to social norms and values and the process of reconciling indigenous and transplanted institutions.

In this section, we summarized relevant literature on social entrepreneurship in subsistence markets, networks, bricolage and institutional entrepreneurship as it relates to the fundamental entrepreneurial challenge of reconciling indigenous and transplanted institutions in Africa. In the next section, we provide an example of a for-profit, social enterprise to help us draw the literature streams together and illustrate the theory of network bricolage.

Honey Care Africa: An Illustrative Example

Honey Care Africa has grown from its establishment in 2000 to become East Africa's largest honey producer with 38% of the domestic market share in Kenya. Having expanded beyond Kenya to Tanzania, South Sudan and the Democratic Republic of the Congo, Honey Care Africa works with 15,000 farmers (43% of whom are women) to enable them to generate additional income (Jiwa, 2007). Founded by Kenyan Farouk Jiwa and now led by Madison Ayer and his team of 35 full-time staff, Honey Care Africa collects, packages, and markets honey primarily for sale in Nairobi supermarkets. It links poverty reduction and environmental conservation by providing beehives and related beekeeping equipment to organizations, communities, and individuals (Jiwa, 2007; Valente, 2010) and has introduced several innovations to the sector, including more productive hives, microfinance funding for individual beekeepers, beekeeping training, prompt cash payments to local farmers, and a guaranteed market for honey producers at fair trade prices. Beekeepers selling to Honey Care Africa average $250 in sales per year (often doubling their previous incomes) with a payback period from purchasing a hive and equipment of approximately 18 months. Further, the practice of beekeeping supports the essential ecological service of pollination for crops and vegetation, which further enhances the incomes of many of the beekeepers who also keep crops. Honey Care Africa collaborates with a network of partners to create value in economic, social, and ecological terms. We suggest that the success of such social enterprise approaches to poverty alleviation in Africa is, in fact, primarily attributable to network bricolage.

TOWARD A THEORY OF NETWORK BRICOLAGE

Based on our review of the literature, we define network bricolage as a process that involves a relational governance structure at the network level and interest alignment and coordination of incentives across network members to yield value. In contrast with core processes of bricolage, which can operate at either the organizational or network level (using resources at hand, combining resources for net purposes, and negotiating meanings in context), we suggest that the two unique core processes of *network bricolage* operate primarily at the network level. Our theory of network bricolage can help explain the effectiveness of social entrepreneurs in subsistence markets in Africa to reconcile indigenous and transplanted institutions. In putting forward this theory, we hope to extend our understanding of entrepreneurship in Africa and contribute to the literature on social entrepreneurship in subsistence markets and institutional entrepreneurship.

We propose that the process of network bricolage can bridge the needs of network members in ways that facilitate access to dispersed resources (Hardy & Maguire, 2008: 201). The capacity of network bricoleurs to facilitate access to disbursed resources by linking across multiple stakeholders is consistent both with recent research on institutional entrepreneurship in the social services sector (Mair & Marti, 2009; Maguire et al., 2004), with more recent characterizations of institutional entrepreneurship as a predominantly relational and collective process (Hardy & McGuire, 2008), and with research on networks in base-of-the-pyramid contexts (Rivera-Santos & Rufín, 2010). Network bricolage explains the process by which social enterprises in Africa can achieve their objectives of simultaneously creating economic, social, and ecological value by reconciling formal and informal institutions present around institutional voids. Figure 1 summarizes our theoretical model. We propose that network bricolage is an effective governance process in low-income economic settings in Africa because its focus is on engagement with and brokering among local resources, institutions and expertise and resources from outside the local context.

This theoretical model of network bricolage captures two distinguishing features of social entrepreneurship in subsistence markets. First, social enterprises are founded on the basis of an opportunity for social, economic, and ecological value creation (Seelos & Mair, 2005) that leverages resources or skills that already exist *in situ* (Baker & Nelson, 2005). Second, because the governance model of social enterprise networks is network based, it can develop and become self-perpetuating by means of bringing diverse actors together in a network to fund, operate, and derive

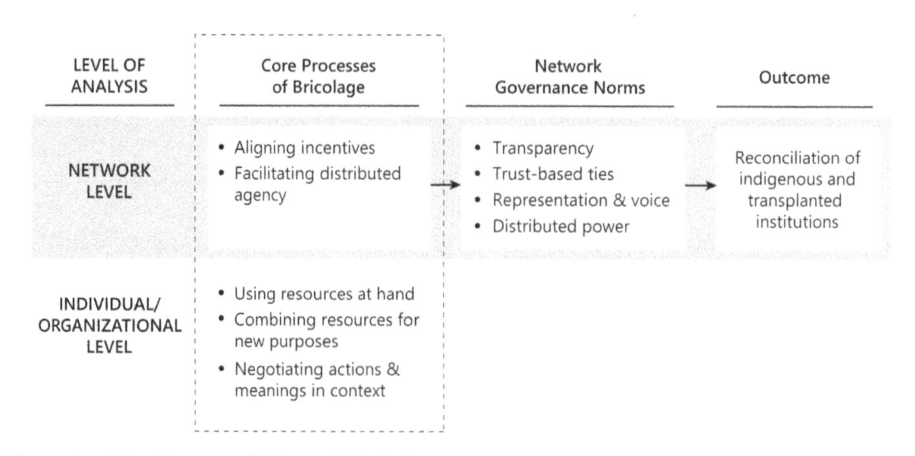

Figure 1. The Process of Network Bricolage.

benefits from the enterprise (Wheeler et al., 2005). Network bricoleurs link diverse participants based on their understanding of others' interests, resources, and beliefs. As Weick (1993: 353) emphasizes, "Exhaustive observation and systematic cataloging of relations and connections (Levi-Strauss, 1996: 10) are necessary for successful bricolage." And as Banerjee and Campbell (2009: 477) recognize, "entrepreneurial agency is distributed across actors." The underlying driver of Honey Care Africa's success in promoting small-scale beekeeping is its network of over 15,000 local farmers and its ties with microfinance organizations, development agencies, local firms, and local communities, which have made it possible to attain its social and economic objectives. Relations and connections were established between Honey Care Africa and the large number of other organizations in its enterprise network based on the CEO's skill in listening, understanding the interests of other organizations, and aligning interests that already existed among the individual organizations. Based on our reviews of the literature, we argue that five core processes of bricolage explain the success of social enterprises in subsistence markets in reconciling indigenous and transplanted institutions. Three core process are present in both organization-level bricolage and network bricolage, and two core processes are uniquely relevant to network-level bricolage. These core processes are outlined below.

Core Processes of Bricolage

Using resources at hand. Applied both at the organizational and the network level, bricolage refers to employing or repurposing resources to solve problems or create new opportunities (Di Domenco, Haugh & Tracey, 2010). At the organizational level, Barney (1997: 142–143) defines resources as "all assets, capabilities, competencies, organizational processes, firm attributes, information, knowledge and so forth that are controlled by its members and that enable the firm to conceive of and implement strategies that improve its efficiency and effectiveness." When considering the network level of analysis, we can also include these tangible resources, as well as intangible resources such as institutional norms and beliefs, inter-organizational relationships and social legitimacy (Desa, 2012; Scott, 2008). The issue of resources is central to the concept of bricolage, with Cunha and Cunha (2007: 52) arguing that bricolage is primarily "a creative approach to problems in which resources play a fundamental role." In an 'engineering' approach (Levi-Strauss, 1966), the assumption is that problems can be solved if enough resources are thrown at it. Although entrepreneurs and bricoleurs in any context are challenged with resource constraints, entrepreneurs and bricoleurs in subsistence markets in Africa face severe limits to many resources, which affect value creation activities and market transactions (Linna, 2013).

The constraints on material resources in subsistence markets in Africa have interesting implications for bricolage. Firstly, African bricoleurs develop a greater depth of knowledge about resources that are on hand. Effective bricolage requires an intimacy with available resources (Duymedjian & Rüling, 2010), which may be extremely limited or scarce (Diomande, 1990). Weick (1993: 352) reinforces this point, emphasizing that "the more fully the materials themselves are understood, the more innovative will the bricoleur be in improvising new designs from this stock of materials." In this context, resourcefulness and the depth of familiarity is more important than the specific resources at hand (Cunha & Cunha, 2007; Gibbert, Hoegl, & Välikangas,

2007). Becoming more intimately familiar with resources at hand, including intangible resources of network members, allows African bricoleurs to redefine what is categorized as a 'useful' resource, allowing a greater diversity of resources to be seen as potentially useful. This includes resources that may have been unrecognized, ignored, discarded or not valued by others (Di Domenco, Haugh & Tracey, 2010). In the illustration provided by Honey Care Africa, flowering plants in ecological reserves were an untapped resource that could be turned into income by poor farmers living on the periphery of the parks. Paradoxically, although African bricoleurs in materially resource constrained contexts may have fewer resources to work with, they also may have fewer limits on the perceived uses to which the resources can be put and may be more able to reject pre-conceived constraints on how resources can be used (Baker & Nelson, 2005).

Secondly, with severe constraints on material resources, African bricoleurs focus greater attention on institutional resources such as relationships, local knowledge, social norms and cultural beliefs (Diomande, 1990). Many intangible social resources, such as social capital and trust, exist in the relations between individuals and organizations that can have significant impact on value creation and distribution (Peredo & Chrisman, 2006). With Africa's entrepreneurial challenge of reconciling local and transplanted institutions in resource constrained environments, bricolage needs to not only consider local material resources that can be understood and used, but also social, institutional and relational resources that can be used to solve coordination failures and create economic, social and ecological value. For example, at the network level, microfinance institutions were reluctant to work with Honey Care Africa when it was first established, until Honey Care Africa proposed a way to collect regular loan repayments on behalf of the microfinance institutions when it collected honey and paid farmers. In this way, Honey Care Africa used the resources already at hand (staff collecting honey and paying farmers cash on the spot) to create an incentive for a network member, the microfinance institution, to add its resources (a loan) to the network.

Third, the use of familiar resources already extant in the local market context helps to reduce what Hodgson (2001: 76) refers to as "the vexed question of distributive fairness within the market order." Thus, "mak[ing] to do with what is at hand" (Levi-Strauss, 1966: 17), Honey Care Africa used the natural Kenyan and East African bee populations, vegetation, farmers, demand in urban supermarkets, non-governmental organizations and microfinance institutions as some of the foundational resources for creating its business and building a network of participants to sustain its function as a source of income. In general, when using resources at hand at the network level, network bricolage succeeds in "creating new ventures out of nothing and defy(ing) conventional assumptions about the role of the environment in determining the success or failure of organizations" (Phillips & Tracey, 2007). Specifically, Honey Care Africa "made use of what was built up locally" (Andersen, 2008: 61) – an abundance of potential for beekeeping, other organizations and untapped middle-class demand – to create a sustainable business, and, as beekeeping requires minimal land, the smallholder farmers have been able to engage in commercial beekeeping on the basis of what is at hand, that is, on the land they already own. In this way bricolage assists in reducing "a different distribution of 'original endowments' – i.e., allocation of ownership of factors of production across the individual members of a particular society" (Hodgson, 2001: 76). Consistent with previous views of bricolage as being oriented toward practical problem solving, the use of resources at hand gains particular traction in contexts where new resource acquisition is problematic, suggesting that network bricolage is especially well suited to African contexts.

Combining existing resources for new purposes. Using resources at hand is insufficient alone for bricolage at either the organizational or network level. Resources must be combined for new purposes to successfully create something out of nothing (Di Domenico, Haugh, & Tracey, 2010). Combining resources in novel ways allows them to address new problems or opportunities for which they were not originally designed (Archer, Baker, & Mauer, 2009). Combining existing resources occurs as a synergistic process that evolves through bottom-up mobilization of network members. This combining of existing resources for new purposes can be undertaken in a number of ways. As Weick (1993: 352) notes, "Through the use of generalization, analogies, and comparisons, the bricoleur assembles new arrangements of elements."

At the network level, network bricolage-based social entrepreneurship can be locally initiated innovations in the pursuit of common goals (Andersen, 2008). Bricolage at the network level can include the active assembly of existing organizations and individual human resources to achieve novel outcomes. Honey Care Africa identified rural subsistence farmers already residing in impoverished areas and worked with various non-governmental organizations to train these farmers in beekeeping as a primary or supplementary source of income. They also worked with microfinance organizations, such as Kiva, to facilitate loans for farmers to purchase hives and equipment. Therefore, network bricolage partially succeeds because it induces a process of combining resources at hand, including existing organizations and human capital, through a bottom-up network approach that produces synergistic partnerships that meet both individual and collective-level goals.

Negotiating actions and meanings in context. The process of bricolage includes negotiating the meanings of resources or practices with local participants who interpret or conceptualize possible solutions fitted to local problems and constraints (Desa, 2012). In contrast with many donor-funded or charitable approaches to poverty alleviation, which can come with a predetermined plan of implementation, bricolage as a process negotiates the meaning of economic and social action in the local context in which the poor negotiate the adversity of their daily lives (McKague, Zietsma & Oliver, 2015). This is particularly relevant for the reconciliation of local and transplanted institutions in Africa. From the perspective of bricolage, resourcefulness is a function of one's knowledge of the immediate environment, including material resources and intangible network resources. Valente's (2012) study of six business–community partnerships in Africa found that understanding local context is essential to negotiating the actions and meaning of sustainable development in the countries in which the partnerships operate. Levi-Strauss (1966) argued that a local orientation to what is at hand may contribute to deeper levels of social knowledge with respect to local resource endowments, and that this deeper knowledge makes more apparent the usefulness of what is available cheaply (Baker 2007: 697). Meaning must also be negotiated in context because bricolage is practice that is grounded in daily activities rather than predesigned policies or plans. In other words, bricolage is situated resourcefulness negotiated in context by local participants who interpret action in terms of local problems and available resources. Contextual or *in situ* problem solving orients social entrepreneurs toward workable rather than theoretically optimized solutions to local constraints, increasing the feasibility of proposed solutions. For example, Honey Care Africa's rural African farmers can adapt beekeeping activities to their current ecological circumstances (their own existing farms) rather than having to adopt entirely new practices or circumstances to enact economic enterprise. Economic activity is negotiated with local participants on the basis of approaches and meaning systems they already possess.

Negotiating actions and meanings in context includes challenging limitations imposed by conventional institutional norms, beliefs and logics (De Domenico, Haugh & Tracy, 2010; Baker & Nelson, 2005). Baker and Nelson (2005: 336) argue that bricolage, at the level of normative and cultural institutions, recognizes the "socially constructed nature of idiosyncratic firm resource environments." At the network level, Honey Care Africa took a trial and error approach to working with non-governmental organizations to train subsistence farmers in beekeeping. Some non-governmental organizations did not understand the logic of Honey Care Africa operating as a business, believing that farmers should receive their hives for free (as had been the case with many aid-funded honey development projects in the past). Through persuasion (Di Domenco, Haugh & Tracey, 2010) and legitimizing their approach through dialogue with non-governmental organizations (McKague, 2011), Honey Care Africa negotiated their actions and the meaning of their social business model in the context of the understandings of the East African NGO community in ways that could be understood by them. If the materials being bricolaged are meanings, this explains why bricoleurs can create something from nothing (Phillips & Tracey, 2007).

Network bricolage also alters the meaning of daily activity from within the network itself. The transformation of Honey Care Africa's honey producers from subsistence farmers to beekeepers has altered their own and community members' perceptions of their roles and identity over time. In generating meaning systems from within the network, bricolage is able to occur outside the formal boundaries of institutionalized arrangements while simultaneously drawing institutions into the network's own meaning systems and practices. Thus, in contrast with pre-conceived externally imposed models of poverty alleviation, a network bricolage approach defines and situates the nature of economic action within the potentialities available from skills and resources at hand.

Unique Processes of Network Bricolage

To date, explanations of bricolage have failed to fully distinguish bricolage at the organizational level from bricolage at the network level of analysis. The core bricolage processes of using resources at hand, combining existing resources for new purposes, and negotiating actions and meanings in context, operate at both levels of analysis. However, reviewing the literature on social entrepreneurship in subsistence markets in Africa in light of the literature on bricolage, networks and institutional entrepreneurship, we distinguish two core processes of bricolage that have unique applications when applied at the network level of analysis.

We suspect that the context of subsistence markets in Africa were uniquely suited to surfacing the concept of network bricolage and the processes involved because this context requires much greater attention to addressing coordination failures, bridging institutional voids and reconciling formal and informal institutional norms and beliefs. The two core processes of network bricolage especially relevant at the network level – customizing incentives to network members' interests and engaging in local participation through distributed agency – are described below.

Customizing incentives to network members' interests. Based on the reviews of our literature, we argue that a core process especially relevant to bricolage at the network level is connecting entrepreneurial enterprises to the "activities and interests of other actors in a field, crafting their [enterprise] to fit the conditions of the field itself" (Maguire et al., 2004: 659). The objectives and value that network actors are interested in creating differs in form across network participants (e.g., improving productivity for rural communities, creating jobs for low-income employees and entrepreneurs, and increasing social and financial return to capital investors, for example). By being locally rooted, network bricoleurs can better understand the interests of various network members so that they are incentivized to contribute their needed resources to the network by receiving returns on the investments that are of interest to them (Rivera-Santos, Rufín, & Kolk, 2012). Honey Care Africa provides on-the-spot cash payments and training to honey producers, which are customized incentives that are highly motivational to subsistence farmers. Honey Care Africa guarantees to buy honey from farmers in cash at prices that are mutually agreed upon in advance (practices previously unheard of in the industry). Microfinance institutions receive low-risk clients who have a high repayment rate due to Honey Care Africa's collection of loan payments at the time of honey sale. Non-governmental organizations who partner with Honey Care Africa and train farmers in beekeeping know that farmers will be able to generate income as a result of their training. Other actors in the network are similarly incentivized with returns that are of interest to them. Notably, the returns do not necessarily have to be in the type of capital that was initially invested. For example, NGOs invest financial resources but seek a return in environmental protection and the social benefit of poverty alleviation (Wheeler, et al., 2005).

At a broader network level, interest alignment among multiple actors is also a key feature of network bricolage. Dialogue among network actors helps create a greater understanding of the interests and resources each actor has and the outcomes each actor is looking for and how the network can be configured to achieve them. Dialogue and interaction about resources available in the network is "based not on an exhaustive and complete understanding of what things *are*, but of how they can be *related* to one another" (Duymedjian & Rüling, 2010, italics in original).

Network bricoleurs can continually align differentiated incentives and interests to mobilize the participation of all collaborating organizations. For example, Honey Care Africa aligns the interests of small-scale farmers and community organizations (for income generation), donor agencies (for environmental protection and poverty alleviation), microfinance organizations (for support to entrepreneurs), and private sector investors (for financial returns). By customizing incentives and aligning interests among members of the network, Honey Care Africa is able to mobilize the required resources needed for the network to prosper and grow. Unlike organizations that catalyze change around a single core vision to which all stakeholders must adhere, organizations engaging in network bricolage in Africa can "connect the dots" across differing interests and customize incentives to each participant's preferences and objectives (Baron, 2006). The process of network bricolage therefore acknowledges differences among network members in their motivations for participation and their valuations of different kinds of social, economic, and ecological capital.

A bricoleur's ability to move from learning about and understanding the various norms, beliefs, cultural assumptions and values of different actors is an important capability for reconciling indigenous and transplanted institutions. This builds on and extends the notion of "cooperative capability" identified by Hansen, Hoskisson & Barney (2008: 196) which includes assessing "potential partners' cooperative resources and capabilities" given the interests and resources of each partner.

Engaging local participation through distributed agency. The second element that is particularly relevant for bricoleurs at the network level is decentralized or distributed decision-making agency. Garud & Karnøe (2005: 88) suggest that

> There is now an emerging perspective that considers agency to be distributed across actors, artifacts, rules, and routines (Hutchins, 1995; Callon and Law, 1997). Such a perspective on agency implies that it would be difficult to attribute the outcomes of strategic actions to any single person. Rather, dynamic interaction between actors … generate an 'action net' within which strategic processes unfold (Czarniawska, 1997).

Rivera-Santos and Rufín (2010) argued that networks in subsistence markets are characterized by a lack of centralization. Garud and Karnøe's (2003) study of bricolage showed that resources were developed or redeployed by "constellations of different players, with the entire bricolage process supporting and demonstrating 'distributed agency'" (Baker & Nelson, 2005: 333). In their study of inclusive networks in subsistence markets, Reficco and Márquez (2012) found that, in contrast to MNCs, which tended to maintain hierarchical control over decisions, members of networks that relinquished some measure of direct control over decisions, coordinated action through aligning incentives among network members.

In Garud and Karnøe's (2003: 296) view of distributed agency, bricolage involves engaging with multiple actors and organizations in a network, "moving ahead on the basis of inputs of actors who possess local knowledge, but through their interactions, are able to gradually transform emerging paths to higher degrees of functionality." Distributed agency, we suggest, is an adaptive economic response to reconciling indigenous and transplanted institutions in Africa where market and government coordination failures and institutional voids predominate. Baker and Nelson (2005), for example, found that bricolage was particularly relevant in highly resource-constrained environments. In the context of market failure and failures of government provisioning of basic needs and services, distributed network agency allows for the access and mobilization of a broader variety of necessary resources, including financial, human, and social capital. Distributed agency also reduces problems periodically associated with other means of achieving social and environmental objectives, including vulnerability to either a culture of dependency (a single multinational corporation or aid agency) (Easterly, 2006) or inequitable income distribution (McKague & Oliver, 2012).

In addition, distributed decision making has the ability to create an environment that encourages network actors to take the initiative and combine their capabilities to overcome obstacles and challenges. In their study of bricolage at the organizational level, Baker and Nelson (2005: 356) observed: "How ... you create something out of nothing is by refusing to treat and therefore see the resources at hand as nothing. This refusal calls upon and provides a context in which firms actively exercise their creative and combinatorial capabilities ... through this process, bricolage is used to create something from nothing." In addition, distributed decision making maximizes network member involvement and ensures a level of freedom for each network member to act according to their interests. Distributed decision making is central to Honey Care Africa's network. Farmers are not locked into any contract with Honey Care Africa after the loan for purchasing their hive (about $60 dollars) is paid off. They are free to sell honey to any buyer, but typically continue to sell to Honey Care Africa. Engaging the participation of local organizations and individuals through distributed agency is also conducive to providing space for actors to express and negotiate their institutional norms and beliefs.

Governance of Network Bricolage

Governance is a means of coordination (Jones, Hesterly, & Borgatti, 1997). For our purposes, we define the governance of a network as the coordination of a group of independent organizations and individuals through informal social systems (as opposed to through formal contracts). What emerges from our analysis of network bricolage is a portrayal of the potential for unique collective-level institutional reconciliation that is novel in terms of its overall constellation of outcomes in subsistence markets, such as those that can be found in some parts of Africa. We categorize the distinctive governance norms of network bricolage into four key elements: governance transparency, trust-based ties, representation and voice, and distributed power, each described below.

Governance transparency. Networks in subsistence markets that coordinate action through aligning incentives (rather than direct control) rely on transparency of action and information to reduce power and information asymmetries and strengthen ties among network members (Reficco & Márquez, 2012). In contrast with charitable or aid agencies, which tend to provide limited feedback mechanisms between the poor and the agency serving them, feedback by means of transparent information sharing can be immediate because the businesses, farmers, microfinance organizations and non-governmental organizations form part of the same network. High levels of feedback, in turn, are conducive to governance transparency. Further, by including a range of actors in the network, more resources can also be brought to bear to examine and monitor outcomes (Hoang & Antoncic, 2003).

Trust-based ties. The engagement of local participation through distributed agency – a core process of network bricolage – can lead to greater trust among network members. Although trust is a multi-dimensional concept, there is a broad understanding among researchers that trust concerns predictability of the behavior of another actor in situations of vulnerability where violation of trust would be costly (Hansen, et al., 2008). Following Rousseau, Sitkin, Burt, and Camerer (1998: 395), trust can be defined as "a psychological state comprising the intention to accept vulnerability based on positive expectations of the intentions of behaviour of another." Although the network literature acknowledges the importance of trust in inter-organizational networks (Brass, Galaskiewicz, Greve, & Tsai, 2004), trust is perhaps particularly crucial in contexts of high uncertainty and low levels of coordination, such as those that can be found in subsistence markets in Africa. Trust enables network members to learn from one another about potential mutual interests. This accelerates joint problem solving, a process that is essential where existing resources or skills are scarce (London, Anupindi, & Sheth, 2010). Trust-based ties also help surface and share hard-to-codify tacit knowledge, which may be essential for effective coordination and value creation (Reficco & Márquez, 2012). As the network is developed and established over time, network members become more socially embedded as they experience reciprocity and cooperative resource sharing (Uzzi, 1997). Trust-based ties also reduce perceived risks and increase perceived stability of value creation activities by network members, thus enabling greater contributions and circulating of resources among network members (Reficco & Márquez, 2012). The self-perpetuating nature and customized incentives of network bricolage also increase the tendency of actors to enter into long-term relationships, which, in turn, contribute to the likelihood of trust-based ties (Rivera-Santos & Rufín, 2010).

Long-term relationships and trust-based ties also increase the ability of network actors rooted in different institutional belief systems to see that alternative taken-for-granted beliefs are possible and acceptable. Trust-based ties create space for self-reflection, adaptation and combining elements of indigenous and transplanted institutions. Alternative institutional norms, rules, beliefs and values are more open to exploration when trust-based ties are present.

The development of trust between network members has generally been regarded as dependent on factors such as the mechanism of governance of their relationship, the social or institutional setting and prior experience between the parties (Hansen, et al., 2008). Governance mechanisms to facilitate the building of trust between network actors embedded in indigenous or transplanted belief systems include both personal and inter-organizational trust relations (direct experience) and reputation (indirect experience) (Dyer and Singh, 1998). If potential transaction partners do not have previous experience of working together, network bricoleurs will need the capability to build trust through creating opportunities for direct experience and personal relations. Building trust is an idiosyncratic and complex process and the greater the network bricoleur's ability to build trust, the greater the chance of bridging, integrating and reconciling the indigenous and transplanted institutional assumptions and worldviews.

Representation and voice. Another important norm to effectively govern the process of network bricolage is ensuring representation and voice from network members, rather than utilizing command and control mechanisms of authority. Reficco and Márquez (2012: 534) in their study of nine enterprise networks in subsistence markets found that governance structures "take into account the interests of all relevant stakeholders and facilitate cooperation." Processes of network bricolage can empower the disadvantaged to exercise a voice in their own economic activities because network members are interdependent and rely on shared consensus for the achievement of goals. Network bricolage processes that are inclusive of all members of the value ecosystem are more likely to generate contributions of complementary resources from network members (Wheeler, et al., 2005). As incentives are individually customized to optimize the needs of each participant in the network, there is little motivation to disrupt or exploit existing network arrangements. Thus, representation is broader and efforts to disable it tend to be unavailing. While no governance model is fully fair and inclusive, the mutual dependencies and social embeddedness of ensuring representation and voice in network bricolage governance tend to discourage capture by ruling elites or intermediaries and motivate network actors to contribute to ongoing network functioning and value creation (McKague & Oliver, 2012).

The governance of network bricolage through enabling representation and voice allows the surfacing and addressing of conflicts among network members that will naturally arise. The weak formal institutional environment and limited enforcement of rules and contracts means that these formal routes to conflict resolution are often ineffective. Ensuring representation and voice allows a process to surface and resolve conflicts among network members in the absence of formal regulatory mechanisms to do so (Reficco & Márquez, 2012).

Distributed power. The membership of enterprise networks in subsistence markets often includes a variety of actors (e.g. social enterprises, MNCs, local chiefs, government agencies, investors, suppliers, distributors, non-governmental organizations, microfinance organizations, community groups, etc.) with highly asymmetrical sets of resources, knowledge and bases of power and legitimacy (Reficco & Márquez, 2012).

Literature on subsistence marketplaces, bricolage and institutional entrepreneurship recognizes the relevance of power relations in any change process (Mair & Marti, 2009). The norms for how power is distributed in a network have important implications for the functioning of the network, the effectiveness in creating and distributing value and the possibility of institutional reconciliation. Although Prahalad (2005: 65) understood the relevance of wealth being created in an "ecosystem" comprised of "symbiotic relationships," the base-of-the-pyramid approach sought to optimize the market system's utility for multinationals and large domestic firms in developing countries. The base-of-the-pyramid approach was interested in the question of "How do we move the composition of the ecosystem towards large firms?" and provides direction on organizing the market ecosystem around multinational "nodal firms" (Prahalad, 2005: 68). Norms governing effective network bricolage may require a more equitable and more inclusive distribution of power than is the case if a multinational firm dominates the network.

Network bricolage can generate a community of practice in which power is decentralized (Reficco and Márquez, 2012). Unlike models of institutional entrepreneurship that emphasize struggle and contestation as the impetus for institutional change (Maguire & Hardy, 2006), power is distributed in the process of network bricolage by means of delegation of resource and market access to the farmers directly responsible for on-the-ground economic activity. Also, unlike more centralized approaches to poverty reduction (direct aid provision, multinational company sales and sourcing), power is distributed through performance accountability throughout the network of constituents who actually implement the network's activities in a mutually interdependent fashion. For example, after receiving training and loans, farmers who provide honey to Honey Care Africa are established as independent business owners and the direct recipients of the income they generate. As the operations grow, any necessity to provide further technical support, growth capital, or access to markets diminishes, and the power distributions across local community enterprises become institutionalized.

Together, these four norms of network governance and the five core processes of bricolage suggest a unique form of enterprise development in particular African contexts that has the potential to significantly improve the probability that different institutional norms, beliefs and values will be negotiated and reconciled.

DISCUSSION

"In Africa", Dia (1994: 33) argues, "mutual legitimation, reconciliation, and harmonious convergence between formal and informal institutions" is essential to organizational performance and success. This view is consistent with institutional theory. In our paper we defined the most important challenge for entrepreneurs in Africa as the reconciliation of informal, locally rooted, indigenous normative and cultural institutions with formal institutions primarily transplanted from outside. To understand the process of how entrepreneurs can understand and address the need for institutional reconciliation, we reviewed the literature on social entrepreneurship in subsistence markets, bricolage, networks and institutional entrepreneurship. The spaces where institutional differences would be most apparent, we argued, were in the context of coordination failures and institutional voids. It is precisely in these spaces that social entrepreneurs in subsistence markets position themselves. Because institutional reconciliation is inherently associated with change, we also reviewed the literature on institutional entrepreneurship for insights in addressing our question. The literature on networks operating in subsistence markets rounded out the theoretical concepts that we collected to help us explain our phenomena of interest.

Through our immersion in the literature, we found that social enterprises operating in subsistence markets can be understood to engage in a process of *network bricolage*. We defined network bricolage as a process that involves interest alignment and a relational governance structure among network actors. Our analysis distinguished core characteristics of network bricolage from organizational-level bricolage (using resources at hand, combining existing resources for new purposes and negotiating meanings in context). Our reading of the literature also identified four norms of network governance that may lead to effective value creation and distribution among network actors: transparency, trust-based ties, representation and voice, and distributed power. Our theory of network bricolage has implications for the existing literature on social entrepreneurship in subsistence markets in Africa and institutional entrepreneurship, as described below.

Implications for Social Entrepreneurship in Subsistence Markets in Africa

Entrepreneurs in Africa, and especially social entrepreneurs working in and around institutional voids in subsistence markets, operate in a context of existing resources and local beliefs and institutions which overlap with formal institutional rules, norms and cultural assumptions. Conventional theories of social entrepreneurship in subsistence markets do not explain the process of how market-based approaches to poverty alleviation succeed in low-income markets in Africa. We have argued that success can be explained by social entrepreneurs that use network bricolage to overcome market and government provisioning failures. A sophisticated understanding of the institutional and cultural context in Africa is therefore required for entrepreneurs to achieve their goals.

The literature suggests that in complex and fluid settings like subsistence markets in Africa, minimal structures or "simple rules" can be effective at coordinating networks of actors (Eisenhart & Sull, 2001: 107). Simple rules or "minimal structures" (Kamoche, & Cunha, 2001) balance the need for both freedom and control. To achieve this balance, simple rules define the objectives, norms, roles, expectations, responsibilities and deadlines for each actor in the network (Brown & Eisenhardt, 1997). How the objectives are achieved is left to the local creativity of each organization or individual. Cunha and Cunha (2007: 64) argue that minimal structures "facilitate bricolage because they create a space for exploration within established boundaries."

The social enterprise literature and the network bricolage model both tend to recognize the importance of new institutions that create markets and encourage market participation by the poor (Mair, Marti, & Ganly, 2007), as well as the importance of beginning with local needs rather than with the assumptions of large centralized planned donor agencies, multinational companies or government decision-making bodies (Seelos & Mair, 2005). However, the social entrepreneurship literature suggests that to collaborate effectively, social entrepreneurial organizations should create networks with "companies which share their social vision" (Mair & Schoen, 2007: 66). The network bricolage model suggests that social and economic value creation can be achieved simultaneously without the need for all members of the network to share the same social mission (Wheeler, et al., 2005). Future research on social entrepreneurship in Africa might take its cue from Seelos and Mair's (2007: 60) observation that governance is enhanced when "the partners explicitly go about maximizing their own private benefits."

With respect to the base-of-the-pyramid (BoP) approach to poverty alleviation, the network bricolage model shares the BoP approach's emphasis on the need to access a wide range of knowledge, information, and resources to create new models of enterprise. However, an essential component of the BoP approach is the instrumental use of the MNC-organized market ecosystem for the utility of the multinational firm (Prahalad, 2005). Much of the BoP literature focuses on recommended strategies for MNCs to create new business ecosystems around themselves. The network bricolage model suggests that distributed and inclusive network approaches to poverty reduction may be as or even more effective than MNC-centric models. A study of the BoP activities of two MNCs by Halme, Lindeman and Linna (2012) found that adopting a bricolage approach was important in overcoming internal obstacles of short-term profit interests and uncertainty avoidance by the MNC. Alternatively, MNC-based BoP initiatives may benefit from developing linkages with community enterprises in Africa as a mechanism for social investment in developing countries, a conclusion supported by research into an MNC's social investment in water provisioning in Nigeria (Nwankwo, Phillips, & Tracey, 2007). These authors found that the MNC, by partnering with local community enterprises, was able to play a meaningful role in local capacity building and empowerment. Thus, the network bricolage model suggests the need for future research on the benefits of more community-based network engagement in poverty alleviation (Peredo & Chrisman, 2006; Singer, 2006).

Implications for Institutional Entrepreneurship

Our preliminary theory of network bricolage has several implications for the literature on institutional entrepreneurship. First, it suggests that underorganized or underdeveloped domains "offer considerable scope for institutional entrepreneurship" (Perkmann & Spicer, 2007: 1115), because network bricoleurs often possess unique localized knowledge about the coordination failures and institutional voids that impede local innovation (Hardy & Maguire, 2008: 200; Maguire et al., 2004). Therefore, in contrast with examinations of institutional entrepreneurship that point to social position, elite status, or field dominance as necessities in catalyzing change, future work on institutional entrepreneurship might consider how network bricoleurs are able to envision and institute change as a product of their unique understanding of the impediments to the change process.

Another implication of our model of network bricolage is the power of practical positive inducements and customized incentives in altering institutional fields. Although considerable attention has been devoted to coercive, mimetic, and normative processes in bringing about institutional change (DiMaggio & Powell, 1983), less attention has been paid to tangible financial and social benefits as a catalyst for institutional change. Future management research in Africa and elsewhere might examine how such material incentives create new rationales surrounding legitimate economic behavior and help to reinforce and instantiate economic change.

The theory of network bricolage explains how innovation may emerge from networked actors who leverage current resources to bring about change. Future research in Africa and elsewhere might apply network bricolage to other governance networks, such as professional associations that rely on networks of individuals to create new social or economic initiatives with limited resources, to determine whether bricolage processes are generalizable across different settings or effective as agents of social and economic reform.

Future theorists might also examine the extent to which network bricolage as an organizing element within markets can redress some of the limitations of markets as a means of welfare improvement. In his exploration of the moral value of market systems, Hodgson (2004: 3) draws attention to the "severely idealized" conceptualization of general market equilibrium in market economies. Future work might begin to address the moral value of network bricolage as an economic arrangement judged, as Hodgson observes, on "the consequentialist dimension of moral assessment – i.e., one wherein actions or institutional practices are judged desirable to the extent they bring about an end deemed morally valuable" (2004: 3).

The literature on institutional entrepreneurship has generated valuable insights into how actors instigate industry or field-level change in developed market contexts (Cantwell, Dunning, & Lundan, 2010; Greenwood & Suddaby, 2006; Huybrechts, 2010; Lounsbury, 2002; Perkmann & Spicer, 2007). What remains less clear is the nature of institutional entrepreneurship in subsistence markets. Therefore, in addition to contributing to understanding the process by which entrepreneurs can reconcile indigenous and transplanted logics, we contribute to the literature on institutional entrepreneurship in two ways: by explaining how institutional entrepreneurship occurs in low-income economies and by showing how institutional entrepreneurship can be characterized and implemented as a collective- or network-level phenomenon in bringing about institutional change.

LIMITATIONS AND FUTURE RESEARCH

A network developed based on bricolage may overcome coordination failures and institutional voids due to social relationships and cohesion among network members built by principles of network governance, including transparency, trust, representation and distributed power. Although Baker and Nelson (2005) suggests that routinization is possible with bricolage, the social embeddedness of actors in a network can also potentially limit the ability of the network to develop more standardized and scalable operating rules and procedures. Growing to benefit a larger number of stakeholders and achieving economies of scale are often necessary to achieve positive social and ecological impact at scale. Further research could further explore the potential tensions between network embeddedness and the ability to scale a social enterprise network.

The number, range and variety of actors in a network is often a source of strength, as multiple resources are required to be shared and coordinated among network members to overcome coordination failures and institutional voids. However, this strength can also become a challenge, as the variety of actors (for-profit and not-for-profit, large and small, local and international) can generate greater chances for miscommunicating, misunderstanding and hard-to-reconcile differences. Further research can be undertaken to understand the tensions between network diversity and coordination efficiency and effectiveness.

CONCLUSION

In resource-constrained and economically uncoordinated contexts such as subsistence markets in Africa, network bricolage can help entrepreneurs broker and reconcile different normative and cultural understandings that may be present in indigenous and transplanted institutions. The theory of network bricolage offers an alternative and potentially effective approach to the problem of poverty reduction and sustainability in subsistence markets in Africa, and the network bricolage model not only provides an important extension to the existing literature on current approaches to social entrepreneurship in these contexts, but also points to the potential importance of collaborative action through distributed goal fulfillment as a source of institutional entrepreneurship. Our theory of network bricolage offers an emerging collaborative approach that has the potential to genuinely benefit the poor, as well as understand the theory and practice of entrepreneurship in Africa, including the need to understand the deeper ontological and epistemological assumptions that underpin informal and formal institutions.

ORCiD

Christine Oliver http://orcid.org/0000-0001-6923-3783

References

Andersen, O. J. (2008). A bottom-up perspective on innovations mobilizing knowledge and social capital through innovative processes of bricolage. *Administration & Society*, *40*(1), 54–78. http://dx.doi.org/10.1177/0095399707311775

Ansari, S., Munir, K., & Gregg, T. (2012). Impact at the 'bottom of the pyramid': The role of social capital in capability development and community empowerment. *Journal of Management Studies*, *49*(4), 813–842. http://dx.doi.org/10.1111/j.1467-6486.2012.01042.x

Archer, G. R., Baker, T., & Mauer, R. (2009). Towards an alternative theory of entrepreneurial success: Integrating bricolage, effectuation and improvisation (summary). *Frontiers of Entrepreneurship Research*, *29*(6), Article 4.

Auerbach, D. (2016). Sustainable Sanitation Provision in Urban Slums: The Sanergy Case Study. In E. Thomas (Ed.), *Broken Pumps and Promises* (pp. 211–216). Cham: Springer International Publishing. http://dx.doi.org/10.1007/978-3-319-28643-3_14

Baker, T. (2007). Resources in play: Bricolage in the toy store (y). *Journal of Business Venturing*, *22*(5), 694–711. http://dx.doi.org/10.1016/j.jbusvent.2006.10.008

Baker, T., Miner, A. S., & Eesley, D. T. (2003). Improvising firms: Bricolage, account giving and improvisational competencies in the founding process. *Research Policy*, *32*(2), 255–276. http://dx.doi.org/10.1016/S0048-7333(02)00099-9

Baker, T., & Nelson, R. E. (2005). Creating something from nothing: Resource construction through entrepreneurial bricolage. *Administrative Science Quarterly*, *50*(3), 329–366. http://dx.doi.org/10.2189/asqu.2005.50.3.329

Banerjee, P. M., & Campbell, B. A. (2009). Inventor bricolage and firm technology research and development. *R & D Management*, *39*(5), 473–487. http://dx.doi.org/10.1111/j.1467-9310.2009.00572.x

Barney, J. B. (1997). *Gaining and Sustaining Competitive Advantage*. Reading, MA: Addison-Wesley.

Baron, R. A. (2006). Opportunity recognition as pattern recognition: How entrepreneurs "connect the dots" to identify new business opportunities. *The Academy of Management Perspectives*, *20*(1), 104–119. http://dx.doi.org/10.5465/AMP.2006.19873412

Birley, S. (1985). The role of networks in the entrepreneurial process. *Journal of Business Venturing*, *1*(1), 107–117. http://dx.doi.org/10.1016/0883-9026(85)90010-2

Boxenbaum, E., & Rouleau, L. (2011). New knowledge products as bricolage: Metaphors and scripts in organizational theory. *Academy of Management Review*, *36*(2), 272–296.

Brass, D., Galaskiewicz, J., Greve, H., & Tsai, W. (2004). Taking stock of networks and organizations: A multilevel perspective. *Academy of Management Journal*, *47*(6), 795–817. http://dx.doi.org/10.2307/20159624

Brown, S. L., & Eisenhardt, K. M. (1997). The art of continuous change: Linking complexity theory and time-paced evolution in relentlessly shifting organizations. *Administrative Science Quarterly*, *42*(1), 1–34. http://dx.doi.org/10.2307/2393807

Burt, R. S. (1995). *Structural Holes*. Cambridge, MA: Harvard University Press.

Callon, M., & Law, J. (1997). After the individual in society: Lessons on collectivity from science, technology and society. *Canadian Journal of Sociology*, *22*(2), 165–182. http://dx.doi.org/10.2307/3341747

Cantwell, J., Dunning, J. H., & Lundan, S. M. (2010). An evolutionary approach to understanding international business activity: The co-evolution of MNEs and the institutional environment. *Journal of International Business Studies*, *41*(4), 567–586. http://dx.doi.org/10.1057/jibs.2009.95

Christensen, L. J., Lehr, D., & Fairbourne, J. (2010). A good business for poor people. *Standford Social Innovation Review*, *8*(3), 44–49.

Cunha, M. P., & Cunha, J. V. (2007). Bricolage in organizations: Concept and forms. In M. A. Rahim (Ed.), *Current Topics in Management* (Vol. 12, pp. 51–69). Piscataway, NJ: Transaction Publishers.

Czarniawska, B. (1997). *Narrating the organization: Dramas of institutional identity*. Chicago: University of Chicago Press.

Dacin, M., Goodstein, J., & Scott, W. R. (2002). Institutional theory and institutional change: Introduction to the special research forum. *Academy of Management Journal*, *45*(1), 45–56. http://dx.doi.org/10.5465/AMJ.2002.6283388

Datta-Chaudhuri, M. (1990). Market failure and government failure. *The Journal of Economic Perspectives*, *4*(3), 25–39. http://dx.doi.org/10.1257/jep.4.3.25

Desa, G. (2012). Resource mobilization in international social entrepreneurship: Bricolage as a mechanism of institutional transformation. *Entrepreneurship Theory and Practice, 36*(4), 727–751. http://dx.doi.org/10.1111/j.1540-6520.2010.00430.x
De Soto, H. (2000). *The mystery of capital: Why capitalism triumphs in the West and fails everywhere else.* New York, NY: Basic Books.
Di Domenico, M., Haugh, H., & Tracey, P. (2010). Social bricolage: Theorizing social value creation in social enterprises. *Entrepreneurship Theory and Practice, 34*(4), 681–703. http://dx.doi.org/10.1111/j.1540-6520.2010.00370.x
Dia, M. (1994). *Africa's Management in the 1990s and Beyond: Reconciling Indigenous and Transplanted Institutions.* Washington, DC: World Bank.
DiMaggio, P., & Powell, W. W. (1983). The iron cage revisited: Institutional isomorphism and collective rationality in organizational fields. *American Sociological Review, 48*(2), 147–160. http://dx.doi.org/10.2307/2095101
Diomande, M. (1990). Business creation with minimal resources: Some lessons from the African experience. *Journal of Business Venturing, 5*(4), 191–200. http://dx.doi.org/10.1016/0883-9026(90)90016-M
Dyer, J. H., & Singh, H. (1998). The relational view: Cooperative strategy and sources of interorganizational competitive advantage. *Academy of Management Review, 23*(4), 660–679.
Sherman, E., & Donnelly, A. C. (2011). *One Acre Fund: Outgrowing the Board.* Evanston, IL: Kellogg School of Management.
Douglas, M. (1986). *How institutions think.* Syracuse, NY: Syracuse University Press.
Duymedjian, R., & Rüling, C. C. (2010). Towards a foundation of bricolage in organization and management theory. *Organization Studies, 31*(2), 133–151. http://dx.doi.org/10.1177/0170840609347051
Easterly, W. (2006). *White man's burden: Why the West's efforts to aid the rest have done so much ill and so little good.* New York: Penguin.
Eisenhardt, K. M., & Sull, D. N. (2001). Strategy as simple rules. *Harvard Business Review, 79* (1), 106–119.
Fisher, G. (2012). Effectuation, causation, and bricolage: A behavioral comparison of emerging theories in entrepreneurship research. *Entrepreneurship Theory and Practice, 36*(5), 1019–1051. http://dx.doi.org/10.1111/j.1540-6520.2012.00537.x
Friedland, R. & Alford, R. R. (1991). Bringing society back in: Symbols, practices, and institutional contradictions. In W. W. Powell & P. J. DiMaggio (Eds.), *The New Institutionalism in Organizational Analysis* (pp. 232–263). Chicago: University of Chicago Pres.
Garud, R., Jain, S., & Kumaraswamy, A. (2002). Institutional entrepreneurship in the sponsorship of common technological standards: The case of Sun Microsystems and Java. *Academy of Management Journal, 45*(1), 196–214. http://dx.doi.org/10.2307/3069292
Garud, R., & Karnøe, P. (2003). Bricolage versus breakthrough: Distributed and embedded agency in technology entrepreneurship. *Research Policy, 32*(2), 277–300. http://dx.doi.org/10.1016/S0048-7333(02)00100-2
Garud, R., & Karnøe, P. (2005). Distributed agency and interactive emergence. In S W. Floyd, J. Roos, C. D. Jacobs & F. W. Kellermans (Eds.), *Innovating Strategy Process* (pp. 88–96). Malden, MA: Blackwell Publishing.
Gibbert, M., Hoegl, M., & Välikangas, L. (2007). In praise of resource constraints. *MIT Sloan Management Review, 48*(3), 15–17.
Gradl, C., Krämer, A., and Amadigi, F. (2010). Partner selection for inclusive business models. *Greener Management International,* 56(1), 2442. http://dx.doi.org/10.9774/GLEAF.3062.2006.wi.00005
Greenwood, R., & Suddaby, R. (2006). Institutional entrepreneurship in mature fields: The big five accounting firms. *Academy of Management Journal, 49*(1), 27–48. http://dx.doi.org/10.5465/AMJ.2006.20785498
Gupta, V., & Perepu, I. (2010). *Living Goods: Developing a Sustainable Business Model to Provide Health Care Services in Uganda.* Hyderabad: IBS Centre for Management Research.
Hall, J. A. 2010. State Failure. In G. Morgan, J. Campbell, C. Crouch, P.H. Kristensen, O. Pedersen, & R. Whitley (Eds.), *The Oxford Handbook of Comparative Institutional Analysis.* New York: Oxford University Press.

Halme, M., and Lindeman, S. (2009, June). *Innovating sustainable energy for the rural BOP: Bricolage and intrapreneurship in ABB's mini-hydro power project in rural Ethiopia.* Paper presented at the Joint action on Climate Change Conference: Alborg.

Halme, M., Lindeman, S., & Linna, P. (2012). Innovation for inclusive business: Intrapreneurial bricolage in multinational corporations. *Journal of Management Studies, 49*(4), 743–784. http://dx.doi.org/10.1111/j.1467-6486.2012.01045.x

Hamann, R., & Boulogne, F. (2008). Partnerships and cross-sector collaboration. In R. Hamann, S. Woolman, & C. Sprague (Eds.), *The business of sustainable development in Africa* (pp. 54–82). Pretoria, South Africa: UNISA Press.

Hansen, M. H., Hoskisson, R. E., & Barney, J. B. (2008). Competitive advantage in alliance governance: Resolving the opportunism minimization–gain maximization paradox. *Managerial and Decision Economics, 29*(2–3), 191–208. http://dx.doi.org/10.1002/mde.1394

Hardy, C., & Maguire, S. (2008). Institutional entrepreneurship. In R. Greenwood, C. Oliver, K. Sahlin & R. Suddaby (Eds.), *The Sage handbook of organizational institutionalism* (pp. 198–217). London: Sage Publications. http://dx.doi.org/10.4135/9781849200387.n8

Hart, S. L. (2005). *Capitalism at the crossroads: The unlimited business opportunities in solving the world's most difficult problems.* Upper Saddle River, New Jersey: Pearson Education.

Hart, S. L., & London, T. (2005). Developing native capability. *Stanford Social Innovation Review, 3*(2), 28–33.

Hoang, H., & Antoncic, B. (2003). Network-based research in entrepreneurship: A critical review. *Journal of Business Venturing, 18*(2), 165–187. http://dx.doi.org/10.1016/S0883-9026(02)00081-2

Hodgson, B. (2001). Can the beast be tamed? Reflections on John McMurtry's "Unequal freedoms: The global market as an ethical system.". *Journal of Business Ethics, 33*(1), 71–78. http://dx.doi.org/10.1023/A:1011972421036

Hodgson, B. (2004). Introduction. In B. Hodgson (Ed.), *The invisible hand and the common good* (pp. 1–10). Berlin: Springer.

Hutchins, E. (1995). *Cognition in the Wild.* Cambridge, MA: MIT press.

Huybrechts, B. (2010). Fair trade organizations in Belgium: University in diversity. *Journal of Business Ethics, 92*(S2), 217–240. http://dx.doi.org/10.1007/s10551-010-0580-4

Jiwa, F. (2007). Honey Care Africa. In J. Fairbourne, S. W. Gibson, & W. G. Dyer (Eds.), *Microfranchising: Creating wealth at the bottom of the pyramid* (pp. 149–163). Northampton, MA: Edward Elgar. http://dx.doi.org/10.4337/9781847205360.00019

Jones, C., Hesterly, W. S., & Borgatti, S. P. (1997). A general theory of network governance: Exchange conditions and social mechanisms. *Academy of Management Review, 22*(4), 911–945.

Kamoche, K., & Cunha, M. P. (2001). Minimal structures: From jazz improvisation to product innovation. *Organization Studies, 22*(5), 733–764. http://dx.doi.org/10.1177/0170840601225001

Karnani, A. & McKague, K. (2014). Job creation in the Mozambican poultry industry. *European Financial Review*, 50–53.

Khanna, T., & Palepu, K. (2005). Strategies that fit emerging markets. *Harvard Business Review, 83*(6), 63–76.

Kolk, A., & Lenfant, F. (2012). Business–NGO collaboration in a conflict setting: Partnership activities in the Democratic Republic of Congo. *Business & Society, 51*(3), 478–511. http://dx.doi.org/10.1177/0007650312446474

Kolk, A., Rivera-Santos, M., & Rufín, C. (2013). Reviewing a decade of research on the "base/bottom of the pyramid" (BOP) concept. *Business & Society, 53*(3), 338–377. http://dx.doi.org/10.1177/0007650312474928

Kubzansky, M., Cooper, A., & Barbary, V. (2011). *Promise and progress: Market-based solutions to poverty in Africa.* Johannesburg, South Africa: Monitor Group.

Levi-Strauss, C. (1966). *The savage mind.* Chicago: University of Chicago Press.

Linna, P. (2013). Bricolage as a means of innovating in a resource-scarce environment: A study of innovator-entrepreneurs at the BoP. *Journal of Developmental Entrepreneurship, 18*(3), 1–23. http://dx.doi.org/10.1142/S1084946713500155

London, T. (2016). *The base of the pyramid promise.* Stanford, CA. Stanford: Business Books.

London, T., & Anupindi, R. (2012). Using the base-of-the-pyramid perspective to catalyze interdependence-based collaborations. *Proceedings of the National Academy of Sciences of the United States of America, 109*(31), 12338–12343. http://dx.doi.org/10.1073/pnas.1013626108

London, T., Anupindi, R., & Sheth, S. (2010). Creating mutual value: Lessons learned from ventures serving base of the pyramid producers. *Journal of Business Research*, *63*(6), 582–594. http://dx.doi.org/10.1016/j.jbusres.2009.04.025

London, T., & Hart, S. L. (2004). Reinventing strategies for emerging markets: Beyond the transnational model. *Journal of International Business Studies*, *35*(5), 350–370. http://dx.doi.org/10.1057/palgrave.jibs.8400099

Lounsbury, M. (2002). Institutional transformation and status mobility: The professionalization of the field of finance. *Academy of Management Journal*, *45*(1), 255–266. http://dx.doi.org/10.2307/3069295

Maguire, S., Hardy, C., & Lawrence, T. (2004). Institutional entrepreneurship in emerging fields: HIV/AIDS treatment advocacy in Canada. *Academy of Management Journal*, *47*(5), 657–679. http://dx.doi.org/10.2307/20159610

Maguire, S., & Hardy, C. (2006). The emergence of new global institutions: A discursive perspective. *Organization Studies*, *27*(1), 7–29. http://dx.doi.org/10.1177/0170840606061807

Mair, J., & Marti, I. (2009). Entrepreneurship in and around institutional voids: A case study from Bangladesh. *Journal of Business Venturing*, *24*(5), 419–435. http://dx.doi.org/10.1016/j.jbusvent.2008.04.006

Mair, J., Martí, I., & Ventresca, M. J. (2012). Building inclusive markets in rural Bangladesh: How intermediaries work institutional voids. *Academy of Management Journal*, *55*(4), 819–850. http://dx.doi.org/10.5465/amj.2010.0627

Mair, J., Marti, I., & Ganly, K. (2007). Institutional voids as spaces of opportunity. *European Business Forum*, *31*, 34–39.

Mair, J., & Schoen, O. (2007). Successful social entrepreneurial business models in the context of developing economies. *International Journal of Emerging Markets*, *2*(1), 54–68. http://dx.doi.org/10.1108/17468800710718895

McKague, K. (2011). Dynamic capabilities of institutional entrepreneurship. *Journal of Enterprising Communities*, *5*(11), 11–28.

McKague, K., & Oliver, C. (2012). Enhanced market practices as redistribution of social control. *California Management Review*, *55*(1), 98–129.

McKague, K., Zietsma, C., & Oliver, C. (2015). Building the social structure of a market. *Organization Studies*, *36*(8), 1063–1093. http://dx.doi.org/10.1177/0170840615580011

McMullen, J. S. (2011). Delineating the domain of development entrepreneurship: A market-based approach to facilitating inclusive economic growth. *Entrepreneurship Theory and Practice*, *35*(1), 185–193. http://dx.doi.org/10.1111/j.1540-6520.2010.00428.x

Mendoza, R. U., & Thelen, N. (2008). Innovations to make markets more inclusive for the poor. *Development Policy Review*, *26*(4), 427–458. http://dx.doi.org/10.1111/j.1467-7679.2008.00417.x

Miller, D. (2012). *Selling solar: The diffusion of renewable energy in emerging markets*. Sterling, Virginia: Routledge.

Milstein, M. B., London, T., & Hart, S. L. (2007). Revolutionary routines: Capturing the opportunity for creating a more inclusive capitalism. In S. K. Piderit, R. E. Fry, & D. L. Cooperrider (Eds.), *Handbook of transformative cooperation: New designs and Dynamics* (pp. 84–106). Standford, California: Standford University Press.

Montgomery, A. W., Dacin, P. A., & Dacin, M. T. (2012). Collective social entrepreneurship: Collaboratively shaping social good. *Journal of Business Ethics*, *111*(3), 375–388. http://dx.doi.org/10.1007/s10551-012-1501-5

Morgan, G. (1980). Paradigms, metaphors, and puzzle solving in organization theory. *Administrative Science Quarterly*, *25*(4), 605–622. http://dx.doi.org/10.2307/2392283

North, D. C. (1990). *Institutions, institutional change and economic performance*. Cambridge, UK: Cambridge University Press. http://dx.doi.org/10.1017/CBO9780511808678

Nwankwo, E., Phillips, N., & Tracey, P. (2007). Social investment through community enterprise: The case of multinational corporations involvement in the development of Nigerian water resources. *Journal of Business Ethics*, *73*(1), 91–101. http://dx.doi.org/10.1007/s10551-006-9200-8

Peredo, A. M., & Chrisman, J. J. (2006). Toward a theory of community-based enterprise. *Academy of Management Review*, *31*(2), 309–328. http://dx.doi.org/10.5465/AMR.2006.20208683

Perkmann, M., & Spicer, A. (2007). Healing the scars of history: Projects, skills and field strategies in institutional entrepreneurship. *Organization Studies*, *28*(7), 1101–1122. http://dx.doi.org/10.1177/0170840607078116

Phillips, N., & Tracey, P. (2007). Opportunity recognition, entrepreneurial capabilities and bricolage: Connecting institutional theory and entrepreneurship in strategic organization. *Strategic Organization*, *5*(3), 313–320. http://dx.doi.org/10.1177/1476127007079956

Porter, M. E. (1981). The contributions of industrial organization to strategic management. *Academy of Management Review*, *6*(4), 609–620.

Prahalad, C. K. (2005). *Fortune at the bottom of the pyramid: Eradicating poverty through profits.* Upper Saddle River, NJ: Wharton School Publishing.

Rangan, V. K., & Lee, K. (2010). *Bridge International Academies: A School in a Box.* Cambridge, MA: Harvard Business School Publishing.

Rao, H., Monin, P., & Durand, R. (2005). Border crossing: Bricolage and the erosion of categorical boundaries in French gastronomy. *American Sociological Review*, *70*(6), 968–991. http://dx.doi.org/10.1177/000312240507000605

Rao, H., Morrill, C., & Zald, M. N. (2000). Power plays: How social movements and collective action create new organizational forms. *Research in Organizational Behavior*, *22*, 237–281. http://dx.doi.org/10.1016/S0191-3085(00)22007-8

Reficco, E., & Márquez, P. (2012). Inclusive networks for building BOP markets. *Business & Society*, *51*(3), 512–556. http://dx.doi.org/10.1177/0007650309332353

Rivera-Santos, M., & Rufín, C. (2010). Global village vs. small town: Understanding networks at the base of the pyramid. *International Business Review*, *19*(2), 126–139. http://dx.doi.org/10.1016/j.ibusrev.2009.07.001

Rivera-Santos, M., Rufín, C., & Kolk, A. (2012). Bridging the institutional divide: Partnerships in subsistence markets. *Journal of Business Research*, *65*(12), 1721–1727. http://dx.doi.org/10.1016/j.jbusres.2012.02.013

Rivera-Santos, M., Holt, D., Littlewood, D., & Kolk, A. (2015). Social entrepreneurship in Sub-Saharan Africa. *The Academy of Management Perspectives*, *29*(1), 72–91. http://dx.doi.org/10.5465/amp.2013.0128

Rosa, J. A. & Viswanathan, M. (2007). Product and market development for subsistence marketplaces: Consumption and entrepreneurship beyond literacy and resource barriers. *Advances in International Management*, *20*, 1–17. http://dx.doi.org/10.1016/S1571-5027(07)20001-4

Rousseau, D. M., Sitkin, S. B., Burt, R. S., & Camerer, C. (1998). Not so different after all: A cross-discipline view of trust. *Academy of Management Review*, *23*(3), 393–404. http://dx.doi.org/10.5465/AMR.1998.926617

Rufín, C., & Rivera-Santos, M. (2012). Between commonweal and competition understanding the governance of public–private partnerships. *Journal of Management*, *38*(5), 1634–1654. http://dx.doi.org/10.1177/0149206310373948

Sarasvathy, S. D. (2001). Causation and effectuation: Toward a theoretical shift from economic inevitability to entrepreneurial contingency. *Academy of Management Review*, *26*(2), 243–263.

Scott, W. R. (2008). *Institutions and organizations* (3rd ed.). Thousand Oaks, CA: Sage.

Scribner, S. (1986). Thinking in action: Some characteristics of practical thought. In R. Wagner & R. Sternberg (Eds.), *Practical intelligence: Nature and origins of competence in the everyday world* (pp. 13–60). Cambridge: Cambridge University Press.

Seelos, C., & Mair, J. (2005). Social entrepreneurship: Creating new business models to serve the poor. *Business Horizons*, *48*(3), 241–246. http://dx.doi.org/10.1016/j.bushor.2004.11.006

Seelos, C., & Mair, J. (2007). Profitable business models and market creation in the context of deep poverty: A strategic view. *The Academy of Management Perspectives*, *21*(4), 49–63. http://dx.doi.org/10.5465/AMP.2007.27895339

Senghor, L. S. (1964). *Liberté I. Négritude et Humanisme.* Paris: Seuil.

Simon, H. A. (1991). Bounded rationality and organizational learning. *Organization Science*, *2* (1), 125–134. http://dx.doi.org/10.1287/orsc.2.1.125

Singer, A. (2006). Business strategy and poverty alleviation. *Journal of Business Ethics*, *66*(2–3), 225–231. http://dx.doi.org/10.1007/s10551-005-5587-x

Sprague, C. (2008). Alternative approaches to reaching the bottom of the pyramid. In R. Hamann, S. Woolman, & C. Sprague (Eds.), *The business of sustainable development in Africa* (pp. 83–96). Pretoria, South Africa: UNISA Press.

Stiglitz, J. (2009). Regulation and failure. In D. Moss & J. Cisternino (Eds.), *New perspectives on regulation* (pp. 11–23). Cambridge MA: The Tobin Project.

Stinchfield, B. T., Nelson, R. E., & Wood, M. S. (2013). Learning from Levi-Strauss' legacy: Art, craft, engineering, bricolage, and brokerage in entrepreneurship. *Entrepreneurship Theory and Practice*, *37*(4), 889–921. http://dx.doi.org/10.1111/j.1540-6520.2012.00523.x

Taylor, F. W. (2004). *Scientific Management*. New York, NY: Routledge. (Original work published 1911)

Thornton, P., & Ocasio, W. (1999). Contingency of power in organizations: Executive succession in the higher education publishing industry, 1958-1990. *American Journal of Sociology*, *105* (3), 801–843. http://dx.doi.org/10.1086/210361

Thornton, P. & Ocasio, W. (2008). Institutional logics. In R. Greenwood, C. Oliver, K. Sahlin & R. Suddaby (Eds.), *The Sage handbook of organizational institutionalism* (pp. 99–129). Thousand Oaks, CA: Sage Publications. http://dx.doi.org/10.4135/9781849200387.n4

Thumbadoo, B., & Wilson, G. L. (2007). *From dust to diamonds: Stories of South African social entrepreneurs*. Johannesburg, South Africa: Macmillan.

Tracey, P., Phillips, N., & Jarvis, O. (2011). Bridging institutional entrepreneurship and the creation of new organizational forms: A multilevel model. *Organization Science*, *22*(1), 60–80. http://dx.doi.org/10.1287/orsc.1090.0522

Uzzi, B. (1997). Social structure and competition in interfirm networks: The paradox of embeddedness. *Administrative Science Quarterly*, *42*(1), 35–67. http://dx.doi.org/10.2307/2393808

Valente, M. (2010). Public and private partnerships for sustainable development in Africa: A process framework. *Journal of African Business*, *11*(1), 49–69. http://dx.doi.org/10.1080/15228911003608538

Valente, M. (2012). Indigenous resource and institutional capital: The role of local context in embedding sustainable community development. *Business & Society*, *51*(3), 409–449. http://dx.doi.org/10.1177/0007650312446680

Viswanathan, M., & Rosa, J. A. (2010). Understanding subsistence marketplaces: Toward sustainable consumption and commerce for a better world. *Journal of Business Research*, *63*, 253–257.

Webb, J. W., Kistruck, G. M., Ireland, R. D., & Ketchen, D. J. J., Jr. (2010). The entrepreneurship process in base of the pyramid markets: The case of multinational enterprise/nongovernment organization alliances. *Entrepreneurship Theory and Practice*, *34*(3), 555–581. http://dx.doi.org/10.1111/j.1540-6520.2009.00349.x

Weber, M. (1997). *The methodology of the social sciences*. New York: Free Press.

Weick, K. E. (1993). Organization redesign and improvisation. In G. Huber and W. H. Glick (Eds.), *Organizational Change and Redesign* (pp. 349–382). New York: Oxford University Press.

Weick, K. E. (1998). Introductory Essay: Improvisation as a mindset for organizational analysis. *Organization Science*, *9*(5), 543–555. http://dx.doi.org/10.1287/orsc.9.5.543

Wheeler, D., McKague, K., Thompson, J., Davies, R., Medalye, J., & Prada, M. (2005). Creating sustainable local enterprise networks. *MIT Sloan Management Review*, *47*(1), 33–40.

Wijen, F., & Ansari, S. (2007). Overcoming inaction through collective institutional entrepreneurship: Insights from regime theory. *Organization Studies*, *28*(7), 1079–1100. http://dx.doi.org/10.1177/0170840607078115

Yunus, M., Moingeon, B., & Lehmann-Ortega, L. (2010). Building social business models: Lessons from the Grameen experience. *Long Range Planning*, *43*(2–3), 308–325. http://dx.doi.org/10.1016/j.lrp.2009.12.005

Zoogah, D. B. (2008). African business research: A review of studies published in the Journal of African Business and a framework for enhancing future studies. *Journal of African Business*, *9* (1), 219–255. http://dx.doi.org/10.1080/15228910802053037

Zoogah, D. B., & Nkomo, S. (2013). Management research in Africa: Past, present, and future. In T. R. Lituchy, B. J. Punnett, & B. B. Puplampu (Eds.), *Management in Africa: Macro and micro perspectives* (pp. 9–31). New York: Routledge.

Zoogah, D. B., Peng, M. W., & Woldu, H. (2015). Institutions, resources, and organizational effectiveness in Africa. *The Academy of Management Perspectives*, *29*(1), 7–31. http://dx.doi.org/10.5465/amp.2012.0033

POSITIVE IMPACT OF ENTREPRENEURSHIP TRAINING ON ENTREPRENEURIAL BEHAVIOR IN A VOCATIONAL TRAINING SETTING

Michael M. Gielnik, Michael Frese, Kim Marie Bischoff, Gordon Muhangi and Francis Omoo

Unemployment among youths is a serious problem in many African countries. Researchers and politicians alike consider entrepreneurship to be part of the solution to the high unemployment rates. In this study, we present the conceptual basis of an action-oriented entrepreneurship training program and provide evidence for its positive impact on trainees' entrepreneurial behavior in a vocational training setting. Furthermore, we present a case study that illustrates how a vocational training institute successfully implemented the training. The case study demonstrates the long-lasting effects achieved by a vocational training institute to promote entrepreneurship among its trainees. Our study shows that entrepreneurship training boosts entrepreneurship among youths, creates jobs, and leads to income generating activities. Furthermore, our study indicates that entrepreneurship training can be successfully integrated into vocational training settings when the training institutions take over responsibility, keep the conceptual core of the training (that is the practical and action-oriented approach of the training), and tailor the overarching framework of the training according to their specific needs.

INTRODUCTION

In this study we describe an entrepreneurship training program, its impact on vocational trainees' entrepreneurial behavior, and how the vocational training institute adopted the training to permanently offer entrepreneurship training to its trainees. Why is this important? This is important for at least three reasons. First, there is a practical reason. Entrepreneurship training can be part of the solution to address the problem of high unemployment rates that many African countries face. Particularly, high unemployment rates among youths constitute a serious challenge for many African economies. Although several African economies have experienced considerable economic growth in recent years, e.g., Ghana 7.6%, Kenya 5.7%, Nigeria 5.4%, Uganda 3.3%, Tanzania, 7.3% (World Bank, 2015b), this has not led to a comparable creation in new employment opportunities for people of the workforce under the age of 30 years. Estimates of unemployment rates among youths go as high as 64%

(Ahaibwe & Kasirye, 2015). Entrepreneurship might constitute a solution to this problem because of the strong impact of entrepreneurship on job creation (Fritsch, 2008; Thurik, Carree, van Stel, & Audretsch, 2008; van Praag & Versloot, 2007). Entrepreneurship is defined as the process of identifying and exploiting business opportunities to introduce new products or services into the market (Shane & Venkataraman, 2000). A prevalent form of entrepreneurship is starting a new business that offers jobs for the entrepreneur and additional employees. Accordingly, many African governments revised their action plans and focused on entrepreneurship as a major way to boost employment creation. For example, the government of Uganda put a particular focus on entrepreneurship in their Second National Development Plan; an important objective is to support entrepreneurship through tax rebates and access to financial services (Uganda Government, 2015). Similarly, policy makers in Tanzania, Kenya, and further African countries changed their approach from establishing large industrial complexes to facilitating the creation of small businesses by private individuals (Nelson & Johnson, 1997; Nkirina, 2010). This resulted in African countries being top in the world regarding the number of regulatory reforms introduced to increase the ease of doing business. In 2013/14, countries in sub-Sahara Africa accounted for the largest number of regulatory reforms worldwide, to facilitate doing business (World Bank, 2015a). By providing access to financial capital and changing regulatory frameworks governments can change contextual factors to improve the business environment for entrepreneurship. However, the effectiveness of contextual changes depends on psychological factors, such as the skills and knowledge of the individual entrepreneurs (de Mel, McKenzie, & Woodruff, 2008; Gielnik & Frese, 2013; Kiggundu, 2002). Without the necessary skills, people will not be able to start a new business – even in the most progressive business environment. Therefore, entrepreneurship training that provides entrepreneurial skills constitutes an important complementary factor empowering people to make use of conducive business environments. Generally, it is the interplay between psychological and contextual factors that results in entrepreneurship (Frese & Gielnik, 2014; Welter, 2010); only if people have the necessary skills, they will successfully engage in entrepreneurship and create new job opportunities. In this paper, we discuss the Student Training for Entrepreneurial Promotion (STEP) as an entrepreneurship training program that is effective in enhancing entrepreneurial skills (Bischoff, Gielnik, & Frese, 2014; Frese, Gielnik, & Mensmann, in press; Gielnik et al., 2015). We demonstrate that STEP is an effective intervention to promote vocational trainees' entrepreneurial behavior. Vocational trainees have skills in their profession. Providing them with entrepreneurship skills in addition to their professional skills gives them the opportunity to benefit from business friendly environments and start their own professional businesses. By starting their own business, they create jobs for themselves and additionally for other people. Thus, STEP might contribute to solving the problem of high unemployment rates among youths.

The second reason is that our study provides a best practice approach how vocational training institutes can sustainably implement entrepreneurship training in their curriculum. Previous research has noted that it might be difficult to include practical entrepreneurship training in an academic setting with a credit system and standardized grading schemes (Rasmussen & Sorheim, 2006; Souitaris, Zerbinati, & Al-Laham, 2007). Entrepreneurship training requires flexibility and an open setting that allow trainees to make mistakes and go back and forth in the entrepreneurial process. In this study, we present the case of a vocational training institute and how it implemented entrepreneurial projects based on STEP in the long-term. The entrepreneurial projects deal with products and services that have been developed by trainees and that have been passed on from cohort to cohort since the launch of the projects. The trainees continuously improve the quality of the products and services in an innovative manner, which constitutes an important aspect of entrepreneurship (Wong, Ho, & Autio, 2005). Practitioners can use this best practice approach as a model for sustainably implementing entrepreneurship training at similar training institutions.

The third reason this study is important is that we discuss the idea of evidence-based entrepreneurship, which has been the basis for designing STEP (Frese, Bausch, Schmidt, Rauch, & Kabst, 2012). Good evidence is also one of the prerequisites suggested by the very ambitious Africa 2063 agenda (DeGhetto, Gray, & Kiggundu, 2016). We suggest that borrowing from the field of evidence-based management (Pfeffer & Sutton, 2006; Rousseau, 2006) and establishing the concept of evidence-based entrepreneurship is useful to guide the decision-making process of selecting the most effective interventions to promote entrepreneurship. Evidence-based management means making use of the current best evidence to make decisions and deriving principles from the best evidence to guide organizational practices (Pfeffer & Sutton, 2006; Rousseau, 2006). Similarly, we follow Frese and colleagues (2012; Glaub, Frese, Fischer, & Hoppe, 2014; Rauch & Frese, 2006) and present evidence-based entrepreneurship as consisting of four principles: identifying the best scientific knowledge and evidence relevant for entrepreneurship, developing theoretical models to explain entrepreneurship, developing manuals of evidence-based practices that guide interventions to promote entrepreneurship, and finally, evaluating the interventions to test the impact of the interventions. In this paper, we discuss how evidence-based entrepreneurship informed this study. We refer to Gielnik et al. (2015) to present the theoretical and methodological underpinnings of STEP (see also Bischoff et al., 2014; Frese et al., 2016). Furthermore, we present the results of the evaluation study to assess the impact of STEP in the context of a vocational training institute. To assess the impact of the training on trainees' entrepreneurial behavior, we conducted a quantitative study. The results showed that STEP had a significant impact on trainees' opportunity identification and entrepreneurial action, which are crucial factors leading to business creation (Gielnik et al., 2015). Furthermore, our case illustrates how STEP led to long-lasting entrepreneurial projects that continuously trained vocational trainees in entrepreneurial skills and behavior. Our study thus demonstrates how the concept of evidence-based entrepreneurship can contribute to designing, evaluating, and implementing effective interventions to promote entrepreneurship.

The theoretical and methodological underpinnings of STEP

We designed STEP as an entrepreneurship training program for undergraduate university students and adapted it to fit the context of vocational training institutes (Bischoff et al., 2014; Frese et al., 2016; Gielnik et al., 2015). Students are an important target group because university and professional training increase the likelihood of starting businesses that are not necessity-based and thus more likely to create higher economic value (van Stel, Storey, & Thurik, 2007). We followed the concept of evidence-based entrepreneurship and used the best scientific knowledge to develop the content and method of the training. Regarding the content, STEP covers topics from the domains of business administration (e.g., financial management and marketing) and psychology (e.g., leadership and action planning). Specifically, STEP includes 12 modules on the topics of (1) identifying business opportunities, (2) marketing, (3) leadership and strategic management, (4) the psychology of planning and implementing plans, (5) financial management, (6) persuasion and negotiation, (7) acquiring starting capital, (8) networking, (9) accounting, (10) personal initiative, (11) business planning, and (12) legal and regulatory issues. We selected the modules on the basis of a comprehensive literature review of relevant topics in entrepreneurship education (Fiet, 2001; Solomon, 2007). The training participants studied the 12 modules in three-hour long weekly sessions over a period of 12 weeks.

Regarding the method, we drew on the entrepreneurship literature that emphasizes the importance of action for entrepreneurship (Carter, Gartner, & Reynolds, 1996; Frese, 2009; McMullen & Shepherd, 2006). Accordingly, STEP puts a particular focus on action to promote entrepreneurship. A prominent theory to understand taking action is action-regulation theory (Frese & Zapf, 1994; Frese, 2009). According to action-regulation theory, action is goal-directed behavior. Two aspects are important when taking action to achieve a goal. The first aspect is the action sequence. The action sequence consists of the different steps involved in taking action. These steps are setting goals, seeking information, forming action plans, executing and monitoring the action, and, eventually, seeking feedback. In order to take action, people must specify what they want to achieve (goal-setting), seek information relevant for goal achievement, specify an action plan of how they want to achieve the goal, execute and monitor the action plan, and gather feedback on whether they have achieved their goal or whether they have to modify their action plans. The second aspect is the operative mental model. The operative mental model is the cognitive representation of action. It comprises people's knowledge about relevant actions, about how to perform the actions, and about the environment in which people operate. The more functionally useful and sophisticated people's operative mental model is, the more efficient their actions will be (Frese & Zapf, 1994).

Action-regulation theory provides a useful framework for developing training interventions to promote taking action (Frese & Zapf, 1994). First, training interventions should consider the action sequence and ensure that participants are able and motivated to set goals, form action plans, execute and monitor the action, and seek relevant feedback after the training. Second, participants should acquire a sophisticated operative mental model that contains relevant knowledge to efficiently perform actions. The knowledge should be action-ready, which means that the knowledge should be easy to apply and inform how things are done. Action-regulation theory suggests several didactical elements to properly consider the action sequence and operative mental model in training. First, training should teach evidence-based action principles. Action principles are heuristics (or rules-of-thumb) derived from theory and scientific evidence. Action principles provide specific knowledge about how to go about and accomplish tasks. Teaching action principles is an efficient way to alter and improve people's operative mental model in a specific area (e.g., starting a business). Action principles and simple rules facilitate taking action because they are easy to apply (Drexler, Fischer, & Schoar, 2014). Second, training should be action-oriented. This means that participants should be instructed to engage in active practicing and learn through action. Actively practicing and repeating the target behavior during training is important for a deep processing and routinization of the training content. Moreover, active practice is key to developing a realistic and sophisticated operative mental model because active practicing is necessary to transform abstract (declarative) knowledge into practical (procedural) knowledge. Finally, action-regulation theory emphasizes the importance of feedback for effective training. Participants should receive positive and negative feedback. Positive feedback has a motivating function because it indicates that participants are making progress and it is a reinforcement for effective actions. Negative feedback provides participants with information about non-functional actions and thus contributes to refining the operative mental model. Negative feedback also has a motivating function because it discloses a gap between the current status and the desired end-state, prompting people to invest additional effort to achieve their goals. A special form of negative feedback is making errors. Action-regulation theory emphasizes the importance of making errors in the training. Reflecting on the reasons for errors (e.g., what was I thinking when I made the error) and reducing negative emotionality that often results from errors lead to a better mental model, new hypotheses, more frequent exploration, and better handling of errors (Heimbeck, Frese, Sonnentag, & Keith, 2003; Keith & Frese, 2005).

STEP follows the guidelines provided by action-regulation theory for developing effective trainings. Specifically, we developed evidence-based action principles for each of the 12 modules. The action principles informed the participants what and how they had to accomplish tasks in the start-up process. For example, the session on financial management included action principles on how to manage debtors, creditors, and cash. It is important to note that all action principles were based on theories and empirical evidence from the entrepreneurship literature (see Gielnik et al., 2015). Thus, the action principles comply with the principles of evidence-based entrepreneurship. Furthermore, STEP has a strong action-orientation. In the training, the participants formed entrepreneurial teams of four to six members, who engaged in the start-up of a real business during the training. In the first session, the entrepreneurial teams received starting capital (approximately US$100) that they had to refund at the end of the training. The teams identified a business opportunity and invested the starting capital to acquire the necessary equipment and raw materials to implement the opportunity. The goal was to start a micro business that generates revenue and profits during the 12 weeks of the training. The teams thus experienced the whole entrepreneurial process and conducted entrepreneurship in a real business environment. During the training sessions, the participants learnt action principles and gave presentations about the progress of their start-ups. The trainers provided positive and negative feedback after each presentation. In case of negative feedback, the trainers pointed to specific action principles to give precise advice how the participants could improve their performance. Furthermore, the trainers emphasized that errors should not be considered detrimental but as an opportunity to learn (Heimbeck et al., 2003; Keith & Frese, 2005). Considering errors as a valuable form of feedback changes participants' mindset towards errors and helps them to develop a positive attitude towards errors (Frese & Zapf, 1994). The training thus included all elements important to enhance participants' operative mental model in an action-oriented manner.

Previous evaluation studies provided evidence for the positive effect of STEP on entrepreneurship (Frese et al., 2016; Gielnik et al., 2015). A long-term evaluation study using a randomized pre-post-test design with a non-treatment control group demonstrated the impact of the training on participants' entrepreneurial action regulation and their subsequent success in entrepreneurship (Gielnik et al., 2015). Measurements shortly after the training revealed that the training increased participants' entrepreneurial self-efficacy, entrepreneurial goal intentions, action planning, and action knowledge (operative mental model). The long-term measurements (12 months after the training) showed that the increase in these factors translated into more entrepreneurial actions and higher start-up rates among the training participants. In summary, the findings indicate that the participants were more likely to take action and create new businesses. These results hold across different cohorts and countries (Frese et al., 2016).

Effects of STEP on entrepreneurship in the context of a vocational training institute

Following the line of reasoning by Gielnik et al. (2015), we hypothesized that STEP has positive effects on trainees' business opportunity identification and entrepreneurial action. We focused on business opportunity identification and entrepreneurial action because Gielnik et al. (2015) have shown that these two factors are antecedents of business creation, mediating the effect of STEP on business creation. STEP has a positive effect on business opportunity identification because during the training, the trainees learn creativity techniques and the importance of identifying customer needs in the modules on identifying business opportunities and marketing (Gielnik et al., 2015). STEP has a positive effect on entrepreneurial action because of the didactical elements included in the training. STEP teaches action-principles, it is action-oriented with a focus on learning through action, and it ensures that trainees improve their operative mental model through positive and negative feedback (Gielnik et al., 2015). Accordingly, we hypothesized:

Hypothesis 1: STEP has a positive effect on business opportunity identification.

Hypothesis 2: STEP has a positive effect on entrepreneurial action.

Besides the positive effects of STEP on opportunity identification and entrepreneurial action, we were interested in how a training institute can sustainably implement STEP. Sustainable implementation is important to offer entrepreneurship training to future cohorts of trainees. We have experienced very successful implementations of the STEP training. However, in some projects, we have also experienced the difficulty of offering the training on a continuous basis without external support. The permanent implementation of the training independent of third party funding has been a major challenge for some partner institutions. We therefore report the case of a vocational training institute and the measures it took to offer entrepreneurship training to its trainees on a self-sustaining basis.

METHOD

Procedure and Sample

The study took place at the Nakawa Vocational Training Institute in Kampala, the capital city of Uganda. With the help of lecturers from the vocational training institute, we informed the vocational trainees about the opportunity to take part in

STEP. The lecturers also distributed brochures and information material about the training. Vocational trainees, who were interested in participating in the STEP training, had to complete an application form and a baseline questionnaire. Participation in STEP was voluntary and for free. The participants received a certificate upon successful completion of the training.

We used a randomized pre-/post-test design with a training and control group to evaluate the impact of STEP on trainees' entrepreneurial behavior. The randomized pre-/post-test design allows researchers to control for methodological artefacts and biases, such as history, testing, maturation, and self-selection, and is thus the gold standard for evaluating the impact of interventions (Campbell, 1957; Reay, Berta, & Kohn, 2009). We collected data with the baseline questionnaire before the training (T1) and with an identical questionnaire after the training (T2). After the first data collection (T1), we randomly assigned the applicants to the training group and the control group.

At T1, 389 vocational trainees completed the application form and baseline questionnaire. The majority of applicants were male (95.6%). Applicants were trained in the following departments: sheet metal and plumbing (18.7%), welding and fabrication (17.9%), electricity (12.4%), machining and fitting (11.7%), brick laying and concrete practice (11.1%), motor vehicle (9.8%), electronics (8.8%), auto-electrical (8.3%), and woodworking (1.3%). Our capacities allowed us to train about half of the applicants in four classes. We randomly selected 183 applicants to form the training group. The remaining 206 applicants formed the control group. We conducted *t*-tests to compare the two groups and test whether the randomization was successful. The *t*-tests revealed that there were no significant differences between the two groups at T1 on any control or main variable, indicating that the two groups were equivalent before the training. We experienced a high drop-out rate of trainees during the training. Qualitative interviews with trainees who decided to discontinue the training showed that the main reasons for dropping-out were timetable clashes and problems of coordinating the training with other duties. At T2, we were able to collect data from 178 participants (training group = 121, control group = 57). T-tests with the respondents and non-respondents to investigate differences on the study variables showed no significant differences between the two groups, suggesting that the drop-out was not systematic and that there were was no response bias.

Measures

In this study, we used the following measures:

Training. We created a binary variable to capture being part of the training group ("1") or control group ("0").

Business opportunity identification. We measured business opportunity identification before (T1) and after the training (T2). We used the measure by Gielnik et al. (2015). We asked three questions to measure business opportunity identification: "How many opportunities for creating a business have you identified ('spotted') within the last three months", "Out of all those opportunities, how many were in your opinion profitable", and "How many opportunities for creating a business have you pursued within the last three months". The participants provided the number of opportunities for each question. Following Gielnik et al. (2015), we recoded numbers larger than 6 as 6 to avoid extreme responses and to approximate a normal distribution. We computed the mean of participants' responses to the three questions to form our scale of business opportunity identification. The internal consistency of the scale was good (Cronbach's Alpha T1 = 0.74 and T2 = 0.78).

Entrepreneurial action. We measured entrepreneurial action before (T1) and after the training (T2). We adapted the interview measure by Gielnik et al. (2015) to develop a questionnaire measure. In the questionnaire, we asked the participants two filter questions. We asked them whether they intended to start a new business within the next 12 months and whether they were starting a new business at the moment. If they affirmed either of the two questions, we asked them "How much effort have you already put into" followed by 12 start-up activities. We derived the start-up activities from the list of start-up activities used by Gielnik et al. (2015). The 12 start-up activities included "checking whether there is a demand or need for your product/service in the market", "finding a place where you will set-up the business", and "getting the equipment, raw materials, or other facilities for your business". We used 5-point Likert scales ranging from "Not at all" to "Very much" to measure participants' effort in the entrepreneurial activities. Participants responding "no" to both filter questions received the minimum score of "1" for each start-up activity because they had not shown any entrepreneurial action. We computed the mean across the 12 start-up activities to form our scale of entrepreneurial action. Cronbach's Alpha at both measurement waves was good (T1 = 0.94, T2 = 0.92).

Control variables. We measured the following control variables because previous research has provided evidence for their influence on entrepreneurship (Davidsson & Honig, 2003). In the baseline questionnaire at T1, we measured family business ownership (whether a member in the participants' family had a business; 0 = no, 1 = yes) and prior business courses taken by the participants (0 = no, 1 = yes).

RESULTS

Table 1 presents the descriptive statistics and correlations of the variables. Training was significantly correlated with business opportunity identification ($r = 0.19$, $p < 0.01$) and entrepreneurial action ($r = 0.17$, $p < 0.05$) after the training (T2). These findings suggest that STEP had a significant impact on business opportunity identification and entrepreneurial action. Family business ownership correlated significantly with entrepreneurial action at T2 ($r = 0.15$, $p < 0.05$) and prior business courses correlated significantly with business opportunity identification at T1 ($r = 0.16$, $p < 0.05$). We therefore included these variables as control variables in our regression analyses to test Hypotheses 1 and 2.

Test of hypotheses

To test Hypotheses 1 and 2, we used linear regression analyses. Hypothesis 1 states that STEP has a positive effect on business opportunity identification. We used business opportunity identification after the training (T2) as the dependent variable and controlled for business opportunity identification before the training (T1) to model

Table 1. Correlations of study variables.

Variables and Scales	M	SD	1	2	3	4	5	6
1. Training	0.68	0.47						
2. Business opportunity identification (T1)	1.79	1.13	0.04					
3. Business opportunity identification (T2)	2.11	1.18	0.19**	0.31**				
4. Entrepreneurial action (T1)	3.23	1.22	−0.03	0.05	0.03			
5. Entrepreneurial action (T2)	3.46	1.11	0.17*	0.15*	0.25**	0.39**		
6. Family business ownership	0.76	0.43	0.07	0.03	−0.05	0.05	0.15*	
7. Prior business courses	0.29	0.45	0.04	0.16*	0.09	0.08	0.06	0.09

Note: * $p < 0.05$, ** $p < 0.01$.

change in business opportunity identification from T1 to T2. Table 2 presents the results. In Model 1, we included the control variables. Business opportunity identification before the training was a significant predictor of business opportunity identification after the training (B = 0.33, β = 0.31, $p < 0.01$). In Model 2, we added training to the equation. Training had a positive and significant effect on business opportunity identification (B = 0.48, β = 0.19, $p < 0.01$). Training explained 4% of the variance in business opportunity identification. The results thus supported Hypothesis 1 that STEP has a positive impact on trainees' business opportunity identification.

Hypothesis 2 states that STEP has a positive effect on entrepreneurial action. We computed linear regression analyses with entrepreneurial action after the training (T2)

Table 2. Effect of STEP on business opportunity identification.

Variables	Model 1			Model 2		
	Business opportunity identification (T2)			Business opportunity identification (T2)		
	B	SE	β	B	SE	β
Intercept	1.63	0.22		1.34	0.24	
Family business ownership	−0.18	0.20	−0.06	−0.22	0.20	−0.08
Prior business courses	0.13	0.19	0.05	0.12	0.19	0.04
Business opportunity identification (T1)	0.33**	0.08	0.31	0.32**	0.08	0.30
Training				0.48**	0.18	0.19
F	6.67			6.93		
R^2	0.10			0.14		
Change in R^2				0.04		

Note: Unstandardized (B) and standardized coefficients (β) are shown; * $p < 0.05$, ** $p < 0.01$.

Table 3. Effect of STEP on entrepreneurial action.

Variables	Model 1			Model 2		
	Entrepreneurial action (T2)			Entrepreneurial action (T2)		
	B	SE	β	B	SE	β
Intercept	2.19	0.26		1.96	0.27	
Family business ownership	0.27	0.19	0.10	0.22	0.19	0.09
Prior business courses	−0.01	0.17	−0.01	−0.02	0.17	−0.01
Entrepreneurial action (T1)	0.34**	0.06	0.38	0.34**	0.06	0.39
Training				0.38*	0.17	0.16
F	10.55			9.43		
R^2	0.16			0.19		
Change in R^2				0.03		

Note: Unstandardized (B) and standardized coefficients (β) are shown; * $p < 0.05$, ** $p < 0.01$.

as the dependent variable and controlled for entrepreneurial action before the training (T1) to model change in the dependent variable. Table 3 displays the results. In Model 1, we included the control variables. Entrepreneurial action before the training was significantly related to entrepreneurial action after the training (B = 0.34, β = 0.38, $p < 0.01$). In Model 2, we entered training into the model. Training had a positive and significant effect on entrepreneurial action (B = 0.38, β = 0.16, $p < 0.05$) explaining 3% of the variance in entrepreneurial action. We therefore found support for Hypothesis 2 that STEP has a positive impact on trainees' entrepreneurial action.

To illustrate the positive impact of STEP on trainees' business opportunity identification and entrepreneurial action, we plotted the means of the training group and the control group before (T1) and after the training (T2). Figure 1 shows the effect of STEP on business opportunity identification. The figure illustrates that there was a strong increase in business opportunity identification from T1 to T2 for the STEP training group. There was almost no change in business opportunity identification

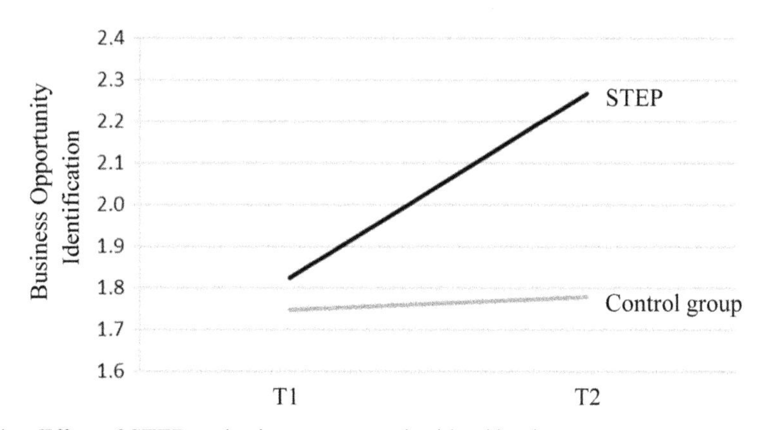

Figure 1. Effect of STEP on business opportunity identification.

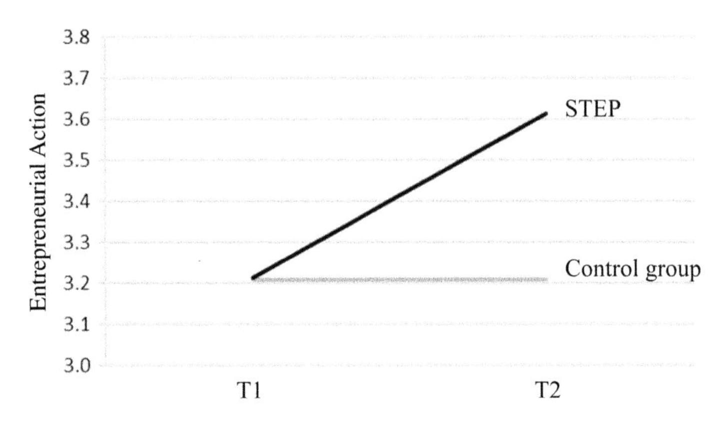

Figure 2. Effect of STEP on entrepreneurial action.

from T1 to T2 in the control group. Figure 2 displays the effect of STEP on entrepreneurial action. The figure shows that trainees in the STEP training group increased in entrepreneurial action from T1 to T2 whereas the participants in the control group showed no change in entrepreneurial action from T1 to T2. The figures demonstrate that the positive effect of STEP on business opportunity identification and entrepreneurial action was due to an increase in the STEP training group (and not due to a decrease in the control group). Consequently, STEP enhanced trainees' business opportunity identification and entrepreneurial action.

Long-term Implementation of STEP: The case of Nakawa Vocational Training Institute

Nakawa Vocational Training Institute (NVTI) was established in 1971 by the government of Uganda. NVTI has nine technical departments (including electronics, electricity, machining and fitting, motor vehicle mechanics, auto electrical, woodworking, sheet metal and plumbing, welding and fabrication, and building and concrete practice) and one auxiliary department for instructors and manager training. It offers its programs in full day basic training programs and evening advanced training programs. The objectives of NVTI are to enhance skills development for workers in enterprises and to impart employable skills to young men and women searching for employment.

Entrepreneurship training started at NVTI in 1998 with training modules developed by UNIDO. These modules were used until 2013 and then replaced by the 12 STEP modules, which strongly emphasize practical and innovative entrepreneurship training. To prepare and familiarize NVTI lecturers with the new didactical approach of STEP, we held a three-day train-the-trainers workshop with 12 lecturers. The aim of the train-the-trainers workshop was to develop the necessary capacity at NVTI for delivering STEP. The group of 12 lecturers was responsible for implementing STEP at NVTI. After the initial implementation of STEP in 2013 (which has been described above), NVTI followed selected groups of the training. One group successfully ran a poultry farm. A second group started their business by selling airtime (i.e., prepaid cards for mobile phones) and then expanded to mobile money operations. A third group ran a business selling juices and a variety of soft drinks. A fourth group started by selling groundnut paste at a market in Nakawa and then expanded their operations to buying groundnuts from upcountry and distributing them to several markets in Kampala. Based on the successful implementation and positive impact of STEP on trainees' entrepreneurial behavior, NVTI decided to offer STEP continuously to their trainees without any further external support. They decided to keep the conceptual core of the training, that is the practical and action-oriented approach of the training, but to change the overarching framework. NVTI observed that teams usually disband after completion of the training. Disbandment of the entrepreneurial teams after the training is part of the concept of STEP. However, NVTI sought to maintain the achievements of the teams. So, instead of beginning anew at each new round of training, new trainees engage in and take over businesses that have been established by previous cohorts. For example, in 2014, the training participants started producing liquid soap (Figure 3). This business was formed by 30 teams with five members each. They raised the starting capital and acquired the necessary facilities to start production of liquid soap at the vocational training institute. The teams introduced the liquid soap into the market, generating a positive cash flow. In 2015, the next cohort of STEP trainees took over and expanded the business now offering STEP detergent and getting wider access to markets in Kampala. Similar large-scale projects introduced by the trainees were modern bee-keeping, rabbit-keeping, and envelope production. In the most recent cohort, STEP trainees proposed establishing additional strong teams in order to deal in juice-making, floriculture, producing charcoal briquettes, mobile photo studio operation, and block and paver making. Changing the overarching framework led to the sustainable success of the businesses and helped NVTI to permanently offer STEP as a practical entrepreneurship training to their trainees. The trainees were successful in creating employment opportunities and generating income. NVTI facilitated this process by helping the trainees to mobilize start-up capital for their businesses, organizing field trips to successful entrepreneurs, and linking STEP trainees to business mentors. Since the first

Figure 3. STEP detergent (liquid soap) produced by students of NVTI.

implementation in 2013, NVTI has trained an additional 400 trainees (200 trainees in 2014 and another 200 trainees in 2015). Furthermore, NVTI introduced 50 trainers from 32 technical institutes located in 26 different districts in Uganda to the STEP methodology.

NVTI reported that three key success factors were crucial for permanently implementing STEP at their institution. First, the positive backup by the institute's administration was important to have the top-down approval for replacing the old entrepreneurship program with the STEP program. Second, STEP was quickly accepted by trainees and trainers because of its focus on practical training and the voluntary participation of trainees and trainers. Third, STEP does not only offer long-term but also short-term benefits to the trainees. There are short-term benefits because trainees generate income already during the training, which is a strong incentive increasing trainees' efforts and commitment. NVTI also reported that the training is particularly effective because trainees realize the importance of start-up capital and that they have to take initiative to raise it by themselves. The most important barriers and obstacles have been limited time to manage the businesses and coordinate the business tasks with the regular courses and teaching plans. Furthermore, more skills on financial management might be necessary to increase trainees' financial literacy. Also, limited start-up capital for the trainees plays a role. Although the trainees learn how to acquire capital during the training, some trainees become demoralized when they realize that their capital base is small and, as a consequence, they abandon the idea of engaging in entrepreneurship.

The long-term plan of NVTI is to train 600 trainees per year at their institution. Furthermore, NVTI seeks to extend the STEP training by 2017 and reach out to further technical institutes around the country, such as vocational training or technical institutes in Lugogo, Jinja, Masulita, and Kabasanda. The plan is to establish a main demonstration center at NVTI and to establish the STEP training and entrepreneurship brooding centers in each region with effect from 2017. In these entrepreneurship brooding centers, the focus will be on training practical, product and service output oriented entrepreneurship and initiate income generating projects in technical and vocational institutions. To support this process, NVTI plans to develop and maintain a network of STEP trainees and STEP trainers from all the 32 technical institutions. NVTI will finance the long-term implementation of STEP at their and other institutions by raising funds from collaborators of NVTI, cost sharing with trainees, collecting donations and grants, negotiating credit purchase of raw materials, and re-investments of profits.

DISCUSSION

In this study, we presented the STEP training, its impact on trainees' entrepreneurial behavior in a vocational setting, and the long-term implementation of the training in the vocational training institute. We found that STEP positively influenced trainees' entrepreneurial behavior in terms of business opportunity identification and entrepreneurial action. These findings corroborate previous evaluation studies showing a positive effect of STEP on entrepreneurship (Bischoff et al., 2014; Frese et al., 2016; Gielnik et al., 2015). Furthermore, we presented a best-practice approach by NVTI on how to permanently implement STEP on a long-term basis. The NVTI case study showed that training and education institutions can institutionalize STEP by keeping the core idea of an action-oriented training approach and by making necessary modifications to the general framework of the training in order to ensure the best fit between the entrepreneurship training and the training institution. We think that our study provides several theoretical and practical contributions.

Theoretical and Practical Contributions

Unemployment, particularly among youths, remains a pressing issue in Uganda and many other African countries (Ahaibwe & Kasirye, 2015). Among other potential solutions, governments have identified entrepreneurship as a leverage point to boost economic development and create new employment opportunities for youths. Governments have applied several top-down strategies to effectively promote business creation among the poor. These strategies include changing laws and regulations to enhance the ease of doing business, expanding access to secondary school education, and providing early stage financing (Reynolds, 2012; World Bank, 2015b). In addition to the top-down strategies, bottom-up strategies provide an effective leverage point to promote entrepreneurship. Bottom-up strategies focus on psychological empowerment (Bischoff et al., 2014; Frese & Gielnik, 2014; Gielnik & Frese, 2013). More specifically, bottom-up strategies aim at enhancing people's active orientation to their role in society by changing their attitudes and increasing their knowledge, skills, and motivation. An active orientation is crucial to achieve entrepreneurial success (Frese, 2009; McMullen & Shepherd, 2006). Consequently, training people to become more active is a powerful means to promote entrepreneurship. In this study, we presented the STEP training as an action-oriented training program to promote entrepreneurial behavior. The findings supported our hypotheses that STEP increases trainees' business opportunity identification and entrepreneurial action. The long-term follow-up study by NVTI showed that the trainees maintained their active orientation and successfully managed businesses in the areas of farming, mobile services, and food processing. This means that STEP was successful in turning trainees into job creators, making it an effective tool to reduce unemployment among youths.

Our study showcased NVTI as a training institute that successfully implemented STEP over several years with only a minimum of external support. We have implemented STEP at several education institutions in Africa (Frese et al., 2016). At some institutions, it has been a problem to permanently offer STEP because of high administrative hurdles and a lack of financial support. The case of NVTI shows that institutions do not only have to adopt an entrepreneurial mindset with regard to training their trainees, but also with regard to implementing new and innovative programs. NVTI showed an active orientation in taking responsibility for the adoption and implementation of STEP after the first round of training in 2013. They decided to adopt STEP as the new entrepreneurship program and replaced the old entrepreneurship program. They kept the core idea of STEP to offer an action-oriented entrepreneurship training to their trainees but adapted the overarching framework of the training to the needs of the institution and developed a new concept to facilitate the implementation of the training at their institution. Adapting the overarching framework to the needs of the institution ensured that STEP could be offered on a long-term and self-sustaining basis. The case of NVTI shows that training institutions have to take several steps in order to successfully implement and independently run STEP. Based on our observations, we conclude that it is a process that requires high levels of psychological ownership of the training (Pierce, Kostova, & Dirks, 2001), personal initiative (Frese & Fay, 2001), and commitment (Hollenbeck & Klein, 1987) by the personnel of the training institution. Furthermore, the institution has to come up with effective strategies and action plans on how to adapt the training to its specific structures and context. Nonetheless, the case of NVTI demonstrates that it is worthwhile engaging in this process because it results in long-lasting positive benefits for trainees and their training in entrepreneurship.

Finally, we think that our study contributes to the literature on evidence-based entrepreneurship. We developed an interdisciplinary, action-oriented entrepreneurship training program, following principles of an evidence-based approach towards entrepreneurship (Frese et al., 2012). Our study can serve as a model for future studies seeking to develop evidence-based interventions in the field of entrepreneurship. Furthermore, we evaluated the training in a randomized controlled field experiment. We think that the concept of evidence-based entrepreneurship is theoretically useful. According to our conceptualization of evidence-based entrepreneurship, evaluating the intervention is an important aspect. Scientifically sound evaluations are important to make the decision whether or not to implement the intervention on a larger scale or on a regular basis. Many training programs cannot be adequately evaluated, because of self-selection and history effects. The self-selection effect leads to certain people participating in a training program while the control group consists of people who do not want to participate. It is obvious that there may be differences in personality, initiative, and interest in the training that may lead to differences later on. Moreover, whenever there is no adequate control group, history effects cannot be controlled for and wrong attributions litter the scientific and unscientific literature on training outcomes. In our study, we used a randomized control group design. Therefore, we can conclude that the increase in entrepreneurial behavior was due to the STEP training and not due to other external circumstances. We therefore provide strong evidence for the positive impact of STEP on entrepreneurial behavior (Reay et al., 2009).

Limitations and Strengths

As in any study, we acknowledge that there are certain limitations. We acknowledge that we provided evidence only from one vocational training institute in the capital city of Uganda. Whether our findings are generalizable and also hold in different regions needs to be established by future research. However, we are confident that STEP has a positive impact across different cohorts and contexts. We have conducted several evaluation studies showing a consistent pattern of results: STEP has positive short- and long-term effects on entrepreneurial behavior (Bischoff et al., 2014; Frese et al., 2016; Gielnik et al., 2015). We also acknowledge that the case of NVTI might be a special case and that it could be difficult to use as a model for future implementation of STEP at other institutions. Every institution has its peculiarities, which need to be taken into consideration. However, across the different implementations of the STEP training program in countries all over Africa (e.g., Uganda, Kenya, Tanzania, Rwanda, Liberia, and Lesotho), we have observed that the institutions are struggling with similar problems when it comes to the self-sustaining and long-term implementation of STEP. These were similar problems reported and dealt with by NVTI. We therefore think that the case of NVTI provides interesting insights into how to overcome administrative and financial problems related to the permanent implementation of STEP.

We also think that our study has several strengths. The solid theoretical conceptualization rooted in evidence-based entrepreneurship (Frese et al., 2012) and strong empirical evidence based on the gold standard in evaluation research (Reay et al., 2009) allow us to draw robust conclusions regarding the effectiveness of the STEP training and its impact on trainees' entrepreneurial behavior. Furthermore, the combination of the quantitative evaluation study with the qualitative case of NVTI provides deeper insights into the successful set-up and continuation of entrepreneurship training at a vocational training institute.

CONCLUSIONS

More and more often, scholars, practitioners, and journalists alike are posing the question whether Africa's youth is a ticking time bomb or an opportunity (Ighobor, 2013). We are convinced that Africa's youth is an opportunity if it gets the necessary skills to create jobs for themselves and other people. Entrepreneurship training, for example the STEP training presented in this study, may be one path to increase youth's entrepreneurial skills and turn them into job creators. Furthermore, it is essential that education and training institutions offer entrepreneurship training as part of their standard curricula. The case of NVTI presented in this study illustrates how such institutions can continuously provide entrepreneurship training to their trainees on top of their regular programs. We are confident that offering entrepreneurship training in addition to governmental top-down strategies to foster entrepreneurship will help to defuse the ticking time bomb and open the avenue to new opportunities.

Funding

This work was supported by the German Academic Exchange Service (DAAD) [grant number ID 50020279 and ID 54391079].

ORCiD

Michael M. Gielnik http://orcid.org/0000-0002-8234-4071
Kim Marie Bischoff http://orcid.org/0000-0003-4404-848X

References

Ahaibwe, G., & Kasirye, I. (2015). *Creating youth employment through entrepreneurship financing: The Uganda Youth Venture Capital Fund. Research Series No. 122*. Kampala, Uganda: Economic Policy Research Centre.

Bischoff, K. M., Gielnik, M. M., & Frese, M. (2014). Entrepreneurship training in developing countries. In W. Reichman (Ed.), *Industrial and Organizational Psychology Help the Vulnerable: Serving the Underserved* (pp. 92–119). Houndmills, UK: Palgrave Macmillan. http://dx.doi.org/10.1057/9781137327734_6

Campbell, D. T. (1957). Factors relevant to the validity of experiments in social settings. *Psychological Bulletin*, *54*(4), 297–312. http://dx.doi.org/10.1037/h0040950

Carter, N. M., Gartner, W. B., & Reynolds, P. D. (1996). Exploring start-up event sequences. *Journal of Business Venturing*, *11*(3), 151–166. http://dx.doi.org/10.1016/0883-9026(95)00129-8

Davidsson, P., & Honig, B. (2003). The role of social and human capital among nascent entrepreneurs. *Journal of Business Venturing*, *18*(3), 301–331. http://dx.doi.org/10.1016/S0883-9026(02)00097-6

DeGhetto, K., Gray, J. R., & Kiggundu, M. N. (2016). The African Union's Agenda 2063: Aspirations, challenges, and opportunities for management research. *Africa Journal of Management*, *2*(1), 93–116. http://dx.doi.org/10.1080/23322373.2015.1127090

de Mel, S., McKenzie, D., & Woodruff, C. (2008). Returns to capital in microenterprises: Evidence from a field experiment. *The Quarterly Journal of Economics*, *123*(4), 1329–1372. http://dx.doi.org/10.1162/qjec.2008.123.4.1329

Drexler, A., Fischer, G., & Schoar, A. (2014). Keeping it simple: Financial literacy and rules of thumb. *American Economic Journal. Applied Economics*, *6*(2), 1–31. http://dx.doi.org/10.1257/app.6.2.1

Fiet, J. O. (2001). The theoretical side of teaching entrepreneurship. *Journal of Business Venturing*, *16*(1), 1–24. http://dx.doi.org/10.1016/S0883-9026(99)00041-5

Frese, M. (2009). Toward a psychology of entrepreneurship - An action theory perspective. *Foundations and Trends in Entrepreneurship*, *5*(6), 437–496. http://dx.doi.org/10.1561/0300000028

Frese, M., Bausch, A., Schmidt, P., Rauch, A., & Kabst, R. (2012). Evidence-based entrepreneurship: Cumulative science, action principles, and bridging the gap between science and practice. *Foundations and Trends in Entrepreneurship*, *8*(1), 1–62. http://dx.doi.org/10.1561/0300000044

Frese, M., & Fay, D. (2001). Personal initiative: An active performance concept for work in the 21st century. *Research in Organizational Behavior*, *23*, 133–187. http://dx.doi.org/10.1016/S0191-3085(01)23005-6

Frese, M., & Gielnik, M. M. (2014). The psychology of entrepreneurship. *Annual Review of Organizational Psychology and Organizational Behavior*, *1*(1), 413–438. http://dx.doi.org/10.1146/annurev-orgpsych-031413-091326

Frese, M., Gielnik, M. M., & Mensmann, M. (2016). Psychological training for entrepreneurs to take action: Contributing to poverty reduction in developing countries. *Current Directions in Psychological Science*, *25*(3), 196–202.

Frese, M., & Zapf, D. (1994). Action as the core of work psychology: A German approach. In H. C. Triandis, M. D. Dunnette, & L. M. Hough (Eds.), *Handbook of Industrial and Organizational Psychology* (Vol. 4, pp. 271–340). Palo Alto, CA: Consulting Psychologists Press.

Fritsch, M. (2008). How does new business formation affect regional development? Introduction to the special issue. *Small Business Economics*, *30*(1), 1–14. http://dx.doi.org/10.1007/s11187-007-9057-y

Gielnik, M. M., & Frese, M. (2013). Entrepreneurship and poverty reduction: Applying I-O psychology to microbusiness and entrepreneurship in developing countries. In J. B. Olson-Buchanan, L. L. Koppes Bryan, & L. Foster Thompson (Eds.), *Using Industrial-Organizational Psychology for the Greater Good: Helping Those Who Help Others* (pp. 394–438). New York: Routledge.

Gielnik, M. M., Frese, M., Kahara-Kawuki, A., Katono, I. W., Kyejjusa, S., Ngoma, M., . . . Dlugosch, T. J. (2015). Action and action-regulation in entrepreneurship: Evaluating a student training for promoting entrepreneurship. *Academy of Management Learning & Education*, *14*(1), 69–94. http://dx.doi.org/10.5465/amle.2012.0107

Glaub, M. E., Frese, M., Fischer, S., & Hoppe, M. (2014). Increasing personal initiative in small business managers or owners leads to entrepreneurial success: A theory-based controlled randomized field intervention for evidence-based management. *Academy of Management Learning & Education*, *13*(3), 354–379. http://dx.doi.org/10.5465/amle.2013.0234

Heimbeck, D., Frese, M., Sonnentag, S., & Keith, N. (2003). Integrating errors into the training process: The function of error management instructions and the role of goal orientation. *Personnel Psychology*, *56*(2), 333–361. http://dx.doi.org/10.1111/j.1744-6570.2003.tb00153.x

Hollenbeck, J. R., & Klein, H. J. (1987). Goal commitment and the goal-setting process: Problems, prospects, and proposals for future research. *The Journal of Applied Psychology*, *72*(2), 212–220. http://dx.doi.org/10.1037/0021-9010.72.2.212

Ighobor, K. (2013). Africa's youth: A "ticking time bomb" or an opportunity? *Africa Renewal*, May 2013, 10. Retrieved from http://www.un.org/africarenewal/magazine/may-2013/africa's-youth-"ticking-time-bomb"-or-opportunity

Keith, N., & Frese, M. (2005). Self-regulation in error management training: Emotion control and metacognition as mediators of performance effects. *The Journal of Applied Psychology, 90* (4), 677–691. http://dx.doi.org/10.1037/0021-9010.90.4.677

Kiggundu, M. N. (2002). Entrepreneurs and entrepreneurship in Africa: What is known and what needs to be done. *Journal of Developmental Entrepreneurship*, *7*(3), 239–258.

McMullen, J. S., & Shepherd, D. A. (2006). Entrepreneurial action and the role of uncertainty in the theory of the entrepreneur. *Academy of Management Review, 31*(1), 132–152. http://dx.doi.org/10.5465/AMR.2006.19379628

Nelson, R. E., & Johnson, S. D. (1997). Entrepreneurship education as a strategic approach to economic growth in Kenya. *Journal of Industrial Teacher Education, 35*(1), 7–21.

Nkirina, S. P. (2010). The challenges of integrating entrepreneurship education in the vocational training system: An insight from Tanzania's Vocational Education Training Authority. *Journal of European Industrial Training*, *34*(2), 153–166. http://dx.doi.org/10.1108/03090591011023998

Pfeffer, J., & Sutton, R. I. (2006). Evidence-based management. *Harvard Business Review, 84*(1), 62–74.

Pierce, J. L., Kostova, T., & Dirks, K. T. (2001). Toward a theory of psychological ownership in organizations. *Academy of Management Review*, *26*(2), 298–310. http://dx.doi.org/10.5465/AMR.2001.4378028

Rasmussen, E. A., & Sorheim, R. (2006). Action-based entrepreneurship education. *Technovation*, *26*(2), 185–194. http://dx.doi.org/10.1016/j.technovation.2005.06.012

Rauch, A., & Frese, M. (2006). Meta-analysis as a tool for developing entrepreneurship research and theory. In J. Wiklund, D. Dimov, J. A. Katz, & D. A. Shepherd (Eds.), *Advances in Entrepreneurship, Firm Emergence and Growth* (Vol. 9, pp. 29–51). Oxford: JAI Press. http://dx.doi.org/10.1016/S1074-7540(06)09003-9

Reay, T., Berta, W., & Kohn, M. K. (2009). What's the evidence on evidence-based management? *The Academy of Management Perspectives*, *23*(4), 5–18. http://dx.doi.org/10.5465/AMP.2009.45590137

Reynolds, P. D. (2012). Entrepreneurship in developing economies: The bottom billions and business creation. *Foundations and Trends in Entrepreneurship*, *8*(3), 141–277. http://dx.doi.org/10.1561/0300000045

Rousseau, D. M. (2006). Is there such a thing as "evidence-based management"? *Academy of Management Review*, *31*(2), 256–269. http://dx.doi.org/10.5465/AMR.2006.20208679

Shane, S., & Venkataraman, S. (2000). The promise of entrepreneurship as a field of research. *Academy of Management Review*, *25*(1), 217–226. http://dx.doi.org/10.5465/AMR.2000.2791611

Solomon, G. (2007). An examination of entrepreneurship education in the United States. *Journal of Small Business and Enterprise Development*, *14*(2), 168–182. http://dx.doi.org/10.1108/14626000710746637

Souitaris, V., Zerbinati, S., & Al-Laham, A. (2007). Do entrepreneurship programmes raise entrepreneurial intention of science and engineering students? The effect of learning, inspiration and resources. *Journal of Business Venturing*, *22*(4), 566–591. http://dx.doi.org/10.1016/j.jbusvent.2006.05.002

Thurik, A. R., Carree, M. A., van Stel, A., & Audretsch, D. B. (2008). Does self-employment reduce unemployment? *Journal of Business Venturing*, *23*(6), 673–686. http://dx.doi.org/10.1016/j.jbusvent.2008.01.007

Uganda Government (2015). Second national development plan (NDPII) 2015/16-2019/20.Kampala: The Republic of Uganda.

van Praag, C. M., & Versloot, P. H. (2007). What is the value of entrepreneurship? A review of recent research. *Small Business Economics*, *29*(4), 351–382. http://dx.doi.org/10.1007/s11187-007-9074-x

van Stel, A., Storey, D. J., & Thurik, A. R. (2007). The effect of business regulations on nascent and young business entrepreneurship. *Small Business Economics*, *28*(2-3), 171–186. http://dx.doi.org/10.1007/s11187-006-9014-1

Welter, F. (2011). Contextualizing entrepreneurship - Conceptual challenges and ways forward. *Entrepreneurship Theory and Practice*, *35*(1), 165–184. http://dx.doi.org/10.1111/j.1540-6520.2010.00427.x

Wong, P. K., Ho, Y. P., & Autio, E. (2005). Entrepreneurship, innovation and economic growth: Evidence from GEM data. *Small Business Economics*, *24*(3), 335–350. http://dx.doi.org/10.1007/s11187-005-2000-1

World Bank. (2015a). *Doing business 2015: Going beyond efficiency*. Washington, DC: World Bank.

World Bank. (2015b). *World Development Indicators 2015*. Washington, DC: World Bank.

Entrepreneurship in Africa: Identifying the Frontier of Impactful Research

Richard A. Devine and Moses N. Kiggundu

This review summarizes literature covering entrepreneurship research in Africa, examining 121 articles published in prominent entrepreneurship and management journals from 2002 to 2015. To do so, this research organizes the work done along three broad themes describing: the African entrepreneur, the entrepreneurial firm, and macro socio-economic conditions. Within this framework, the review examines entrepreneurial attributes with regard to gender, age, education, and work behavior. The topics explored that are relevant to the entrepreneurial firm include organizational forms (e.g., SMEs and family businesses), financial and social capital, as well as the informal economy. Macro socio-economic conditions with respect to the various circumstances African entrepreneurs are subject to are then considered. Issues typical to Africa concerning poverty, corruption, internationalization, and environmental concerns are also examined. In an effort to facilitate future work, this research highlights knowledge gaps concerning the theoretical nature of most of work done, which has primarily been focused within Anglophone African countries. This review concludes by considering what needs to be done to improve the quality of entrepreneurship studies within the African context.

INTRODUCTION

Entrepreneurship in Africa is considered a means by which the African population can foster country development and alleviate poverty (Ortmans, 2015). As it happens, sub-Saharan Africa contains the highest number of individuals engaged in nascent entrepreneurship (14.1%) or early stage entrepreneurial activity (26%) in the world (Global Entrepreneurship Monitor, 2015). Also fascinating is the recognition that Africa leads the world with the highest participation rates of women in early stage entrepreneurial activity (24.6%), with the next highest occurring in Latin America (16.1%) (Global Entrepreneurship Monitor, 2015). Despite steady growth in gross domestic product (GDP) and an increase in entrepreneurship rates, overall GDP by country in Africa remains among the lowest relative to other regions of the world (World Bank, 2013). Against this backdrop, academic interest with regard to entrepreneurship in Africa has been increasing (e.g., Rivera-Santos, Holt, Littlewood, and Kolk, 2015; Khayesi, George, and Antonakis, 2014; Daspit and Long, 2014). However, to the best of the authors' knowledge, there has been no attempt at a review of this literature since a *Journal of Developmental Entrepreneurship* review piece by Kiggundu (2002a) nearly 15 years ago. In recognition of this need, this review aims to systematically summarize the current state of the African entrepreneurship literature.

Entrepreneurship is defined as, "the scholarly examination of how, by whom, and with what effects opportunities to create future goods and services are discovered, evaluated, and exploited" (Shane and Venkataraman, 2000: 218). In Africa, entrepreneurship is examined amidst the individual entrepreneur, small and medium enterprises (SMEs), and family businesses, as well as within the informal and formal sectors of the economy, among other forms (Kiggundu, 2002a). Although there have been various initiatives to encourage research in Africa, including the establishment of the Global Entrepreneurship Monitor (GEM) in 1999, the majority of entrepreneurship research takes place within a U.S. context (Terjesen, Hessels, and Li, 2016). Perhaps one of the greatest impediments to scientific inquiry regarding entrepreneurship in Africa is the lack of access to the frontiers of recent research. As such, it is partly the aim of this review to facilitate inquiry across the African continent. However, this review is not meant to be exhaustive, but rather descriptive of extant work. This review still contains gaps, but it provides researchers with a renewed base for exploring the entrepreneurship literature in Africa. In keeping with this purpose, this review points to the need for developing theoretically and empirically rich studies as a path toward better understanding entrepreneurship in Africa.

The remainder of this paper is organized as follows. In the next section, the systematic review process is summarized and the theoretical, empirical, and geographical nature of the work being published is detailed. This review then describes extant research along the three broad themes of the African entrepreneur, the entrepreneurial firm, and macro socio-economic conditions. In the last sections, directions for future research are discussed.

STATE OF AFRICAN ENTREPRENEURSHIP RESEARCH

Article Identification

This review aims to examine the management literature and identify impactful entrepreneurship research in the African context at the individual, firm, and environmental level. To do so, searches were conducted employing a systematic review process (e.g., Tranfield, Denyer, and Smart, 2003; Rauch and Frese, 2007; Terjesen et al., 2016), using the *Thomson Reuters Web of Science*, *ProQuest*, *Academic Search Complete*, and *Business Source Complete* databases. The databases were searched using the following keywords: *entrepreneur, entrepreneurs, entrepreneurial, entrepreneurship, small business, family business, informal sector, intrapreneur, intrapreneurship, new firm, new ventures, venture, venturing, spin-off/spinoff, start-up/startup*, along with the keyword *Africa* within the time frame 2002 to 2015. As a result, the entrepreneurship literature reviewed herein this article is inclusive of many areas of research. Since this review was primarily intended to identify high quality empirical and theoretical work in management related journals, our results were kept limited to impactful journals. However, *ProQuest* was used to identify any relevant dissertations and this review also includes work that is more phenomenologically driven.

In the interest of ensuring that no relevant articles were missed, separate searches were conducted in top entrepreneurship and management journals. In executing this, searches were done in *Journal of Business Venturing*, *Entrepreneurship Theory & Practice (ET&P)*, *Journal of Small Business Management (JSBM)*, *Small Business Economics (SBE)*, *Journal of Developmental Entrepreneurship (JDE)*, *World Development (WD)*, *Journal of International Business Studies (JIBS)*, *Journal of Management (JOM)*, *Academy of Management Journal (AMJ)*, and *Strategic Management Journal (SMJ)*, which are the same journals that contribute much of the final sample. From these searches, 121 articles published in prominent entrepreneurship and management journals from 2002 to 2015 were identified for inclusion. In the next section, key descriptives of the sample with regard to the journal outlets and various metrics of the studies are explored, including their composition, theoretical perspectives, methodologies used, and regions studied.

Journal Coverage

The journals that were identified as publishing the most research involving entrepreneurship in Africa are *WD*, *JDE*, *SBE*, *ET&P*, and *JSBM*. Only occasional pieces occurred in *SMJ* or *JIBS*, suggesting that the majority of research regarding entrepreneurship in Africa appears in entrepreneurship journals or on the fringe of mainstream management journals. While this is also generally true for entrepreneurship research (Keupp and Gassmann, 2009; Shane, 2012), it also points to Africa as an understudied research context. It may also point to the possibility that unlike in the U.S. and Europe, entrepreneurship research in Africa has not yet been mainstreamed (Fayolle and Riot, 2015).

Overview of Reviewed Research

The general levels of analysis studied across the African entrepreneurship literature are depicted in Table 1 (e.g., the entrepreneur, the firm, and the environment) with findings represented according to the attributes, antecedents, and outcomes of the levels being explored (e.g., Terjesen et al., 2016). At the individual level (e.g., the entrepreneur), minority, women, and youth entrepreneurs, and personality attributes are of common interest. At the firm level, topics include small and medium enterprises, and family businesses, as well as types of firms, including informal and socially oriented ventures. In the external environment, poverty, corruption, internationalization, and environmental concerns are of particular interest. Table 1 helps to more concisely articulate the characteristics and research questions that are being explored within each level of analysis. While some topics exist across levels of analysis (e.g., social networks), other topics are examined exclusive to specific levels of analysis (e.g., psychological traits, country infrastructure). The sampling of research questions along with the theoretical perspectives referenced in the table help to clarify the type of inquiry that has taken place at each level of analysis. We notice that despite reviewing over a decade of recent research, African entrepreneurship still appears in its early stages. Also observed is that not much research has utilized multi-level approaches to exploring entrepreneurship in the African context. Table 2 further details the landscape of the research, listing the number of studies (out of the total 121) that each methodological positioning (e.g., qualitative, quantitative, and mixed-method)

Table 1. Research Article Contents.

	Entrepreneur	Firm	Environment
Attributes	Psychological traits (e.g., cognitive abilities, locus of control, self-efficacy), education, gender, age, prior experience, entrepreneur type (e.g., informal, diaspora, family business), social networks	Business type (e.g., informal, diaspora, family business, social ventures, international), size, social networks, financing, management practices	Infrastructure, culture, government stability, regulation, rule of law, government services
Research Questions	How does motivation affect business success? How do goal intentions and positive fantasies affect new venture creation? How should female leaders be developed? Are metrics used to measure entrepreneurship related constructs biased against women?	Are informal ventures exploiting child labor? Does early internationalization help legitimacy? What characteristics of sibling teams affect business success? Are small firms credit constrained? Does network embeddedness constrain nonprofit firms?	Has Africa fostered development? What is the role of government? Are property rights properly enforced? How can Africa better facilitate innovation? How can government services be better managed? What type of challenges does the African context pose?
Sample Citations	Frese et al. 2007; Gielnik et al. 2014; Bullough et al. 2015; Dawa and Namatovu, 2015	Webbink et al. 2012; Wood et al. 2011; Farrington et al. 2012; Vandenberg, 2003; Kistruck and Beamish, 2010	Frese and Friedrich, 2002; Watkins, 2007; Brown, 2015; Agbo et al. 2008; Sievers and Vandenberg, 2007; Murisa and Chikweche, 2013
Antecedents	Education, gender, age, prior experience, entrepreneur type (e.g., informal, diaspora, family business), social networks	Size, social networks, financing, organizational form (e.g., IJV)	Economic freedom, financing, entry mode, social networks
Research Questions	How does prior business experience influence the ability to introduce new innovations? How does education and drive affect performance? Do female entrepreneurs have trouble securing financing? How do family networks affect business and growth?	Are small firms less likely to use government services? How do network ties affect internationalization? What type of effect does capital have on business success in the short and long term? How do joint ventures with large multinationals affect status?	How does economic freedom affect the survival of foreign enterprises in Africa? How does capital availability affect small business startup rates? Can alternative forms of entry be used to overcome market inefficiencies? How does FDI affect entrepreneurial activity? How do diaspora networks affect entrepreneurship?

Sample Citations	Unger et al. 2009; Robson et al. 2012; Welsh et al. 2013; Khavul et al. 2009	Obeng and Blundel, 2015; Gimede, 2004; Karlan et al. 2015; Hearn, 2015	Demirbag, Apaydin, and Tatoglu, 2011; Pretes, 2002; Meyer et al. 2009; Washington and Chapman, 2014; Kshetri, 2013
Outcomes	Work/life balance, improving infrastructure, corruption	CSR, corruption, financial performance, growth, survival, business formalization	Employment growth, new business creation, CSR, income inequality
Research Questions	How do female entrepreneurs achieve work/life balance and how does this affect their children? What are some of the outcomes of social entrepreneurs' activities? Do entrepreneurs contribute to corruption or are they victims of it?	Do small firms understand corporate social responsibility? How does competition drive informal entrepreneurs to formalize? How do firm characteristics affect incidence and intensity of performance?	How does economic growth and regulation affect employment? How important are deregulation and political stability for new business development? Does FDI improve CSR conditions? Does entrepreneurship affect income inequality?
Sample Citations	Schindehutte et al. 2003; Nelson et al. 2013; Ufere et al. 2012	Liedholm, 2002; Demuijnck and Ngnodjom, 2013; Sonobe et al. 2011; Masakure et al. 2008	Mahadea, 2012; Munemo, 2012; Bardy et al. 2012; Kimhi, 2010
Theoretical Perspectives	Resource based view, Social capital theory, learning theory	Institutional theory, social capital theory, agency theory	Institutional theory, social capital theory

Table 2. Research by Different Approaches and Time Frame.

	Level of Analysis			Study Year		
Method	Entrepreneur	Firm	Environment	2002 –2006	2007 –2011	2012 –2015
Quantitative	18	40	17	13	25	37
Qualitative	14	11	16	5	17	19
Mixed-method	2	1	2	1	2	2
Phenomenological	20	29	27	16	27	33

Note: Studies are classified according to level of analysis and general methodological positioning of the research. Level of analysis and study year groupings are not mutually exclusive. Phenomenological is used as a separate category to describe how many studies in Africa lack theory.

accounted for across levels of analysis (e.g., entrepreneur, firm, and the environment). Study year and level of analysis are separate categories and are not mutually exclusive in order to depict the timeline and level of analysis for each of the methods. Furthermore, phenomenological stands apart from the other categories as its 'method' to describe how much published research is lacking theory. Lastly, Table 3 classifies the studies reviewed according to subcontinental regions with a special category that indicates the number of studies conducted in francophone countries. The categories are not mutually exclusive since many studies use multi-country samples.

Theoretical Perspectives

The majority of the entrepreneurship research conducted in Africa is lacking theoretical development and is mostly phenomenological (See Table 2). However, among the studies that utilize specific theories, social capital theory, resource based theory (RBT), and institutional theory are most prevalent (See Table 1).

Methodologies

The studies reviewed show that a myriad of data collection methods and analytic techniques have been used. Collection methods include case studies (Wheeler, McKague,

Table 3. Research by Region.

	North Africa	East Africa	Southern Africa	West Africa	Francophone
Number of Studies	40	56	72	62	41

Note: Categories are not mutually exclusive since some studies were conducted across regions in addition to within region. North Africa is the northern part of the continent, excluding sub-Saharan Africa. East Africa is used to refer to the countries of Kenya, Tanzania, and Uganda. Southern Africa is inclusive of Angola, Botswana, Lesotho, Malawi, Mozambique, Namibia, South Africa, Swaziland, Zambia, and Zimbabwe. West Africa refers to the western subcontinent of Africa, excluding the Maghreb (formerly known as the Barbary Coast). Francophone indicates the number of studies in the sample that were conducted in predominantly French language countries.

Thomson, Davies, Medalye, and Prada, 2005), questionnaires (Khayesi, George, and Antonakis, 2014; Daspit and Long, 2014), interviews (Robinson, Davidsson, Mescht, and Court, 2007), experiments (Glaub, Frese, Fischer, and Hoppe, 2014), and archival data (Acquaah, 2009). While most of the research conducted was quantitative in nature, a number of studies were qualitative, with some employing mixed methods (see Table 2). Data analytic techniques commonly included ordinarily least squares (OLS) regression (Woodward, Rolfe, Ligthelm, and Guimaraes, 2011), with probit and logit models also being utilized (Robson, Akuetteh, Westhead, and Wright, 2012; Grimm, Knoringa, and Lay, 2012). For example, Amin and Islam (2015) used OLS regression to analyze World Bank surveys in a study examining labor productivity between large and small informal firms. Khavul, Perez-Nordtvedt, and Wood (2010) employed hierarchical moderated regression to examine the internationalization behavior of international new ventures (INVs). And Robson and Obeng (2008) used ordered logit models to examine entrepreneurs' barriers to growth in Ghana.

Regions

In the studies examined for this review, every region of Africa is included (See Table 3). The large majority of work conducted covers sub-Saharan Africa and mostly anglophone countries. Few studies exclusively examined francophone countries, with the inclusion of these countries mostly segmented to multi-country samples. This may be due to language differences since the review did not include publications in French. Language limitations may also apply to North Africa where the dominant languages are Arabic and French rather than English. Across the regions, southern Africa receives the most attention, due in large part to South Africa's developing economy (World Bank, 2013). Table 3 brings attention to the need for more research involving northern Africa as well as francophone Africa. Currently, there is little literature suggesting meaningful differences between African regions as opposed to Africa as a whole (e.g., Asiedu, 2002), in terms of entrepreneurship. Since regional integration is an important consideration (e.g., Foroutan, 1992; Kiggundu and Deghetto, 2015), research examining regional differences in entrepreneurship is warranted.

AFRICAN ENTREPRENEURS

Individual level research accounted for 28% of the studies examined in this review. Examining entrepreneurship at the individual level often entails ways in which entrepreneurs differ in terms of personality, thought processes, education, prior experience, and other individual characteristics. African entrepreneurship research follows these same themes, but also gives due consideration to groups of entrepreneurs that are particularly critical to their countries' developing infrastructures (e.g., women and diaspora entrepreneurs).

Marginalized Entrepreneurs

Across all levels of analysis, studies often examine categories of entrepreneurs (e.g., women, youth, diaspora). Given the inequality that the institutional frameworks in

Africa sometimes facilitate (Seekings and Nattrass, 2008), inquiry into disadvantaged classes of society is warranted. Although entrepreneurship among females is prevalent and young people are relatively overrepresented in Africa, both groups remain marginalized (Brixiová, Ncube, and Bicaba, 2015).

Women. Studies have sought to identify how so many women remain engaged and persist in entrepreneurship despite the vast amount of challenges (Adom and Williams, 2012; Yusuff, 2013). Unfair treatment is represented in the unequal rights conferred to women both socially (Manuh, 1998) and legally (Lastarria-Cornhiel, 1997; Yusuff, 2013). Female entrepreneurs must contend with limited property rights and in many ways need to be more savvy than their male counterparts to remain competitive. The literature supports this contention and recognizes that while women entrepreneurs are disadvantaged, there is untapped potential for women to act in an even more critical role for economic development (Adom, 2015).

Recognizing the amplified challenges female entrepreneurs encounter, research reveals that personal issues, management skills, and financing serve as impediments to women entrepreneurs (Welsh, Memili, Kaciak, and Ahmed 2013). Even further, women interviewed also report experiencing gender discrimination with regard to government policy, customary laws, access to financing (Asiedu, Kalonda-Kanyama, Ndikumana, and Nti-Addae 2013), and bureaucratic hurdles (Chea, 2008). Some findings are more controversial, with the suggestion that male ownership matters in terms of work productivity (e.g., Woodward, Rolfe, Ligthelm, and, Guimaraes, 2011), that males plan more than females (Yusuf and Saffu, 2005), and that sons rather than daughters benefit more coming from a family background of entrepreneurship (Aterido and Hallward-Driemeier, 2011). However, given the exceptional entrepreneurship rates among African women, there are a number of factors to their benefit and a lot left unsaid about their ability to persevere.

For example, studies have found that women are more innovative than men (Aterido, Beck, and Iacovone, 2013; Chea, 2008) and use external financing less because they often choose to enter sectors where there is less need for capital access (Aterido et al., 2013). Women are able to prevail by gaining support through education, prior work experience, and their families (Welsh et al., 2013; Otoo, Fulton, Ibro, and Lowenberg-Deboer, 2011). On this point, women often engage in entrepreneurship because they are necessity driven and need to provide for their families, although they have become more opportunity driven over time (Adom and Williams, 2012). Indeed, necessity and opportunity are not mutually exclusive. For example, Njoroge (2015) chronicled starting his data recovery services business in Kenya out of necessity when his computer crashed in his final year of university and then building it into a growing business concern operating in East Africa with gross revenue of over US$1 million and 70 employees. Moreover, the impact on the children of entrepreneurial mothers is reported to be a positive one, as women serve as role models and provide their children with a blueprint of entrepreneurial behavior (Schindehutte, Morris, and Brennan, 2003). Women are also able to leverage their social networking abilities and use these skills to grow their businesses (Dawa and Namatovu, 2015; Chea, 2008). In keeping with this advantage, network marketing is one such avenue that has proved beneficial to African women, as Avon[1] gives impoverished women a detailed framework for success and a subsequent opportunity at a better income (Scott, Dolan, Johnstone-Louis, Sugden, and Wu, 2012). In sum, women have proven themselves quite competent with regard to entrepreneurship, but it also recognized that training is necessary to facilitate their development into entrepreneurial leaders (Bullough, de Luque, Abdelzaher, and Heim, 2015).

Youth. Withstanding the fact that Africa has the greatest number of individuals aged between 15 and 24 in the world (African Economic Outlook, 2012), unemployment among African youth is in excess of 60%. As a result of the high unemployment among young Africans, entrepreneurship is viewed as a means to empower youth and foster development (Williams and Hovorka, 2013). In this endeavor, young entrepreneurs face a number of obstacles, as their social class, education, and family backgrounds bear on their ability to identify and act on opportunities (Beeka and Rimmington, 2011). Also, young entrepreneurs often lack the skills to succeed in entrepreneurship, and particularly struggle to identify worthwhile opportunities (Brixiová, Ncube, and Bicaba, 2015; Beeka and Rimmington, 2011). Since there is little opportunity provided to this group with regard to training and support, this proves detrimental (Brixiová et al., 2015). Research shows that employment and self-employment prospects increase dramatically with education and training (Calves and Schoumaker, 2004; Williams and Hovorka, 2013). Furthermore, that African youth would be well-served with access to training that caters to improving their intuition and entrepreneurial mindsets (Beeka and Rimmington, 2011; Brixiová et al., 2015).

Education

Education along with training and development is viewed as a means to alleviate poverty and unemployment with regard to youth and as a way to empower each country to overcome developmental hurdles (Watkins, 2013). Access to education and professional development can equip Africans with the skillset to identify opportunities, innovate, grow their businesses, and ultimately increase performance (Robson, Haugh, and Obeng, 2009; Unger, Keith, Hilling, Gielnik, and Frese, 2009). Robson and Obeng (2008) even demonstrated the importance of education above that of gender and age in predicting the likelihood of prevailing against business barriers, with education being valuable to success. While the literature in this area appears to be at a consensus toward the positive effects of education on entrepreneurship (e.g., Robson et al., 2009; Unger et al., 2009), some work has also considered potentiality detrimental effects of entrepreneurship education (De Clercq, Lim, and Oh, 2014), with some studies suggesting that education may deter individuals from certain cultures (De Clercq, Lim, and Oh, 2014). More specifically, entrepreneurship education may make individuals more aware of the associated risks that self-employment carries, which may in turn funnel individuals from a conservative background into more stable career options (De Clercq et al., 2014).

Behavior and Personality Attributes

The ways in which entrepreneurs differ from other individuals is a topic of frequent interest to academics (e.g., McGrath, MacMillan, and Scheinberg, 1992; Busenitz and Barney, 1997). Seeking what makes successful entrepreneurs different from the rest, scholars have found significant relationships for such traits as self-efficacy, motivation, locus of control, initiative, cognitive ability, human capital, and proactive planning (Escher, Grabarkiewicz, Frese, van Steekelenburg, Lauw, and Friedrich, 2002; Krauss, Frese, Friedrich, and Unger, 2005; Frese et al., 2007; Urban 2008). Planning and good health have also been positively linked to new venture creation (Chao, Szrek, Pereira, and Pauly, 2010; Gielnik et al., 2014). In a study by Urban (2008), entrepreneurial self-efficacy emerged as more important than culture in predicting entrepreneurial intentions, suggesting that entrepreneurial behavior is more indicative of individual traits as opposed to cultural values. Entrepreneurs use these skillsets to solve everyday career challenges along with the ethical dilemmas that face them on a daily basis (Robinson, Davidsson, Mescht, and Court 2007). From these studies reviewed, it is clear that entrepreneurs possess different traits and skillsets than non-entrepreneurs (Frese et al., 2007), have a greater tolerance for risk and are more oriented toward and for an entrepreneurial mindset (Krauss, Frese, Friedrich, and Unger, 2005; Urban, 2008). Even further, evidence suggests that entrepreneurs are more innovative than other individuals and that this ability becomes honed over time as it is even sharper in habitual entrepreneurs relative to more novice entrepreneurs (Robson, Akuettah, Westhead, and Wright, 2012).

Diaspora

Fascinating inquiry is also taking place with regard to diaspora entrepreneurship, which describes entrepreneurs who are living outside of their original homeland (Halkias, Harkiolakis, Thurman, Rishi, Ekonomou, Caracatsanis, & Akrivos, 2009). There are around 30 million Africans in the African diaspora and their relevance for African development is captured in the estimated US$40 billion they contribute yearly in remittances (International Fund for Agricultural Development, 2015). Much of these contributions come through entrepreneurial efforts (Newland and Tanaka, 2010). Even more compelling is that actual remittance numbers may be in excess of US$160 billion, with most of the money unable to be tracked since is it mostly sent through informal channels (Doyle, 2013). Some African countries have developed governmental organizations to encourage diasporas to make charity donations back to their communities (Kshetri 2013). This acts as proof that Africa benefits from connections to more developed countries in interesting ways and not just monetarily, but also through access to knowledge, both novel and industry specific (Levin and Barnard, 2013). Diaspora entrepreneurs help the economy and infrastructure through their ability to transfer institutional practices of more advanced host countries back home (Kshetri, 2013). Since diaspora entrepreneurs are more likely to be exporters of goods and knowledge, they also contribute to the internationalization of their host economies (Boly, Coniglio, Prota, and Seric 2014). In these regards, African diaspora contribute significantly to their home and host country's development.

Research has also tracked the return of diaspora, who are also more inclined to engage in entrepreneurship upon their return (Marchetta, 2012). It is found that their migration experience helps their survival chances as entrepreneurs (Marchetta, 2012), potentially due to cultural enrichment while abroad. Other studies have focused on the specific contexts of Lebanon and Greece, recognizing that Lebanese entrepreneurs have had positive effects on sub-Saharan African economies (Ahmed, Zgheib, Kowatly, and Rhetts, 2012). Similarly, Greece has served as a landing point for many African immigrants and refugees, who start businesses and send substantial portions of earnings back home (Halkias et al., 2009). We note that even with the right personal attributes, entrepreneurs cannot be successful unless they operate within well established, functioning and strategically managed firms.

THE ENTREPRENEURIAL FIRM

Firm level research accounts for a large portion of the studies being conducted with regard to African entrepreneurship and about 43% of the literature in this review (See Table 2 above). Issues being considered at the firm level include organizational forms (e.g., family business, SMEs), type of entrepreneurship (e.g., socially oriented, informal), as well as the effects of social networks and capital access. These topics have remained areas of inquiry for some time, since African firms have difficulty sustaining operations and contending with the constraints of their environments (Kiggundu, 2002a). African entrepreneurs must lean on family members and their social networks to maintain hope of survival in a challenging environment (Deberry-Spence and Elliot, 2012). Additionally, entrepreneurs who do succeed with family ventures or informal operations often have trouble sustaining entrepreneurship any other way (Kiggundu, 2002a). In this section, these themes along with aspects of the entrepreneurial firm in Africa are further discussed.

Family Business

Family enterprises are a driving force for African economies. In South Africa alone, family businesses comprise an estimated 80% of all firms and account for 50% of the economic growth (Visser and Chiloane-Tsoka, 2014). Family businesses also frequently operate within the informal economy, allowing them to skirt regulation and inefficient formal institutions (Khavul, Bruton, and Wood, 2009). However, research on family business in Africa depicts more of a necessity driven motivation for this organizational form, given that family firms face a number of challenges. For example, family business networks can facilitate moral hazard and create circumstances that prompt dysfunction in the business (Khayesi, George, and Antonakis, 2014; Daspit and Long, 2014). While these businesses can leverage family and community ties to grow (Khayesi et al., 2014), they also need community ties in order to offset the burden that family ties can create (Khavul et al., 2009). Specifically, scholars have noted that African family businesses incur an undue responsibility to provide for extended family members (Luke and Munshi, 2006; Khavul et al., 2009). Though family firms experience benefits with regard to leveraging community and political ties, tie utilization has diminishing returns to performance (Acquaah, 2011b). Particularly, family firm networks have an inverted U-shaped relationship with performance while nonfamily firm networks display a more linear relationship with performance (Acquaah, 2011b). Both organizational forms (i.e. family and nonfamily firms), however, appear to have their own advantages with regard to network utilization (Acquaah, 2011a; 2011b).

It is clear that family businesses bring unique considerations to bear (Adendorff and Halkias, 2014). Family firms facilitate a family legacy of entrepreneurship (Morris, Williams, Allen, and Avila, 1997), which can employ children born into these families from a young age (e.g., Webbink, Smits, and de Jong, 2012). Also interesting are the steps taken by family firms to combat the "cousin consortium", whereby distant relatives can step in to a family firm after the death of a male owner since women are granted few ownership privileges (Smith, 2009). A striking observation that Smith (2009) noted is that family firms have an incentive for multiple male owners to protect against this free-riding relative problem, whereas family firms have been traditionally viewed as a prevalent business form in developing economies in order to avoid opportunism in the institutional structures (Burkart, Panunzi, and Shleifer, 2003). Other research has considered sibling team success in family business, finding that diverse skills, strategic leadership and their physical resources positively correlate with performance. Another study found that the tenor of owner-successor relationship is important to the success of firm succession (Venter, Boshoff, and Maas 2005).

Social Networks

Social capital, community, kinship ties, and social networks are common themes that run through the African entrepreneurship literature (e.g., Kiggundu, 2002a; Khavul et al., 2009; Khayesi et al., 2014). Prior research has indicated that African entrepreneurs experience difficulty creating and maintaining effective social networks (Kiggundu, 2002a). However, recent research has been less concerned with their existence, and points more to their mostly positive consequences. Though this review has partially documented the positive and negative network implications for family firms (Khavul et al.; Khayesi et al.; Daspit and Long, 2014), research indicates that nonfamily firms benefit more broadly (Acquaah, 2011b; 2012). African entrepreneurial firms that take advantage of community networks are not, however, shielded from community demands that can later increase (Khayesi and George 2011). For the most part, social networks provide enduring benefits to nonfamily firms (Acquaah, 2011b) and also foster market entry and survival of female run ventures (Yusuff 2013; Dawa and Namatovu 2015). Research has also indicated that local network positioning can positively affect firms' innovation (Gebreeyesus and Mohnen 2013) and even pointed to lack of social capital as being partly responsible for the scarcity of black entrepreneurs in South Africa (Preisendorfer, Bitz, and Bezuidenhout, 2012). Expert interviews maintained that blacks lack the social networks and support needed to better facilitate starting a career in entrepreneurship (Preisendorfer et al., 2012).

Informal Business

Business in the informal economy contributes roughly 50% of sub-Saharan Africa's GDP and accounts for 80% of the workforce (African Development Bank, 2013). The informal economy offers impoverished Africans an opportunity to earn a decent wage, which they may not be able to accomplish through formal channels. The informal economy is unable to be regulated by governments and is untaxed, so African entrepreneurs avoid costs related to pensions, insurance, social benefits, and corruption (Ufere, Perelli, Boland, and Carlsson, 2012; African Development Bank, 2013). In this regard, operating in the informal economy enables informal businesses to experience more growth than they would otherwise (Khavul et al., 2009). Although informal channels offer needy Africans a way forward, there is obvious incentive for the government to offer these firms avenues to transition into more productive formal entrepreneurship (Bradford, 2007; Sheriff and Muffatto, 2014). Fostering this transition to formalization can be helped through government incentive programs (Bradford, 2007), but informal firms are also driven to formalization to avoid the tight competition that exists in the informal economy (Sonobe, Akoten, and Otsuka, 2011). More recent research suggests that informal entrepreneurs are primarily necessity-driven and that shop owner entrepreneurs are opportunity-driven (Achua and Lussier 2014). Achua and Lussier (2014) proposed a learning curve effect whereby informal businesses progress from street walkers to street corners before ultimately owning a store. As expected, factors such as human capital, industry, tenure, infrastructure access, and living conditions influence the market entry and success of informal firms (Gulyani, Talukdar, and Jack, 2010). However, this is not to say that there are not a large number of challenges facing entrepreneurs in the informal economy (Deberry-Spence and Elliot, 2012).

Problems hampering informal entrepreneurs are vast, success can be location dependent and informal business are constrained in a number of ways (Liedholm 2002; Grimm, Knorringa, and Lay, 2012; Amin and Islam, 2015). Urban and commercially located firms grow at a faster rate compared with those in rural locations, but demand for informal firms' goods is reported to be income-inelastic, effectively constraining growth beyond a certain point (Bohme and Thiele, 2012). This type of hurdle hinders even the most motivated informal entrepreneurs (Grimm et al., 2012). In addition, informal businesses are also size constrained (Amin and Islam, 2015). Though poor performance of informal businesses is said to be reflective of size, small firms typically have higher productivity than larger firms, indicating that efficiency is a concern as informal businesses grow larger (Amin and Islam, 2015). Interestingly, their informal status does not restrict their capacity to organize in solidarity and assert their ability to use public space to earn a profit, as they will sometimes do to counteract government controls (Brown, 2015). Although the informal economy offers opportunity to Africans who would not otherwise have it, low returns to these base-of-the-pyramid producers by intermediaries reselling their wares in developed markets signifies the issues these entrepreneurial firms endure (Kistruck, Beamish, Qureshi, and Sutter 2013).

Financial Resources

Despite any difficult obtaining financial resources, it is apparent that Africans are undeterred from entering entrepreneurship (Achua and Lussier, 2014). Previous research maintains that the extent to which African entrepreneurs are financially constrained is questionable (Kiggundu, 2002a; Vandenberg 2003). This is supported by the observation that Africans need few resources to enter into the very prevalent informal means of entrepreneurship (Marsden, 1992). However, evidence from East Africa suggests that start-up grants and financing are useful to starting and growing businesses (Pretes, 2002). Also, the availability of financing has the ability to help communities alleviate poverty (Hilson and Ackah-Baidoo 2011). For example, returns to capital in Ghana's informal sector show returns ranging in excess of 50–250% (Udry and Anagol 2006). Nonetheless, formal institutions struggle with handling economic development and deciding how to allocate resources to achieve financial sustainability (Annim, 2012). Kabango and Paloni (2011) found that financial liberalization in Malawi, which was supposed to increase industrialization, instead depressed firm entry and industry concentration. Another study found that fraudulent behavior on the part of loan applicants was quite common (Harrison and Krauss 2002). Even private microfinance entrepreneurs cited economic, political, and infrastructure impediments as challenges to effectively providing poorer citizens with access to capital (Murisa and Chikweche 2013).

Even though African entrepreneurial firms clearly have financial challenges, as evidenced, it seems as though recent research lacks insight on how best to progress. In a recent policy experiment, Karlan, Knight, and Udry (2015) exposed Ghanaian firms to either a cash or consulting treatment, whereby they sought to examine any change effects experienced as a result of the contribution. Surprisingly, they found that although the treatments had the expected results with changed business practices and sparked investment, businesses soon reverted back to their prior business practices (Karlan, Knight, and Udry, 2015). Another approach suggested by Ali and Peerlings (2011) advocates business clustering in Africa, where there is an interconnected geographic concentration of businesses and suppliers, contending that such clustering lowers entry barriers and reduces the initial capital required to start a business (Ali and Peerlings, 2011).

Social Entrepreneurship

Social entrepreneurship is generally defined as a business enterprise that is oriented toward finding solutions to social and/or environmental problems (Doherty, Haugh, and Lyon, 2014) and in Africa, it has specific relevance (Rivera-Santos et al., 2015). It is apparent that Africa is in need of development, as an estimated 48% of the population live in poverty, despite growing GDP (Brookings Institution, 2013). Correspondingly, there are several characteristics about Africa that predispose it for a disproportionately higher amount of social enterprise (Rivera-Santos et al., 2015). The level of poverty and informal business in Africa, along with its colonial history and ethnic identity, encourages African entrepreneurs to self-identity as acting in the public good (Rivera-Santos et al., 2015). Rivera-Santos et al. (2015) observe that many African entrepreneurs self-identify as social ventures given that sub-Saharan Africans share a collectivist worldview. On this point, social entrepreneurship is viewed as a way in which Africans develop their societies and employ young people while bringing about livable wages and positive social change (Katzenstein and Chrispin, 2011). For example, Nelson, Ingols, Christian-Murtie, and Myers (2013) chronicled the social entrepreneur, Susan Murcott, who dedicated her life to developing infrastructure for clean drinking water in Ghana. In hopes of better delivering on the promises of social enterprises, research has offered some useful direction.

A general consensus holds that for-profit social enterprises are the most promising organizational form for bringing sustainable development (Kistruck and Beamish, 2010; Littlewood and Holt, 2015). Compared with nonprofit organizations, for profit organizations are less accountable to network and cultural pressures (Kistruck and Beamish, 2010). Wheeler, McKague, Thomson, Davies, Medalye, and Prada (2005) propose that social enterprises should be anchored by a successful for-profit business and that sustainable social enterprises involve networks of communities, businesses, and local institutions. Building on this, Elmes, Jiusto, Whiteman, Hershey, and Guthey (2012) advanced the importance of a place-based approach to social entrepreneurship, where the location drives the need for any specific development or essential resources. In this way, individual social enterprises are able to definitively target community needs in a refined approach not achievable by larger bureaucratic nongovernmental organizations (NGOs) or nonprofits (Elmes et al., 2012; Littlewood and Holt, 2015)

SME Considerations

SMEs comprise an estimated 95% of the enterprises in Africa (Fjose, Grunfeld, and Green, 2010) and, as such, are an important source of growth for African development. Absence of key infrastructures such as access to electricity and finance are seen as large challenges that SMEs can help overcome (Fjose et al., 2010). Along these lines, although entrepreneurial characteristics have been found to be important, location is an important characteristic of increased performance (Masakure, Cranfield, and Henson, 2008). Basic infrastructures such as internet and access to global markets are viewed as means to increase innovation, performance as well overcome size, resource, and experience constraints (Moodley 2003; Regnier 2009; Goedhuys and Sleuwaegen 2010). Another study went as far to say that formal infrastructure that provides stability could be considered a source of competitive advantage (Webb, Morris, and Pillay 2013). Undoubtedly, governments that provide firms with secure property rights and sufficient architecture provide firms with greater incentive and stability (Deininger and Byerlee, 2012). Trulsson (2002) identified major SME growth constraints in Tanzania to be access to finance, financial management, market competition, human resources, the environment, infrastructure, government policy, and social networks. Despite the myriad hardships, SMEs find ways by which to circumvent their situations.

Franchising is one mechanism through which African firms leverage their circumstances (Welsh, Alon, and Falbe, 2006). Franchisees in emerging markets are able to take advantage of ongoing support, corporate marketing, innovation, and advanced market research (Welsh, Alon, and Falbe, 2006). Alternatively, emerging markets like Africa offer franchisors a growing middle class, a large youth population, and liberalizing economies (Welsh, Alon, and Falbe, 2006; Kiggundu and Deghetto, 2015). Another approach that African SMEs take to bypass infrastructural concerns is through partnering with multinational firms (MNEs) (Acquaah, 2009; Hearn, 2015). Acquaah (2009) found that firms are likely to pursue different strategies with international joint venture (IJV) partners depending on whether or not the firm comes from an emerging or developed economy. Particularly, with partners from emerging markets, firms are likely to pursue efficiency strategies that increase strategic positioning. On the other hand, firms pursue market effectiveness strategies when coupled with partners from developed economies. Hearn (2015) proposes that IJVs help increase the status of developing country firms.

MACRO SOCIO-ECONOMIC CONDITIONS

The macro socio-economic environment for Africa encompasses both African entrepreneurs and their respective firms. Moreover, socio-economic conditions broadly describe the state of Africa's infrastructure and methods by which the government is working to achieve progressive development. Research covering these conditions comprises about 29% of the studies examined in this review. From these, major themes emerged concerning government assistance, institutions, government policy, internationalization, and poverty, which are presented below.

Government Assistance

It is broadly acknowledged that governments that help facilitate efficient formal institutions, such as financial and educational systems are better suited for entrepreneurship (De Clercq, Lim, and Oh, 2013). Though this may be generally true, governments must also consider more carefully how to design programs that specifically spur entrepreneurial initiatives. However, countries struggle with how to administer government assistance, with resources often not being put to their most effective use (Sievers and Vandenberg 2007). For example, Rijkers, Laderchi, and Teal (2010) found that assistance programs do not often affect small firms in the intended manner. They found that firms receiving program assistance appear to experience an earnings premium as a result of education and not through the adoption of new technology or increased labor productivity (Rijkers et al., 2010). Likewise, another study found that many governmental assistance programs are not well conceived in that many small firms will not use them since they do not meet their needs (Obeng and Blundel, 2015). More explicitly, programs are poorly marketed and fail to offer entrepreneurial training (Obeng and Blundel, 2015). Research has proposed that such programs can be helpful and has offered broad suggestions for their improvement (Ladzani and van Vuuren, 2002).

A study by Sievers and Vandenberg (2007) suggests that assistance programs need to be driven by demand and offer more than basic management training. They advise that successful programs should allow for linkages between firms, program providers, and financial institutions (Sievers and Vandenberg, 2007). Ladzani and van Vuuren (2002) also support this premise that entrepreneurial training programs need to be more comprehensive. In an experimental study, Glaub, Frese, Fischer, and Hoppe (2014) reported that a training intervention among entrepreneurs increased personal initiative behavior and led to an entrepreneurial mindset, which, subsequently, had a positive effect on performance. Mano, Iddrisu, Yoshino, and Sonobe (2012) also support that government assistance programs could focus on problems within the firm by familiarizing business owners with standard business practices, in turn improving performance.

Internationalization

Although improving, infrastructure has been found to dampen firm productivity by an estimated 40% (World Bank, 2013). Recognizing that Africa lags in terms of infrastructure, firm internationalization is important for increasing the pace of industrialization in Africa. Likewise, it may be in the best interests of many firms to go international. In this respect, current research seems to support this observation (Gimede, 2004; Omer, van Burg, Peters, and Visser, 2015). Omer et al. (2015) provided evidence that internationalization helps SMEs avoid government constraints in order to accelerate growth. Internationalization allows firms to break into foreign markets and create larger information networks to more easily export (Gimede, 2004). Also, firms that internationalize early and with clear goals are able to increase their legitimacy (Wood, Khavul, Perez-Nordtvedt, Prakhya, Dabrowski, and Zheng, 2011) and can better implement their strategic goals when they attain temporal fit (Khavul,

Perez-Nordtvedt, & Wood 2010). Though African firms have clear incentive to partner with international firms in order to bring their products to the global market, MNEs also prefer joint ventures when entering markets with poor institutional frameworks (Meyer, Estrin, Bhaumik, and Peng 2009). These firm arrangements have benefits for both partners, and give foreign MNEs access to new markets, new resources, and local knowledge with minimum risk(s) (Meyer et al., 2009). While African firms can alleviate some of the difficulties their home countries present through internationalization, lack of government support can still hurt export efficiency (Omer et al., 2015).

Corruption and Poverty

Africa is home to over 300 million poor people and reducing poverty has been a slow process, especially in less developed economies and rural areas (World Bank, 2016). Though the percentage of poor has fallen 13 percentage points over the last 20 years, the population has grown and Africa is also home to several countries boasting some of the world's highest rates of income inequality (World Bank, 2016). This state of affairs highlights the critical need for entrepreneurship. Entrepreneurship grants opportunity to Africa's impoverished and has been helping to alleviate income inequality, in urban and rural Africa (Kimhi, 2010). The landscape and its demographics also offers opportunity to foreign companies that invest or locate operations in Africa (Bardy, Drew, and Kennedy, 2012). Even further, foreign direct investment (FDI) and international business can improve social conditions (Bardy et al., 2012). Since foreign firms from developed economies are often subject to higher standards of social responsibility, they may be able to diffuse some practices to indigenous firms (Bardy et al., 2012). Nonetheless, it is clear that African firms struggle to overcome the challenges of poverty.

A study by Deberry-Spence and Elliot (2012) distinctly chronicles some daily issues entrepreneurs encounter in underdeveloped countries. In their study, one example comes from a jewelry maker in Ghana, who describes a long commute to his marketplace where he finds urine puddles, litter, and people sleeping on his shop porch. Sometimes the entrepreneur finds his shop vandalized, with appliances unplugged and without electricity or running water (Deberry-Spence and Elliot, 2012). Adding to the challenges of poverty, Kistruck, Beamish, Qureshi, and Sutter (2013) found that bottom-of-the-pyramid producers are often not afforded fair wages when their goods are sold in developed markets, due to limited trade linkages. Foreign firms can either contribute to this environment or help host countries to institutionalize more beneficial business practices (Luiz and Stewart, 2014). However, according to Demuijnck and Ngnodjom, (2013), most African firms do not understand socially responsible business practices, which poses a problem for improved infrastructure and institutions. As a result, it is apparent that poverty is deeply rooted in Africa, and subsequently burdens the entry and performance of entrepreneurs. This suggests that poverty is more than income and assets; it is also a mindset.

Environmental Concerns

A prominent theme throughout the African entrepreneurship literature emerges as a focus on the African context, its infrastructure, institutions, culture, and government policy. Small businesses need better working conditions and Africa has failed to facilitate development despite several countries' attempts to implement structural adjustment programs (Frese and Friedrich 2002). Recent research maintains that government reforms are necessary in order to improve these conditions, citing that political stability and entry deregulation have a positive effect for creating an environment conducive to new firm entry (Munemo, 2012). Similarly, Mahadea (2012) found that unemployment and regulation are positively correlated, indicating that countries with high degrees of regulation hurt both employment numbers and potential economic growth. Despite acknowledging the problems that infrastructure poses to entrepreneurship, many African countries lack foresight on how to remedy their situations (Deininger and Byerlee, 2012).

Government plays an important role in the development of entrepreneurship and also toward the impact that entrepreneurs are able to have on economic growth (Watkins, 2007; Bradford, 2007). However, policy needs to be better informed. For example, Rijkers and Soderbom (2013) remark how little incentive there is for non-farm enterprises in rural Africa. Since rural areas revolve around farms, development is curbed outside of urban centers. Major disadvantages are present for entrepreneurs when there are not adequate resources, including education, financing, regulation, and protection of property rights (Trulsson, 2002; Deininger and Byerlee, 2012). Alternatively, Goodstein and Velamuri (2009) contend that some failing policies are a consequence of power dynamics in post-colonial settings, whereby states use their power to dominate various institutional sectors in an attempt to reinforce legitimacy. Taken together, research in this area succeeds in recognizing troubles that African entrepreneurship encounters, but does little in the way of proposing potential reform. Foreign firms conducting business in Africa present an avenue for growth that could be promising or potentially troublesome, however.

Foreign MNEs and FDI offer the promise of more sustainable development for many countries in Africa. Amidst this opportunity, is the reality that these foreign firms can either contribute to more sustainable development or exploit the setting to their advantage (Luiz and Stewart, 2014). Though these actions are not mutually exclusive, government policy needs to be carefully oriented toward advocating economic growth and institutional improvements. For instance, Demirbag, Apaydin, and Tatoglu (2011) describe how Japanese MNEs are able to take advantage of weak institutions and low economic freedom in North Africa. Kshetri (2011) recognizes that foreign firms exploit Africa for its resources, in terms of natural resources (e.g., oil) and also labor resources (e.g., an inexpensive labor force). Similarly, Chinese entrepreneurs have been quite successful in Africa since they have better access to capital from home and are able to take more risks in attaining success (Shen, 2012). Conversely, FDI does not necessarily have to be one-sided and can often have valuable spillover effects, spurring economic growth and entrepreneurial activity (Washington and Chapman, 2014). Even further, 85% of the resource flows from the U.S. to Africa are from private sources, which is indicative of the opportunity for investment as well as the importance of FDI to development (Agbo, Agwale, Ezeugwu, Semete, Swai, Ikeme, and Somiari, 2008).

FUTURE RESEARCH CONSIDERATIONS

This review has summarized the last 15 years of African entrepreneurship research, which, while fragmented, is a diverse literature spanning different levels of analysis (e.g., the entrepreneur, the firm, and the environment). It is apparent that while research involving African entrepreneurship is diverse, it is still not given due consideration with respect to its large implications. Africa is a large geographical area, but only a small fraction of the entrepreneurship research taking place occurs within an African context, with other parts of the world being overrepresented. Entrepreneurship presents an opportunity for improved infrastructure, sustainable development, and poverty reduction and this makes it more critical to facilitate inquiry into the continent. While there are a number of avenues for future research, a few important themes emerge from this review.

Theory and Research Methodologies

As mentioned, much of the entrepreneurship literature in Africa lacks theoretical grounding. Even among the 121 studies reviewed here, many of which were empirically rigorous (62%), only 45 studies utilized a specific theoretical perspective (37%; see Table 2). This means that phenomenological studies make up much of the sample examined here (63%; see Table 2). The larger implication of this is that the literature is lacking a more intimate understanding of the African context. This is at least partly the reason for the fragmentation of the literature observed in this review. Without theory informing the development of new research, the literature lacks awareness of how specific mechanisms operate in African businesses, and how they more meaningfully differ from organizational behavior in other parts of the world. Given the context that Africa provides, which is one of a resource munificent environment steeped in a post-colonial setting with poverty and authoritarian governments, with recent sparks of reforms and progress, there would be the expectation that new theoretical contributions could emerge.

The authors expect that there are many contributions to still be made with regard to the already employed resource based view, as well as social capital, and institutional theories. For example, do informal entrepreneurs maintain competitive advantages through sales of substitutable goods? How do informal entrepreneurs' social networks affect the move toward more formal channels of entrepreneurship? How do institutional norms and values diffuse between entrepreneurs of different African tribes, races or communities? Also, opportunity recognition, entrepreneurial exit, and habitual entrepreneurship are frequently considered topics in the entrepreneurship literature that have not yet received adequate attention in Africa. Organizational theories such as power and resource dependence, transaction cost, agency, and organizational ecology would also be beneficial to gaining perspective on the African context. As we understand, institutional development and residual ideologies of colonialism have made it difficult for Africans to navigate their environments. As such, new contributions in this area could shed light on how entrepreneurs could better mobilize and overcome the institutional and infrastructural challenges of their environment.

Although a variety of methods and data analysis techniques were used in the studies reviewed here, most frequently archival and questionnaire based data collection along with employing regression, African entrepreneurship literature could benefit from more ethnography and case study based research. A lot of what makes the entrepreneurial process in Africa unique may be lost when reduced to a quantitative approach. Entrepreneurs should be given voice to tell their stories and then use them as a basis for more theoretical or quantitative analyses (e.g. Sutton, Short,

McKenny, & Namatovu, 2015). For example, we know very little about the succession, transfer and development of entrepreneurial capabilities within families and across generations, and the effects, if any on poverty alleviation in different African settings. More research focused on a deeper understanding may also partly address the greater philosophical debate as to what constitutes evidence. Fayolle and Riot (2015) address a similar point as they make light of the institutionalization of entrepreneurship research and the corresponding need for entrepreneurship scholars to think outside the box. More theoretical and grounded approaches to African entrepreneurship research along with longitudinal, event history, and multi-level models, which remain underexplored, present further opportunity for future research. In addition to theory development, researchers should use more innovative multitrait, multimethod, comparative and interdisciplinary approaches to the study of entrepreneurship in Africa or when comparing Africa with other (emerging) economies in the world.

Education, Technology, Development, and Training

There is growing interest in developing programs to select, educate, develop, and train entrepreneurs (e.g., Rijkers et al., 2010). Some of these programs are offered through universities, governments, and local or international organizations (e.g., International Labor Organization). However, many of them are expensive. While a few studies have examined these programs in the African context within the last 15 years (e.g., Glaub et al., 2014; Obeng and Blundel, 2015), the literature still lacks insight on how to execute these programs differently and with better results (Glaub and Frese, 2011). For example, is there a template for best practices elsewhere? Would entrepreneurs benefit from a targeted approach differentiated by individual and demographic information? Recent research has commented that many programs are not well designed to meet the needs of different groups of entrepreneurs (Obeng and Blundel, 2015) and that such assistance programs should better address the challenges that entrepreneurs may encounter in their careers (Mano et al., 2012).

The World Bank has shown interest in the issue recently. The organization further cites that it has not yet been determined if entrepreneurial success can be taught (Kigotho, 2014). Additionally, what is currently being taught is not well known (Kigotho, 2014). Undergoing case studies in Ghana, Kenya, and Mozambique, World Bank researchers report that programs are reliant on private and international support, there is little coordination across entrepreneurial education efforts, programs are not evidence based, and a significant gap exists between what is taught and what the local population values (Robb, Valerio, and Parton, 2014). Robb et al. 2014 cite the importance of building entrepreneurial mindsets, tailored and practice oriented programs, comprehensive avenues for tackling local constraints such as financing, and creating program evaluation to monitor the efficacy of assistance efforts. Moving forward, future research should consider how to address these relevant concerns.

The Association of African Business Schools (www.aabschools.com), representing over 30 of the top business schools on the continent, is in the process of launching a continent-wide accreditation program to enable business schools to have a renewed focus on relevance of the African context and more impact in the operating environment. The new focus is intended to shape entrepreneurship and innovation for Africa's future. It is also expected to promote excellence through industry-academia collaboration, capacity building and quality improvement so as to enable business schools to support inclusive social economic growth by linking education, technology, innovation and entrepreneurship. It is expected that emerging African entrepreneurs will be better positioned to use such linkage (e.g., mobile technology, opening new markets, e-commerce) to take advantage of the digital dividends (Peña-López, 2016) – faster growth, more jobs, better services – to overcome the most problematic factors for doing business, and invest in key growth sectors of the African economies such as natural resources, infrastructure, agribusiness, tourism, social and community services.

Policy and Practice

Based on this review, there are a number of policy suggestions that can be made from synthesizing this literature. Broadly, government policies should take into consideration small business enterprise growth. Recurring issues for entrepreneurial firms in the African context involve infrastructure, property rights, financing, and various forms of government support. These fundamental problems affect many aspects of entrepreneurs' firms. More compelling, is that many infrastructural concerns can be remedied through governments protecting property rights and providing entrepreneurs with support and basic access to financing. As noted, growth prospects can be stark for entrepreneurs unless they are working with larger companies through joint ventures or franchising (e.g., Welsh et al., 2006; Hearn, 2015). Of further relevance to private property concerns is the challenge that women entrepreneurs face with regard to ownership. This point addresses a larger struggle for equal rights and basic human rights that is endemic across the continent. Despite the fact that Africa has one of the world's highest entrepreneurship rates among women, many African countries do not make it easier on them, with women not often not being legally allowed to own or inherit property (Dawa and Namatovu, 2015). Given that there is a significant African youth population that is unemployed, it is apparent that government resources should be directed toward capitalizing on such unmet potential (Kew, Namatovu, and Aderinot, 2015).

Policy concerns that involve corruption, poverty, and the environment can at least be partly addressed through giving entrepreneurs the resources they need to thrive. For example, internationalization offers promise to African firms that are hoping to overcome environmental constraints. Internationalization allows firms to access new markets, technology, increase growth prospects, and diversify risk, among other benefits (Meyer et al., 2009). However, many governments in Africa do not make it straightforward for firms (Omer et al., 2015). To this point, a larger problem that arises from this review that impedes social and economic progress is the issue of corruption. While there is some literature that explains the type of ethical behavior that multinational firms confront when operating in other countries (e.g., Rodriguez, Uhlenbruck, and Eden, 2005; Rodriguez, Siegel, Hillman, and Eden, 2006), it is more a recognition that the problem exists as opposed to a prescriptive approach to remedying it. One approach may come through pro-market reforms, which orient the government toward a capitalistic economy and potentially hold increased promise for foreign direct investment and struggling entrepreneurial firms (Cuervo-Cazurra and Dau, 2009). As Luiz and Stewart (2014) suggest, multinational companies have the opportunity to contribute to the institutionalizing of more ethical foundations within the countries they conduct business, which effects both policy and practice and makes a stronger case for economic liberalization. The recent arrival of more than a million Chinese migrants seeking business opportunities in urban and remote rural corners of Africa promises to change the entrepreneurial landscape and create unique opportunities for entrepreneurial research (French, 2014). The suggestion by Luiz and Stewart (2014) that foreign companies can positively influence the institutional framework through socially responsible behavior brings to bear the awareness that multinationals hold a significant amount of power in their ability to both economically contribute to the continent while institutionalizing positive business practices (Chakrabarty and Bass, 2014).

The quality of available data for entrepreneurial research in Africa is steadily improving. For example, the World Bank's annual doing business reports on regulatory quality for SMEs (www.doingbusiness.org), the enterprises survey (www.enterprisesurveys.org) and the World Economic Forum's annual Global Competitiveness Reports (www.weforum.org/reports) which provides data on determinants of global competitiveness as well as the most problematic factors for doing business in African economies together provide macroeconomic, social and firm level data for longitudinal and comparative study of entrepreneurship in Africa. These databases provide information about the entrepreneur, entrepreneurial firm, quality of public administration (regulation, corruption, institutions, etc.), infrastructure, technology, social development, access to credit and trading across borders.

It is clear from the literature, that African entrepreneurs face a number of environmental constraints. A recent issue of *Africa Journal of Management* (2015) featured stories from managers who describe previous issues with protection and isolationism (Njonjo, 2015), free trade (Shah, 2015), the pitfalls of bureaucracy (Bagalwadi, 2015), as well as hard to navigate regulations (Gibson, 2015). Others elaborate the importance of seizing opportunities (Musani, 2015), building trust (Kinoti, 2015), and firm diversification (Gadhoke, 2015). Many of these same problems and lessons are showcased in the research discussed here. Deberry-Spence and Elliot (2012) articulate the infrastructural constraints that lead to everyday challenges and part of the lesson within these managerial stories and entrepreneurial accounts is the importance of perseverance. While this insight brings the analysis back to the individual, the burgeoning informal sector and high rates of women in entrepreneurship also build evidence that Africans are necessity-driven (Adom and Williams, 2012) and find ways to thrive despite their environments. Outside of baseline recommendations of obtaining available education, persevering, continuing professional development, and maintaining social networks, successful entrepreneurs should work to advance the institutional landscape through advocacy of free trade (Njonjo, 2015), regional integration (Shah, 2015), and contributing to the moral and ethical fabric of society (e.g., Luiz and Stewart, 2014).

CONCLUSION

This review endeavored to synthesize the last 15 years of entrepreneurship research in Africa in order to facilitate future work. Examining Table 3, it is observed that research in Africa has increased over the years and has even experienced a recent spike. However, the fragmentation of the literature is revealed along with gaps in theory and research methodologies that future research should address. While this review highlights what has been done, it similarly draws attention to what we do not yet know and even that several topical research questions remain unanswered. For example, do entrepreneurial firms create jobs and what are the conditions for this? What is the link between entrepreneurship and productivity and innovation? Entrepreneurship in Africa needs to embrace innovation, drawing on the ideas of an ecosystem whereby ideas are generated and implemented in the form of new and value-adding products, processes and services in the marketplace. Are there ethnic groups that are more entrepreneurial than others? Do entrepreneurs cause harm to the environment? Also, future work should elaborate the role of intra-region entrepreneurship (Kiggundu and Deghetto, 2015) or intra-Africa diaspora entrepreneurship, those who move from one African country to set up business in another. As it stands, there are few studies that articulate diaspora entrepreneurship (e.g., Halkias et al., 2009) along with the contributions of Chinese and other southeast Asian entrepreneurs arriving to conduct business on the continent (e.g., Shen, 2012; French, 2014). Despite that its rate of entrepreneurship is higher relative to other parts of the world (Global Entrepreneurship Monitor, 2015) and that the informal sector accounts for a large portion of GDP (African Development Bank, 2013), entrepreneurs in Africa struggle to conduct business and thrive (Deberry-Spence and Elliot, 2012). Entrepreneurship may well be oversold as a panacea for Africa's ills (e.g., unemployment, inequality, low productivity, disconnect from global value chains, etc.). If research can provide insight into entrepreneurship in Africa, then the literature should continue to develop drawing on the themes and suggestions provided in this review.

NOTE

1. Avon is a direct selling or network marketing company that specializes in beauty and personal care products.

References

Achua, C. F., & Lussier, R. N. (2014). Entrepreneurial drive and the informal economy in Cameroon. *Journal of Developmental Entrepreneurship, 19*(04), 1450024. http://dx.doi.org/10.1142/S1084946714500241

Acquaah, M. (2009). International joint venture partner origin, strategic choice, and performance: A comparative analysis in an emerging economy in Africa. *Journal of International Management, 15*(1), 46–60. http://dx.doi.org/10.1016/j.intman.2008.06.001

Acquaah, M. (2011a). Business strategy and competitive advantage in family businesses in Ghana: The role of social networking relationships. *Journal of Developmental Entrepreneurship, 16*(01), 103–126. http://dx.doi.org/10.1142/S1084946711001744

Acquaah, M. (2011b). Utilization and value of social networking relationships in family and nonfamily firms in an African transition economy. *European Management Journal, 29*(5), 347–361. http://dx.doi.org/10.1016/j.emj.2011.03.002

Acquaah, M. (2012). Social networking relationships, firm-specific managerial experience and firm performance in a transition economy: A comparative analysis of family owned and nonfamily firms. *Strategic Management Journal, 33*(10), 1215–1228. http://dx.doi.org/10.1002/smj.1973

Adendorff, C., & Halkias, D. (2014). Leveraging ethnic entrepreneurship, culture and family dynamics to enhance good governance and sustainability in the immigrant family business. *Journal of Developmental Entrepreneurship, 19*(02), 1450008. http://dx.doi.org/10.1142/S1084946714500083

Adom, K., & Williams, C. C. (2012). Evaluating the motives of informal entrepreneurs in Koforidua, Ghana. *Journal of Developmental Entrepreneurship, 17*(01), 1250005. http://dx.doi.org/10.1142/S1084946712500057

Adom, P. K. (2015). Asymmetric impacts of the determinants of energy intensity in Nigeria. *Energy Economics*, *49*, 570–580. http://dx.doi.org/10.1016/j.eneco.2015.03.027

African Development Bank. (2013, March). Recognizing Africa's Informal Sector. *African Development Bank Group*. Retrieved from http://www.afdb.org/en/blogs/afdb-championing-inclusive-growth-across-africa/post/recognizing-africas-informal-sector-11645/

African Economic Outlook. (2012). Promoting Youth Employment. Washington, DC: OECD. Retrieved from https://www.oecd.org/site/devyewa/Pocket%20Edition%20AEO2012-EN.pdf

Agbo, E. C., Agwale, S., Ezeugwu, C. O., Semete, B., Swai, H., Ikeme, A., & Somiari, R. I. (2008). Biotechnology innovation in Africa. *Science*, *321*(5897), 1778–1778. http://dx.doi.org/10.1126/science.321.5897.1778a

Ahmed, Z. U., Zgheib, P. W., Kowatly, A. K., & Rhetts, P. (2012). The history of overseas Lebanese entrepreneurs operating worldwide. *Journal of Management History*, *18*(3), 295–311. http://dx.doi.org/10.1108/17511341211236237

Ali, M., & Peerlings, J. (2011). Value added of cluster membership for micro enterprises of the handloom sector in Ethiopia. *World Development*, *39*(3), 363–374. http://dx.doi.org/10.1016/j.worlddev.2010.07.002

Amin, M., & Islam, A. (2015). Are large informal firms more productive than the small informal firms? Evidence from firm-level surveys in Africa. *World Development*, *74*, 374–385. http://dx.doi.org/10.1016/j.worlddev.2015.05.008

Annim, S. K. (2012). Microfinance efficiency: Trade-offs and complementarities between the objectives of microfinance institutions and their performance perspectives. *European Journal of Development Research*, *24*(5), 788–807. http://dx.doi.org/10.1057/ejdr.2011.60

Asiedu, E. (2002). On the determinants of foreign direct investment to developing countries: Is Africa different? *World Development*, *30*(1), 107–119. http://dx.doi.org/10.1016/S0305-750X(01)00100-0

Asiedu, E., Kalonda-Kanyama, I., Ndikumana, L., & Nti-Addae, A. (2013). Access to credit by firms in Sub-Saharan Africa: How relevant is gender? *The American Economic Review*, *103*(3), 293–297. http://dx.doi.org/10.1257/aer.103.3.293

Aterido, R., & Hallward-Driemeier, M. (2011). Whose business is it anyway? *Small Business Economics*, *37*(4), 443–464. http://dx.doi.org/10.1007/s11187-011-9375-y

Aterido, R., Beck, T., & Iacovone, L. (2013). Access to finance in sub-Saharan Africa: Is there a gender gap?. *World Development*, *47*, 102–120. http://dx.doi.org/10.1016/j.worlddev.2013.02.013

Bagalwadi, P. (2015). DHL: Addressing the skills gap in East Africa. *Africa Journal of Management*, *1*(4), 437–439. http://dx.doi.org/10.1080/23322373.2015.1105451

Bardy, R., Drew, S., & Kennedy, T. F. (2012). Foreign investment and ethics: How to contribute to social responsibility by doing business in less-developed countries. *Journal of Business Ethics*, *106*(3), 267–282. http://dx.doi.org/10.1007/s10551-011-0994-7

Beeka, B. H., & Rimmington, M. (2011). Entrepreneurship as a career option for African youths. *Journal of Developmental Entrepreneurship*, *16*(01), 145–164. http://dx.doi.org/10.1142/S1084946711001707

Bohme, M., & Thiele, R. (2012). Is the informal sector constrained from the demand side? Evidence for six West African capitals. *World Development*, *40*(7), 1369–1381. http://dx.doi.org/10.1016/j.worlddev.2011.12.005

Boly, A., Coniglio, N. D., Prota, F., & Seric, A. (2014). Diaspora investments and firm export performance in selected sub-Saharan African countries. *World Development*, *59*, 422–433. http://dx.doi.org/10.1016/j.worlddev.2014.02.006

Bradford, W. D. (2007). Distinguishing economically from legally formal firms: Targeting business support to entrepreneurs in South Africa's townships. *Journal of Small Business Management*, *45*(1), 94–115. http://dx.doi.org/10.1111/j.1540-627X.2007.00201.x

Brixiová, Z., Ncube, M., & Bicaba, Z. (2015). Skills and youth entrepreneurship in Africa: Analysis with evidence from Swaziland. *World Development*, *67*, 11–26. http://dx.doi.org/10.1016/j.worlddev.2014.09.027

Brookings Institution. (2013). Africa's Challenge to End Extreme Poverty by 2030: Too Slow or Too Far Behind? Retrieved from http://www.brookings.edu/blogs/up-front/posts/2013/05/29-africa-challenge-end-extreme-poverty-2030-chandy

Brown, A. (2015). Claiming the streets: Property rights and legal empowerment in the urban informal economy. *World Development*, *76*, 238–248. http://dx.doi.org/10.1016/j.worlddev.2015.07.001

Bullough, A., de Luque, M. S., Abdelzaher, D., & Heim, W. (2015). Developing women leaders through entrepreneurship education and training. *The Academy of Management Perspectives*, *29*(2), 250–270. http://dx.doi.org/10.5465/amp.2012.0169

Burkart, M., Panunzi, F., & Shleifer, A. (2003). Family firms. *The Journal of Finance*, *58*(5), 2167–2201. http://dx.doi.org/10.1111/1540-6261.00601

Busenitz, L. W., & Barney, J. B. (1997). Differences between entrepreneurs and managers in large organizations: Biases and heuristics in strategic decision-making. *Journal of Business Venturing*, *12*(1), 9–30. http://dx.doi.org/10.1016/S0883-9026(96)00003-1

Calves, A.-E., & Schoumaker, B. (2004). Deteriorating economic context and changing patterns of youth employment in urban Burkina Faso: 1980–2000. *World Development*, *32*(8), 1341–1354. http://dx.doi.org/10.1016/j.worlddev.2004.03.002

Chakrabarty, S., & Bass, A. E. (2014). Institutionalizing ethics in institutional voids: Building positive ethical strength to serve women microfinance borrowers in negative contexts. *Journal of Business Ethics*, *119*(4), 529–542. http://dx.doi.org/10.1007/s10551-013-1833-9

Chao, L.-W., Szrek, H., Pereira, N. S., & Pauly, M. V. (2010). Too sick to start: Entrepreneur's health and business entry in townships around Durban, South Africa. *Journal of Developmental Entrepreneurship*, *15*(02), 231–242. http://dx.doi.org/10.1142/S108494671000152X

Chea, A. C. (2008). Factors that influence the survival of women-owned small business start-ups in the city of Tema, Ghana. *International Business Research*, *1*(3), 130–144. http://dx.doi.org/10.5539/ibr.v1n3p130

Cuervo-Cazurra, A., & Dau, L. A. (2009). Promarket reforms and firm profitability in developing countries. *Academy of Management Journal*, *52*(6), 1348–1368. http://dx.doi.org/10.5465/AMJ.2009.47085192

Daspit, J. J., & Long, R. G. (2014). Mitigating moral hazard in entrepreneurial networks: Examining structural and relational social capital in East Africa. *Entrepreneurship Theory and Practice*, *38*(6), 1343–1350. http://dx.doi.org/10.1111/etap.12128

Dawa, S., & Namatovu, R. (2015). Social networks and growth of female-owned ventures: A sub-Saharan Africa perspective. *Journal of Developmental Entrepreneurship*, *20*(02), 1550009. http://dx.doi.org/10.1142/S1084946715500090

De Clercq, D., Lim, D. S., & Oh, C. H. (2013). Individual-level resources and new business activity: The contingent role of institutional context. *Entrepreneurship Theory and Practice*, *37*(2), 303–330. http://dx.doi.org/10.1111/j.1540-6520.2011.00470.x

De Clercq, D., Lim, D. S., & Oh, C. H. (2014). Hierarchy and conservatism in the contributions of resources to entrepreneurial activity. *Small Business Economics*, *42*(3), 507–522. http://dx.doi.org/10.1007/s11187-013-9515-7

DeBerry-Spence, B., & Elliot, E. A. (2012). African microentrepreneurship: The reality of everyday challenges. *Journal of Business Research*, *65*(12), 1665–1673. http://dx.doi.org/10.1016/j.jbusres.2012.02.007

Deininger, K., & Byerlee, D. (2012). The rise of large farms in land abundant countries: Do they have a future? *World Development*, *40*(4), 701–714. http://dx.doi.org/10.1016/j.worlddev.2011.04.030

Demirbag, M., Apaydin, M., & Tatoglu, E. (2011). Survival of Japanese subsidiaries in the middle east and North Africa. *Journal of World Business*, *46*(4), 411–425. http://dx.doi.org/10.1016/j.jwb.2010.10.002

Demuijnck, G., & Ngnodjom, H. (2013). Responsibility and informal CSR in formal Cameroonian SMEs. *Journal of Business Ethics*, *112*(4), 653–665. http://dx.doi.org/10.1007/s10551-012-1564-3

Doherty, B., Haugh, H., & Lyon, F. (2014). Social enterprises as hybrid organizations: A review and research agenda. *International Journal of Management Reviews*, *16*(4), 417–436. http://dx.doi.org/10.1111/ijmr.12028

Doyle, M. (2013). Africans' Remittances Outweigh Western Aid. Retrieved from http://www.bbc.com/news/world-africa-22169474

Elmes, M. B., Jiusto, S., Whiteman, G., Hersh, R., & Guthey, G. T. (2012). Teaching social entrepreneurship and innovation from the perspective of place and place making. *Academy of Management Learning & Education, 11*(4), 533–554. http://dx.doi.org/10.5465/amle.2011.0029

Escher, S., Grabarkiewicz, R., Frese, M., van Steekelenburg, G., Lauw, M., & Friedrich, C. (2002). The moderator effect of cognitive ability on the relationship between planning strategies and business success of small scale business owners in South Africa: A longitudinal study. *Journal of Developmental Entrepreneurship, 7*(3), 305–318. Retrieved from http://search.proquest.com/docview/208430168/abstract/5902EABE44164E42PQ/1?accountid=4840

Fayolle, A., & Riot, P. (2015). *Rethinking Entrepreneurship: Debating Research Orientations.* New York, NY: Routledge.

Fjose, S., Grunfeld, L., & Green, C. (2010). *SMEs and growth in sub-Saharan Africa: Identifying SME roles and obstacles to SME growth.* Oslo: MENON Business Economics.

Foroutan, F. (1992). *Regional integration in sub-Saharan Africa: experience and prospects.* Wahintgton DC: The World Bank.

French, H. W. (2014). *China's second continent: How a million migrants are building a new empire in Africa.* New York, NY: Alfred A. Knopf.

Frese, M., & Friedrich, C. (2002). From the editors of the special issue on entrepreneurship in Africa. *Journal of Developmental Entrepreneurship, 7*(3), 1–5. Retrieved from http://www.evidence-based-entrepreneurship.com/content/publications/240.pdf

Frese, M., Krauss, S. I., Keith, N., Escher, S., Grabarkiewicz, R., Luneng, S. T., … Friedrich, C. (2007). Business owners' action planning and its relationship to business success in three African countries. *The Journal of Applied Psychology, 92*(6), 1481–1498. http://dx.doi.org/10.1037/0021-9010.92.6.1481

Gadhoke, T. (2015). Multi-sector approach ensures Mukwano group thrives despite tough climate. *Africa Journal of Management, 1*(4), 440–445. http://dx.doi.org/10.1080/23322373.2015.1105463

Gebreeyesus, M., & Mohnen, P. (2013). Innovation performance and embeddedness in networks: Evidence from the Ethiopian footwear cluster. *World Development, 41*, 302–316. http://dx.doi.org/10.1016/j.worlddev.2012.05.029

Gibson, I. (2015). What you see is not what you get. *Africa Journal of Management, 1*(4), 427–431. http://dx.doi.org/10.1080/23322373.2015.1105468

Gielnik, M. M., Kramer, A. C., Kappel, B., & Frese, M. (2014). Antecedents of business opportunity identification and innovation: Investigating the interplay of information processing and information acquisition. *Applied Psychology, 63*(2), 344–381. http://dx.doi.org/10.1111/j.1464-0597.2012.00528.x

Gimede, V. (2004). Export propensities and intensities of small and medium manufacturing enterprises in South Africa. *Small Business Economics, 22*(5), 379–389. http://dx.doi.org/10.1023/B:SBEJ.0000022212.08739.54

Glaub, M., & Frese, M. (2011). A critical review of the effects of entrepreneurship training in developing countries. *Enterprise Development and Microfinance, 22*(4), 335–353. http://dx.doi.org/10.3362/1755-1986.2011.035

Glaub, M. E., Frese, M., Fischer, S., & Hoppe, M. (2014). Increasing personal initiative in small business managers or owners leads to entrepreneurial success: A theory-based controlled randomized field intervention for evidence-based management. *Academy of Management Learning & Education, 13*(3), 354–379. http://dx.doi.org/10.5465/amle.2013.0234

Global Entrepreneurship Monitor. (2015, March). *Global Entrepreneurship Monitor 2014 Global Report.* London: GEM.

Goedhuys, M., & Sleuwaegen, L. (2010). High-growth entrepreneurial firms in Africa: A quantile regression approach. *Small Business Economics, 34*(1), 31–51. http://dx.doi.org/10.1007/s11187-009-9193-7

Goodstein, J. D., & Velamuri, S. R. (2009). States, power, legitimacy, and maintaining institutional control: The battle for private sector telecommunication services in Zimbabwe. *Organization Studies, 30*(5), 489–508. http://dx.doi.org/10.1177/0170840609104395

Grimm, M., Knorringa, P., & Lay, J. (2012). Constrained gazelles: High potentials in West Africa's informal economy. *World Development, 40*(7), 1352–1368. http://dx.doi.org/10.1016/j.worlddev.2012.03.009

Halkias, D., Harkiolakis, N., Thurman, P., Rishi, M., Ekonomou, L., Caracatsanis, S. M., & Akrivos, P. D. (2009). Economic and social characteristics of Albanian immigrant entrepreneurs in Greece. *Journal of Developmental Entrepreneurship, 14*(02), 143–164. http://dx.doi.org/10.1142/S108494670900120X

Gulyani, S., Talukdar, D., & Jack, D. (2010). *Poverty, living conditions, and infrastructure access: a comparison of slums in Dakar, Johannesburg, and Nairobi.* (Policy Research working paper; no. WPS 5388). World Bank. Retrieved from https://openknowledge.worldbank.org/handle/10986/3872

Harrison, D. E., & Krauss, S. I. (2002). Interviewer cheating: Implications for research on entrepreneurship in Africa. *Journal of Developmental Entrepreneurship, 7*(3), 319–330. Retrieved from http://search.proquest.com/docview/208439824?pq-origsite=gscholar

Hearn, B. (2015). Institutional influences on board composition of international joint venture firms listing on emerging stock exchanges: Evidence from Africa. *Journal of World Business, 50*(1), 205–219. http://dx.doi.org/10.1016/j.jwb.2014.04.006

Hilson, G., & Ackah-Baidoo, A. (2011). Can microcredit services alleviate hardship in African small-scale mining communities?. *World Development, 39*(7), 1191–1203. http://dx.doi.org/10.1016/j.worlddev.2010.10.004

International Fund for Agricultural Development. (2015). *In all of Western Africa ... 70 per cent of payments are handled by one money transfer operator.* Retrieved from https://www.ifad.org/topic/resource/tags/remittances/2039663

Kabango, G. P., & Paloni, A. (2011). Financial liberalization and the industrial response: Concentration and entry in Malawi. *World Development, 39*(10), 1771–1783. http://dx.doi.org/10.1016/j.worlddev.2011.04.001

Karlan, D., Knight, R., & Udry, C. (2015). Consulting and capital experiments with microenterprise tailors in Ghana. *Journal of Economic Behavior & Organization, 118*, 281–302. http://dx.doi.org/10.1016/j.jebo.2015.04.005

Katzenstein, J., & Chrispin, B. R. (2011). Social entrepreneurship and a new model for international development in the 21st century. *Journal of Developmental Entrepreneurship, 16*(01), 87–102. http://dx.doi.org/10.1142/S1084946711001720

Keupp, M. M., & Gassmann, O. (2009). The past and the future of international entrepreneurship: A review and suggestions for developing the field. *Journal of Management, 35*(3), 600–633. http://dx.doi.org/10.1177/0149206308330558

Kew, J., Namatovu, R., Aderinto, R., & Chigunta, F. (2015). Africa's young entrepreneurs: Unlocking the potential for a bright future. Ottawa, Canada; International Development Research Centre (IDRC). Retrieved from https://www.idrc.ca/sites/default/files/sp/Documents%20EN/Africas-Young-Entrepreneurs-Unlocking-the-Potential-for-a-Brighter-Future.pdf

Khavul, S., Bruton, G. D., & Wood, E. (2009). Informal family business in Africa. *Entrepreneurship Theory and Practice, 33*(6), 1219–1238. http://dx.doi.org/10.1111/j.1540-6520.2009.00342.x

Khavul, S., Perez-Nordtvedt, L., & Wood, E. (2010). Organizational entrainment and international new ventures from emerging markets. *Journal of Business Venturing, 25*(1), 104–119. http://dx.doi.org/10.1016/j.jbusvent.2009.01.008

Khayesi, J. N., & George, G. (2011). When does the socio-cultural context matter? Communal orientation and entrepreneurs' resource accumulation efforts in Africa. *Journal of Occupational and Organizational Psychology, 84*(3), 471–492. http://dx.doi.org/10.1111/j.2044-8325.2011.02029.x

Khayesi, J. N., George, G., & Antonakis, J. (2014). Kinship in entrepreneur networks: Performance effects of resource assembly in Africa. *Entrepreneurship Theory and Practice, 38*(6), 1323–1342.

Kiggundu, M. N. (2002a). Entrepreneurs and entrepreneurship in Africa: What is known and what needs to be done. *Journal of Developmental Entrepreneurship, 7*(3), 239–258. Retrieved from http://search.proquest.com/docview/208434519?pq-origsite=gscholar

Kiggundu, M. N. (2002b). *Managing globalization in developing countries and transition economies: Building capacities for a changing world.* Westport, Connecticut: Greenwood Publishing Group.

Kiggundu, M. N., & Deghetto, K. (2015). Regional integration: Review of the management literature and implications for theory, policy, and practice. *Africa Journal of Management, 1*(4), 303–332. http://dx.doi.org/10.1080/23322373.2015.1106717

Kigotho, J. (2014). *Effects of corporate governance on financial performance of companies quoted at Nairobi securities exchange.* Nairobi: University of Nairobi.

Kimhi, A. (2010). Entrepreneurship and income inequality in southern Ethiopia. *Small Business Economics, 34*(1), 81–91. http://dx.doi.org/10.1007/s11187-009-9196-4

Kinoti, Y. G. (2015). *The effect of non-performing loans on the size of the loan portfolio in commercial banks in Kenya.* Nairobi: University of Nairobi.

Kistruck, G. M., & Beamish, P. W. (2010). The interplay of form, structure, and embeddedness in social intrapreneurship. *Entrepreneurship Theory and Practice, 34*(4), 735–761. http://dx.doi.org/10.1111/j.1540-6520.2010.00371.x

Kistruck, G. M., Beamish, P. W., Qureshi, I., & Sutter, C. J. (2013). Social intermediation in base-of-the-pyramid markets. *Journal of Management Studies, 50*(1), 31–66. http://dx.doi.org/10.1111/j.1467-6486.2012.01076.x

Krauss, S. I., Frese, M., Friedrich, C., & Unger, J. M. (2005). Entrepreneurial orientation: A psychological model of success among southern African small business owners. *European Journal of Work and Organizational Psychology, 14*(3), 315–344. http://dx.doi.org/10.1080/13594320500170227

Kshetri, N. (2013). The diaspora as a change agent in entrepreneurship-related institutions in Sub-Saharan Africa. *Journal of Developmental Entrepreneurship, 18*(03), 1350021. http://dx.doi.org/10.1142/S1084946713500210

Ladzani, W. M., & van Vuuren, J. J. (2002). Entrepreneurship training for emerging SMEs in South Africa. *Journal of Small Business Management, 40*(2), 154–161. http://dx.doi.org/10.1111/1540-627X.00047

Lastarria-Cornhiel, S. (1997). Impact of privatization on gender and property rights in Africa. *World Development, 25*(8), 1317–1333. http://dx.doi.org/10.1016/S0305-750X(97)00030-2

Levin, D. Z., & Barnard, H. (2013). Connections to distant knowledge: Interpersonal ties between more- and less-developed countries. *Journal of International Business Studies, 44* (7), 676–698. http://dx.doi.org/10.1057/jibs.2013.28

Liedholm, C. (2002). Small firm dynamics: Evidence from Africa and Latin America. *Small Business Economics, 18*(1), 225–240. http://dx.doi.org/10.1023/A:1015147826035

Littlewood, D., & Holt, D. (2015). Social Entrepreneurship in South Africa: Exploring the influence of environment. *Business & Society*, 1–37. http://dx.doi.org/10.1177/0007650315613293

Luiz, J. M., & Stewart, C. (2014). Corruption, South African multinational enterprises and institutions in Africa. *Journal of Business Ethics, 124*(3), 383–398. http://dx.doi.org/10.1007/s10551-013-1878-9

Luke, N., & Munshi, K. (2006). New roles for marriage in urban Africa: Kinship networks and the labor market in Kenya. *The Review of Economics and Statistics, 88*(2), 264–282. http://dx.doi.org/10.1162/rest.88.2.264

Mahadea, D. (2012). Prospects of entrepreneurship to the challenge of job creation in South Africa. *Journal of Developmental Entrepreneurship, 17*(04), 1250020. http://dx.doi.org/10.1142/S1084946712500203

Mano, Y., Iddrisu, A., Yoshino, Y., & Sonobe, T. (2012). How can micro and small enterprises in Sub-Saharan Africa become more productive? The impacts of experimental basic managerial training. *World Development, 40*(3), 458–468. http://dx.doi.org/10.1016/j.worlddev.2011.09.013

Manuh, T. (1998). Women in Africas development: Overcoming obstacles pushing for progress. *Africa Recovery, 12*(1), 11–22. Retrieved from http://www.popline.org/node/532184

Marchetta, F. (2012). Return migration and the survival of entrepreneurial activities in Egypt. *World Development, 40*(10), 1999–2013. http://dx.doi.org/10.1016/j.worlddev.2012.05.009

Marsden, K. (1992). African entrepreneurs-pioneers of development. *Small Enterprise Development, 3*(2), 15–25. http://dx.doi.org/10.3362/0957-1329.1992.015

Masakure, O., Cranfield, J., & Henson, S. (2008). The financial performance of non-farm microenterprises in Ghana. *World Development, 36*(12), 2733–2762. http://dx.doi.org/10.1016/j.worlddev.2007.12.005

McGrath, R. G., MacMillan, I. C., & Scheinberg, S. (1992). Elitists, risk-takers, and rugged individualists? An exploratory analysis of cultural differences between entrepreneurs and non-entrepreneurs. *Journal of Business Venturing*, *7*(2), 115–135. http://dx.doi.org/10.1016/0883-9026(92)90008-F

Meyer, K. E., Estrin, S., Bhaumik, S. K., & Peng, M. W. (2009). Institutions, resources, and entry strategies in emerging economies. *Strategic Management Journal*, *30*(1), 61–80. http://dx.doi.org/10.1002/smj.720

Moodley, S. 2003. *The development of an incubator system to promote entrepreneurship for technikon fashion design graduates*. (Unpublished doctoral dissertation). Durban Institute of Technology, Durban. Retrieved from http://ir.dut.ac.za/bitstream/handle/10321/76/Moodley_2003.pdf?sequence=5

Morris, M. H., Williams, R. O., Allen, J. A., & Avila, R. A. (1997). Correlates of success in family business transitions. *Journal of Business Venturing*, *12*(5), 385–401. http://dx.doi.org/10.1016/S0883-9026(97)00010-4

Munemo, J. (2012). Entrepreneurship in developing countries: Is Africa different? *Journal of Developmental Entrepreneurship*, *17*(01), 1250004. http://dx.doi.org/10.1142/S1084946712500045

Murisa, T., & Chikweche, T. (2013). Entrepreneurship and micro-finance in extreme poverty circumstances – challenges and prospects: The case of Zimbabwe. *Journal of Developmental Entrepreneurship*, *18*(01), 1350001. http://dx.doi.org/10.1142/S1084946713500015

Musani, R. (2015). For cosmetics manufacturing firms in the EAC "Localizing" is the key to regional relevance. *Africa Journal of Management*, *1*(4), 384–389. http://dx.do.org/10.1080/23322373.2015.1105453

Nelson, T., Ingols, C., Christian-Murtie, J., & Myers, P. (2013). Susan Murcott and Pure Home Water: Building a sustainable mission-driven enterprise in Northern Ghana. *Entrepreneurship Theory and Practice*, *37*(4), 961–979. http://dx.doi.org/10.1111/j.1540-6520.2011.00448.x

Newland, K., & Tanaka, H. (2010). *Mobilizing diaspora entrepreneurship for development*. Washington DC: Migration Policy Institute.

Njonjo, P. (2015). Coca-Cola: A multinational's perspective on East African integration. *Africa Journal of Management*, *1*(4), 396–405. http://dx.doi.org/10.1080/23322373.2015.1105450

Njoroge, G. (2015). For the EAC, products are visibility. *Africa Journal of Management*, *1*(4), 416–420. http://dx.doi.org/10.1080/23322373.2015.1105466

Obeng, B. A., & Blundel, R. K. (2015). Evaluating enterprise policy interventions in Africa: A critical review of Ghanaian small business support services. *Journal of Small Business Management*, *53*(2), 416–435. http://dx.doi.org/10.1111/jsbm.12072

Omer, N., Van Burg, E., Peters, R. M., & Visser, K. (2015). Internationalization as a "work-around" strategy: How going abroad can help SMEs overcome local constraints. *Journal of Developmental Entrepreneurship*, *20*(02), http://dx.doi.org/10.1142/S1084946715500119

Ortmans, J. (2015). *Entrepreneurs Called to Ignite Economic Growth for Africa and Beyond*. Kansas City, Missouri: The Kauffman Foundation. Retrieved from http://www.kauffman.org/blogs/policy-dialogue/2015/july/entrepreneurs-called-to-ignite-economic-growth-for-africa-and-beyond

Otoo, M., Fulton, J., Ibro, G., & Lowenberg-DeBoer, J. (2011). Women entrepreneurship in West Africa: The cowpea street food sector in Niger and Ghana. *Journal of Developmental Entrepreneurship*, *16*(01), 37–63. http://dx.doi.org/10.1142/S1084946711001732

Peña-López, I. 2016. World Development Report 2016: Digital Dividends. Retrieved from http://ictlogy.net/bibliography/reports/projects.php?idp=2958

Preisendorfer, P., Bitz, A., & Bezuidenhout, F. J. (2012). In search of black entrepreneurship: Why is there a lack of entrepreneurial activity among the black population in South Africa? *Journal of Developmental Entrepreneurship*, *17*(01), 1250006. http://dx.doi.org/10.1142/S1084946712500069

Pretes, M. (2002). Microequity and microfinance. *World Development*, *30*(8), 1341–1353. http://dx.doi.org/10.1016/S0305-750X(02)00044-X

Rauch, A., & Frese, M. (2007). Let's put the person back into entrepreneurship research: A meta-analysis on the relationship between business owners' personality traits, business creation, and success. *European Journal of Work and Organizational Psychology*, *16*(4), 353–385. http://dx.doi.org/10.1080/13594320701595438

Regnier, P. (2009). South-South trade and appropriate technology transfers among agro-food SMEs: The case of Southeast Asia and Western Africa. *Journal of Developmental Entrepreneurship, 14*(02), 121–142. http://dx.doi.org/10.1142/S1084946709001193

Rijkers, B., Laderchi, C. R., & Teal, F. (2010). Who benefits from promoting small enterprises? Some empirical evidence from Ethiopia. *World Development, 38*(4), 523–540. http://dx.doi.org/10.1016/j.worlddev.2009.10.007

Rijkers, B., & Soderbom, M. (2013). The effects of risk and shocks on non-farm enterprise development in rural Ethiopia. *World Development, 45*, 119–136. http://dx.doi.org/10.1016/j.worlddev.2012.10.013

Rivera-Santos, M., Holt, D., Littlewood, D., & Kolk, A. (2015). Social entrepreneurship in sub-Saharan Africa. *The Academy of Management Perspectives, 29*(1), 72–91. http://dx.doi.org/10.5465/amp.2013.0128

Robb, A., Valerio, A., & Parton, B. (2014). *Entrepreneurship education and training: Insights from Ghana, Kenya, and Mozambique.* Washington DC: World Bank Publications.

Robinson, D. A., Davidsson, P., Van Der Mescht, H., & Court, P. (2007). How entrepreneurs deal with ethical challenges – An application of the business ethics synergy star Technique. *Journal of Business Ethics, 71*(4), 411–423. http://dx.doi.org/10.1007/s10551-006-9148-8

Robson, P. J., & Obeng, B. A. (2008). The barriers to growth in Ghana. *Small Business Economics, 30*(4), 385–403. http://dx.doi.org/10.1007/s11187-007-9046-1

Robson, P. J., Haugh, H. M., & Obeng, B. A. (2009). Entrepreneurship and innovation in Ghana: Enterprising Africa. *Small Business Economics, 32*(3), 331–350. http://dx.doi.org/10.1007/s11187-008-9121-2

Robson, P. J., Akuetteh, C. K., Westhead, P., & Wright, M. (2012). Exporting intensity, human capital and business ownership experience. *International Small Business Journal, 30*(4), 367–387. http://dx.doi.org/10.1177/0266242610364426

Rodriguez, P., Uhlenbruck, K., & Eden, L. (2005). Government corruption and the entry strategies of multinationals. *Academy of Management Review, 30*(2), 383–396. http://dx.doi.org/10.5465/AMR.2005.16387894

Rodriguez, P., Siegel, D. S., Hillman, A., & Eden, L. (2006). Three lenses on the multinational enterprise: Politics, corruption, and corporate social responsibility. *Journal of International Business Studies, 37*(6), 733–746. http://dx.doi.org/10.1057/palgrave.jibs.8400229

Schindehutte, M., Morris, M., & Brennan, C. (2003). Entrepreneurs and motherhood: Impacts on their children in South Africa and the United States. *Journal of Small Business Management, 41*(1), 94–107. http://dx.doi.org/10.1111/1540-627X.00069

Scott, L., Dolan, C., Johnstone-Louis, M., Sugden, K., & Wu, M. (2012). Enterprise and inequality: A study of Avon in South Africa. *Entrepreneurship Theory and Practice, 36*(3), 543–568. http://dx.doi.org/10.1111/j.1540-6520.2012.00507.x

Seekings, J., & Nattrass, N. (2008). *Class, Race, and Inequality in South Africa.* New Haven, CT: Yale University Press.

Shah, J. (2015). Leveling the field: Why harmonization is imperative to successful integration. *Africa Journal of Management, 1*(4), 411–415. http://dx.doi.org/10.1080/23322373.2015.1105469

Shane, S., & Venkataraman, S. (2000). The promise of entrepreneurship as a field of research. *Academy of Management Review*, 25(1), 217–226.

Shane, S. (2012). Reflections on the 2010 AMR decade award: Delivering on the promise of entrepreneurship as a field of research. *Academy of Management Review, 37*(1), 10–20. http://dx.doi.org/10.5465/amr.2011.0078

Shen, L. (2012). What makes China's investment successful in Africa: The entrepreneurial spirit and behavior of Chinese enterprises in transitional times. *Journal of Developmental Entrepreneurship, 17*(04), 1250025. http://dx.doi.org/10.1142/S1084946712500252

Sheriff, M., & Muffatto, M. (2014). Reviewing existing policies for unleashing and fostering entrepreneurship in selected African countries. *Journal of Developmental Entrepreneurship, 19*(03), 1450016. http://dx.doi.org/10.1142/S1084946714500162

Sievers, M., & Vandenberg, P. (2007). Synergies through linkages: Who benefits from linking micro-finance and business development services? *World Development, 35*(8), 1341–1358. http://dx.doi.org/10.1016/j.worlddev.2007.04.002

Smith, G. D. (2009). East Africa: Extended families with many rights. *Entrepreneurship Theory and Practice*, *33*(6), 1239–1244. http://dx.doi.org/10.1111/j.1540-6520.2009.00343.x

Sonobe, T., Akoten, J. E., & Otsuka, K. (2011). The growth process of informal enterprises in Sub-Saharan Africa: A case study of a metalworking cluster in Nairobi. *Small Business Economics*, *36*(3), 323–335. http://dx.doi.org/10.1007/s11187-009-9222-6

Sutton, T., Short, J. C., McKenny, A. F., & Namatovu, R. (2015). Institutional factors affecting expansion within the East African community: An analysis of managers' personal stories. *Africa Journal of Management*, *1*(4), 365–383. http://dx.doi.org/10.1080/23322373.2015.1109850

Terjesen, S., Hessels, J., & Li, D. (2016). Comparative international entrepreneurship: A review and research agenda. *Journal of Management*, *42*(1), 299–344. http://dx.doi.org/10.1177/0149206313486259

Tranfield, D., Denyer, D., & Smart, P. (2003). Towards a methodology for developing evidence-informed management knowledge by means of systematic review. *British Journal of Management*, *14*(3), 207–222. http://dx.doi.org/10.1111/1467-8551.00375

Trulsson, P. (2002). Constraints of growth-oriented enterprises in the southern and eastern African region. *Journal of Developmental Entrepreneurship*, *7*(3), 331–339. Retrieved from http://search.proquest.com/docview/208440747?pq-origsite=gscholar

Udry, C. R. & Anagol, S. (2006). *The return to capital in Ghana*. (Yale University Economic Growth Center Discussion Paper, 932). New Haven, CT: Yale University.

Ufere, N., Perelli, S., Boland, R., & Carlsson, B. (2012). Merchants of corruption: How entrepreneurs manufacture and supply bribes. *World Development*, *40*(12), 2440–2453. http://dx.doi.org/10.1016/j.worlddev.2012.05.025

Unger, J. M., Keith, N., Hilling, C., Gielnik, M. M., & Frese, M. (2009). Deliberate practice among South African small business owners: Relationships with education, cognitive ability, knowledge, and success. *Journal of Occupational and Organizational Psychology*, *82* (1), 21–44. http://dx.doi.org/10.1348/096317908X304361

Urban, B. (2008). The prevalence of entrepreneurial orientation in a developing country: Juxtapositions with firm success and South Africa's innovation index. *Journal of Developmental Entrepreneurship*, *13*(04), 425–443. http://dx.doi.org/10.1142/S108494670800106X

Valerio, A., Parton, B., & Robb, A. (2014). *Entrepreneurship education and training programs around the world: Dimensions for success.* Washington DC: World Bank Publications. http://dx.doi.org/10.1596/978-1-4648-0202-7

Vandenberg, P. (2003). Adapting to the financial landscape: Evidence from small firms in Nairobi. *World Development*, *31*(11), 1829–1843. http://dx.doi.org/10.1016/j.worlddev.2003.04.003

Venter, E., Boshoff, C., & Maas, G. (2005). The influence of successor-related factors on the succession process in small and medium-sized family businesses. *Family Business Review*, *18*(4), 283–303. http://dx.doi.org/10.1111/j.1741-6248.2005.00049.x

Visser, T., & Chiloane-Tsoka, E. (2014). An exploration into family business and SMEs in South Africa. *Problems and Perspectives in Management*, *12*(4), 427–432. Retrieved from http://www.businessperspectives.org/journals_free/ppm/2014/PPM_2014_04_spec.issue2_Visser.pdf

Washington, M. L., & Chapman, Z. (2014). Entrepreneurial activity as an externality of inward foreign direct investment in emerging economies: Panel data from Argentina, Brazil, Colombia and South Africa. *Journal of Developmental Entrepreneurship*, *19*(01), 1450004. http://dx.doi.org/10.1142/S1084946714500046

Watkins, B. D. (2007). On government programs that increase small firms' access to capital. *Journal of Small Business Management*, *45*(1), 133–136. http://dx.doi.org/10.1111/j.1540-627X.2007.00203.x

Watkins, K. (2013). *Too Little Access, Not Enough Learning: Africa's Twin Deficit in Education*. Washington, DC: The Brookings Institution. Retrieved from http://www.brookings.edu/research/opinions/2013/01/16-africa-learning-watkins

Webb, J. W., Morris, M. H., & Pillay, R. (2013). Microenterprise growth at the base of the pyramid: A resource-based perspective. *Journal of Developmental Entrepreneurship*, *18*(04), 1350026. http://dx.doi.org/10.1142/S108494671350026X

Webbink, E., Smits, J., & de Jong, E. (2012). Hidden child labor: Determinants of housework and family business work of children in 16 developing countries. *World Development*, *40*(3), 631–642. http://dx.doi.org/10.1016/j.worlddev.2011.07.005

Welsh, D. H., Alon, I., & Falbe, C. M. (2006). An examination of international retail franchising in emerging markets. *Journal of Small Business Management*, *44*(1), 130–149. http://dx.doi.org/10.1111/j.1540-627X.2006.00158.x

Welsh, D. H., Memili, E., Kaciak, E., & Ahmed, S. (2013). Sudanese women entrepreneurs. *Journal of Developmental Entrepreneurship*, *18*(02), 1350013. http://dx.doi.org/10.1142/S1084946713500131

Wheeler, D., McKague, K., Thomson, J., Davies, R., Medalye, J., & Prada, M. (2005). Creating sustainable local enterprise networks. *MIT Sloan Management Review*, *47*(1), 33–40. Retrieved from http://search.proquest.com/docview/224962126?pq-origsite=gscholar

Williams, M., & Hovorka, A. J. (2013). Contextualizing youth entrepreneurship: The case of Botswana's young farmers fund. *Journal of Developmental Entrepreneurship*, *18*(04), 1350022. http://dx.doi.org/10.1142/S1084946713500222

Wood, E., Khavul, S., Perez-Nordtvedt, L., Prakhya, S., Velarde Dabrowski, R., & Zheng, C. (2011). Strategic commitment and timing of internationalization from emerging markets: Evidence from China, India, Mexico, and South Africa. *Journal of Small Business Management*, *49*(2), 252–282. http://dx.doi.org/10.1111/j.1540-627X.2011.00324.x

Woodward, D., Rolfe, R., Ligthelm, A., & Guimaraes, P. (2011). The viability of informal microenterprise in South Africa. *Journal of Developmental Entrepreneurship*, *16*(01), 65–86. http://dx.doi.org/10.1142/S1084946711001719

World Bank. (2013). *Fact Sheet: Infrastructure in Sub-Saharan Africa*. Washington, D.C. World Bank. Retrieved from http://go.worldbank.org/SWDECPM5S0

World Bank. (2016). *While poverty in Africa has declined, number of poor has increased.* Washington, D.C. World Bank. Retrieved from http://www.worldbank.org/en/region/afr/publication/poverty-rising-africa-poverty-report.

Yusuf, A., & Saffu, K. (2005). Planning and performance of small and medium enterprise operators in a country in transition. *Journal of Small Business Management*, *43*(4), 480–497. http://dx.doi.org/10.1111/j.1540-627X.2005.00148.x

Yusuff, O. S. (2013). The dynamics of strategic entry and motivations of Yoruba female textile traders in the Balogun Market, Lagos State, Nigeria. *Journal of Developmental Entrepreneurship*, *18*(02), 1350012. http://dx.doi.org/10.1142/S108494671350012X

Index

For Product Safety Concerns and Information please contact our EU
representative GPSR@taylorandfrancis.com
Taylor & Francis Verlag GmbH, Kaufingerstraße 24, 80331 München, Germany

www.ingramcontent.com/pod-product-compliance
Ingram Content Group UK Ltd.
Pitfield, Milton Keynes, MK11 3LW, UK
UKHW051831180425
457613UK00022B/1197

* 9 7 8 0 3 6 7 5 3 0 6 6 2 *